Visitor's Guide
SOUTH AFRICA

AFRICA

ATLANTIC
OCEAN

South Africa

HOW TO USE THIS GUIDE

This MPC Visitor's Guide has been designed in an easy-to-use format. Each chapter covers an itinerary in a natural progression which gives all background information to help the visitor enjoy a trip. MPC's distinctive margin symbols, the important place names printed in bold and a comprehensive index enables the reader to find the most interesting places to visit with ease.

At the end of each chapter, an Additional Information section gives specific details including addresses and opening times for places of interest, making this guide a complete sightseeing companion.

The Facts for Visitors at the end of the guide gives practical information including a comprehensive hotel and self-catering accommodation listing, and useful tips to help plan a holiday both prior to travel and during a stay.

Acknowledgements

The publishers would like to thank the South African Tourist Board (SATOUR) for their kind assistance in providing the excellent selection of photographs which made this book possible. Thanks are also due to the people of South Africa for their friendship and hospitality during our research work.

Published by
Moorland Publishing Co Ltd., Ashbourne, Derbyshire DE6 1HD England
Published in the USA by
Hunter Publishing Inc, 300 Raritan Center Parkway, Edison, NJ 08818

ISBN 0-86190-555-5
© Moorland Publishing Company Limited 1996

British Library Cataloguing in Publication Data:
A catalogue record for this book is available from the British Library.

Colour origination by: GA Graphics, Stamford, Lincs.
Printed in Hong Kong by: South China Printing Co. (1988) Ltd.

While every care has been taken to ensure that the information in this book is accurate, the publisher and author accept no responsibility for any loss, injury or inconvenience sustained by anyone using this guide.

Cover photograph: Table Mountain and the city of Cape Town.
Back Cover (clockwise): Rolling dunes of the Kalahari; Cape Town in the spring, Blyde River Canyon; Namaqualand wildflowers; Sudwala Caves. Title page: African elephant.

KEY TO SYMBOLS USED IN TEXT MARGIN AND ON MAPS

✽	Garden	♦	Mosque
⌂	Castle/Fortification	♦	Church/Ecclesiastical site
✳	Other Place of Interest	⌂	Building of interest
⚞	Nature reserve/Animal interest	⊓	Archaeological site
♠	Parkland/Forest	⚑	Museum/Art Gallery
⚘	Beautiful view/Scenery	⚐	Recommended walk
⚒	Skiing	⚑	Cave
⌐	Golf	➤	Birdlife
⚓	Beach	⚓	Watersports
⬛	Hindu temple	⬤	Fishing/Aquatiic interest

Visitor's Guide to
SOUTH AFRICA

Poppi Smith and Angela Gama

MPC

Contents

South Africa

BOTSWANA

NAMIBIA

*Kalahari Gemsbok
National Park*

NORTH

Vrybu

Kuruman

Upington

*Richtersveld
National Park*

*Augrabies Falls
National Park*

Kimberle

Alexander Bay

Port Nolloth

Pofadder

NORTHERN CAPE

Goegap Nature Reserve

Springbok

Brandvlei

De Aar

Britstown

Garies

Victoria West

Middleb

Calvinia

Vanrhynsdorp

*Tankwa-Karoo
National Park*

ATLANTIC OCEAN

Clanwilliam

Karoo Nature Park

Beaufort West

Citrusdal

Moorreesburg

WESTERN CAPE

*Saldanha Bay
West Coast
National Park*

Touws River

Worcester

Oudtshoorn

CAPE TOWN

Strand

George

Muizenburg

*Cape of Good Hope
Nature Reserve*

*False
Bay*

Caledon

*De Hoop
Nature Reserve*

WELCOME TO SOUTH AFRICA

When former President FW de Klerk unveiled the beginnings of a 'new South Africa' — free from apartheid and discrimination, he also opened the doors on a country which is now emerging as one of eco-tourism's best-kept secrets. South Africa is a nation of diverse contrasts, and its advertising slogan — *a world in one country* — is a fitting description for this land of exceptional beauty.

From the magnificent game parks where animals roam free, and where tourists can experience easy sightings of the 'big five'; to the mineral deposits of gold and diamonds; across the vast expanses of deserted, white sandy beaches and crystal blue water — this is truly a country with something for everybody.

Numerous sporting activities are available including hiking and walking trails of varying lengths, white-water rafting, golfing, mountaineering, and some of the best scuba diving in the world. Visitors can enjoy the rocks and caves of spectacular mountain ranges and witness fine examples of 'Bushman' art depicting the lifestyles of ancient people dating back thousands of years.

The many tribes and people who have settled in South Africa have left as their legacy a fascinating cultural mix. It is worth reading up on the history before travelling in order not to arrive with the impression that the past is only about apartheid. Many bloody battles were fought between the white settlers, the Boers and the Zulus, and it was only in the twentieth century that laws were introduced where people were segregated according to their colour.

The new South Africa is attempting to combine ancient African tribal traditions with a new fast-moving westernised society. The people's love of this spectacular country, together with the pride they take in demonstrating their friendliness and hospitality towards visitors, will go a long way to make this happen.

South Africans are living in exciting times. With the first democratic government in place, a sense of patriotism exists which was never present before. The new flag is seen everywhere as people declare for the first time — 'South African and proud of it'.

Although tourism is still in its relative infancy, visitors have always been greeted with warmth and enthusiasm. Here, one can enjoy the true essence of Africa, together with the luxury of a sophisticated world. South Africa is now open for visitors keen to enjoy a wealth of new experiences hosted by smiling people from a diversity of cultures. Many educational tribal villages have opened up throughout the Republic to preserve different traditions and to demonstrate these cultures to other tribes and tourists.

The mix of western and African, combined with First and Third World is fascinating. Visitors are often amazed at the advanced infrastructure already established in the cities which co-exists in harmony with the country's charm and natural wonders.

South Africa is now a land of choices. It is an ideal holiday destination offering a temperate climate, superb scenery, fascinating flora and fauna, unspoiled beaches and unsurpassed beauty.

History

The earliest inhabitants of South Africa were the Khoisan, a nomadic people who lived in the south-west of the country. They were made up of the San (or Bushmen) who are believed to have descended from the Stone Age, and the Khoikhoi. Until 2,000 years ago, these people were the only-known inhabitants of South Africa, after which Bantu-speaking migrants began to arrive from other parts of the continent and over the centuries settled in many parts of the country.

There were four main groups of Bantu settlers which included the Nguni-speaking group (made up of the Xhosa and Zulu tribes), the Sotho-Tswana, the Tosonga and Venda speaking people.

In 1488, the Portuguese navigator Bartholomew Diaz was the first European to land in South Africa at Mossel Bay in the Cape. The coastline was used both as a trading post and for navigational purposes until 1652, when Jan van Riebeek arrived with a mandate from the Dutch East India Company to institute a market garden in order to supply provisions to passing ships. Along with his settlers, he soon established contact with the Khoisan during their visits into the interior of the country and traded with them for cattle.

The Dutch quickly seized control of large areas of the Bushmen's land, whilst developing their own close-knit self-sufficient community using slaves imported from other parts of Africa and south-east Asia. They created the language of Afrikaans — a Dutch dialect, their own sect of the Dutch Reformed Church and relied on slave labour to work the land for them. They became known as the 'Boers' — the Afrikaans word for farmer.

Subsequent interbreeding between the whites, Hottentots and the slaves resulted in a new indigenous group known as the coloureds.

As the Dutch settlers spread further east, they encountered various Bantu settlers who were expanding westwards. At the Great Fish River, near present-day Port Elizabeth, they encountered tens of thousands of Xhosa and in 1779, the first of a series of frontier wars broke out. The boundary for the Cape Colony was disputed for many years during these Bantu wars.

Between 1678 and 1700, 225 French Huguenots, fleeing religious persecution in France, swelled the number of white settlers in the Cape. There they used their expertise to develop the fledgling wine industry.

The British began their occupation of the Cape in 1795 when the Dutch East India Company liquidated and British troops took control of the area, after which ownership of the colony passed between Holland and Britain until it was finally ceded to the British in 1814.

The first British Governor was the Earl of Caledon whose initial task was to establish a new and updated legal system and find a solution to the problems with the slave community.

In 1820, the British set out to re-enforce their numbers in the Cape and 5,000 Britons known as 'the 1820 settlers' landed in Algoa Bay (now Port Elizabeth). Most were farming people and they established their homes in the area, while acting as a human buffer zone against the Xhosa tribes along the Great Fish River. Their lifestyle was harsh, basic provisions (including water) were scarce and the settlers suffered constant raids by the Xhosas. However, life did gradually improve and by 1825, the British settlers had begun to have considerable impact on the colonial, the Boer and Bantu societies.

During this period, on the other side

Above left: Bushman wearing traditional beadwork. Above right: Xhosa women in the Eastern Cape.
Opposite: Fine example of Bushman rock art depicting an ancient hunting scene.

of the Great Fish River, Shaka, the Zulu King had forged vast numbers of Zulu-speaking clans into a mighty nation, thereby forcing other indigenous black groups to scatter northwards. He waged a merciless war on other tribes for their land, and by 1828 he controlled a vast area of South Africa. The battles became known as the Zulu Wars and raged for many years as a result of the brutal Shaka's seemingly unquenchable desire for more land.

Government reforms continued under British rule and in 1807 the slave trade was finally decreed illegal throughout South Africa. However, it was not until almost thirty years later that a further law was passed to free slaves already held in captivity.

In 1835, 12,000 Boers began the historical Great Trek — the migration of countless Afrikaner families northwards from the Cape to uncharted territory, in search of a land of their own, away from British interference and rule. They faced incredible hardship as they drove into the heart of the continent and, during the course of their travels through Natal, were frequently attacked by Zulus. Most trekked northwards across the Vaal River and settled in what became the Transvaal region. They became known as the Voortrekkers (meaning the 'first trekkers').

One group, under the leadership of Piet Retief, decided to establish a republic in Natal and sought the permission of Zulu King Dingaan, Shaka's successor, to control large areas of central and southern Natal. Dingaan double-crossed them, and the company of 500 unarmed men was murdered by Zulu warriors. This led to the Battle of Blood River when, in 1835 a group of 460 Voortrekkers overpowered the Zulus. Dingaan was overthrown and the Republic of Natal was founded.

Over the next few years approximately 15,000 farmers migrated from the Cape to settle in the new lands. Although the Boer settlers wanted legal title to the land in Natal, the British refused and they defeated the Afrikaners in 1843 declaring Natal a district of the Cape Colony.

The majority of the settlers soon left the area and joined the Voortrekkers on their continued migration north.

During this period, the population of Durban grew quickly to a busy port city of over 50,000. British immigrants established sugar plantations and labourers were indentured from India, initially on a temporary basis, but many decided stayed to create a further aspect of South Africa's racial spectrum which is still evident today.

The British then came into serious conflict with the Zulus over their land in Natal and in the Anglo-Zulu war of 1879, suffered one of their worst defeats. The Zulus were finally defeated later that year and Zululand was divided into thirteen chiefdoms. Three years later, after the death of the Zulu leader Cetshwayo, the British incorporated the Zulu territories into Natal.

Between 1848 and 1850, the British annexed additional territories, including the Orange Free State. It was only in 1850, when the British decided against colonising further areas of Southern Africa, that they signed a treaty recognizing the Afrikaner state of the Orange Free State. However, in 1877 the British annexed the Republic of Transvaal, blaming the Boers for their inability to control the area.

The discovery of diamonds in the Kimberley area in 1869, followed a few years later by the discovery of gold on the Witwatersrand, heralded the beginning of an economic boom in South Africa and acted as a worldwide magnet to fortune hunters, labourers and investors. The world's largest manmade hole was created at Kimberley when a hill, rich in diamonds, was excavated to form the Big Hole of Kimberley. Demand for labour in the mines exceeded supply, and blacks demanded higher wages and better working conditions.

The Boers held a deep resentment towards the British and the annexation of their republic, and in 1880 they declared war on the British in what became the First Boer War. After three months of bloody battle the Boers regained control of the Transvaal.

The political importance of the Transvaal was highlighted after the discovery of gold in 1886. This brought prospectors from all over the world in search of riches and it was these immigrant workers who established the early foundations of the city of Johannesburg. As a result, a period of social and political turmoil began, fuelled by a resentment towards the *uitlanders* (foreigners) as their presence weakened the influence of the Boer farmers within the state. By 1892, over 10,000 inhabitants of the Transvaal were foreigners who were demanding equal rights with the Boers. The British again saw an opportunity to retake the Transvaal and attempted this in the Jameson Raid. This move, along with a further attempt by Dr. Leander Jameson failed, so the British started moving additional troops to Southern Africa to protect the rights of the *uitlanders*.

The President of the Transvaal, Paul Kruger, issued an ultimatum to British to cease the troop movements, and when this was ignored, the Second Boer War began. It lasted two years during which time the British suffered the highest losses ever sustained in any colonial war. During the war, the British interned thousands of

Afrikaner women and children in concentration camps and destroyed their homes and land. The camps were filthy and overcrowded and caused the death of over thirty thousand prisoners, many of whom were children. This subsequently led to decades of resentment between the two white groups.

Finally, in 1902, the entire sub-continent became British territory at the signing of the Treaty of Vereenigning. The Treaty decreed that the Boers should surrender all their land to the British, although they retained the right to live there.

After the war, British South Africa comprised of the Cape Province, the Orange Free State, Natal and Transvaal. In 1910, the Union of South Africa was established and united these four colonies under the leadership of General Louis Botha of the newly formed South African (National) Party.

Almost immediately African workers were precluded from most skilled categories of work and amidst continued protests by non-whites, the South African Native National Congress (later renamed the African National Congress — ANC) was formed. Its aim was to unite South Africa and to fight for equal rights.

One of the cornerstones of segregation was passed in 1913 — the Native Land Act — which reserved traditional territories for black Africans. In 1923, this was consolidated by the Native (Urban Areas) Act which forced Africans into 'native locations', now more commonly known as townships.

The National Party was formed in 1914 by supporters of the Afrikaner, General Hertzog, who had been forced out of General Louis Botha's cabinet. Initially, the party aimed to serve the interests of the Afrikaner farmer, but it soon received the support of the white working-class who resented the fact that mine owners were giving jobs to the lower-paid black workers in preference to them.

In the 1930s, legislations were introduced reserving certain jobs for whites only, and restricting black workers against security of tenure. During the depression of the 1930s, Hertzog was forced into a coalition with General Jan Smuts to form the United Party, while dissatisfied Nationalists, led by Daniel Malan, broke away and formed a purified National Party.

When World War II began in 1939, it renewed the animosity between the English and Afrikaners, and Hertzog broke with Smuts refusing to support South Africa's entry into the war on Britain's side.

The resulting labour shortage brought thousands of Africans into the cities, and it was primarily white reaction against this which secured victory for Malan's National Party in 1948.

Their policies of segregation between whites and blacks — apartheid — won support with large numbers of whites and during the following years, over one hundred laws were passed making colour segregation a statutory law. These included the Prohibition of Mixed Marriages, the Population Registration Act, the Immorality Act and the Separate Amenities Act. Areas around large cities became black townships, in which basic accommodation was constructed to house blacks, while increased restrictions were placed on all non-whites. These moves were the fundamentals of apartheid rule and excluded blacks, coloureds and Asians from having any political or economic influence in South Africa.

After 1950, ethnic groups were often forcibly removed from cities and dumped on barren land with few or no amenities. The areas which were allocated to them accounted for only thirteen percent of the land in South Africa, and they were only allowed into the 'white' cities to work.

In response to this, the Pan African Congress (PAC) was established in 1959 by radical blacks, who broke away from the ANC in a determined effort to create a new South Africa, free from whites. They adopted the slogan of 'One settler, one bullet' in the later 1970s.

The following year, the PAC called for a mass protest against the pass laws which legally required blacks to carry a pass book at all times. The authorities' response to the march resulted in the Sharpeville massacre, where sixty-nine unarmed blacks were killed and a further 180 injured by gunfire.

Both the PAC and ANC organisations were subsequently banned forcing them into their own guerilla war. The ANC formed *Umkonto we Sizwe* ('Spear of the Nation') to wage a series of attacks on government buildings, while the PAC formed its own military wing, *Poqo* ('we go it alone'). Most of the leaders were either forced into exile or, like Nelson Mandela, were tried and sentenced to life imprisonment.

The withdrawal of foreign investment heightened as a result of the Sharpeville incident and South Africa became further isolated after their withdrawal from the Commonwealth in 1961. The National Party set about winning increased support among the English-speaking South African community while Steve Biko's Black Consciousness Movement revived the demoralised black resistance in the late 1960s.

In 1976, when Soweto's black students took to the streets protesting against the introduction of Afrikaans being taught in their schools, it was Biko's name on their lips. The following year, Biko died whilst in the custody of the secret police and his followers were rounded up.

The Black Consciousness Movement was banned and its leaders were arrested and detained without trial.

In the early 1970s, the National Party now more powerful than ever, was rocked by the collapse of the Portuguese colonies of Mozambique and Angola. This heightened the threat of cross-border guerrilla raids and the government reacted by intervening in the civil war in Angola.

During the 1970s a number of homelands were given independent status, including Ciskei, Bophuthatswana, Transkei and Venda.

Political and social reforms were long overdue, and when P W Botha came to power in 1978, he gave black South Africans the right to buy their own property in townships.

A new constitution was instituted in 1984, establishing a tri-cameral parliament which included whites, coloureds and Indians, but which still totally excluded blacks from any involvement in central government. The new government started to rescind some apartheid laws, including the Pass Laws, the Mixed Marriages Act and the Immorality Act.

However, black opposition to white rule grew stronger, and rebellion flared across the country as blacks burned down schools and homes in protest. A state of emergency was declared and security forces were deployed to control townships across the country. Twenty-four thousand blacks were soon in detention — many of whom were schoolchildren. Shockwaves spread throughout the world as international organisations, horrified by television pictures of South African security forces in violent clashes with blacks, withdrew their interests in the country. Years of isolation followed when it became unacceptable to have any links with South Africa — either economic, political or sporting.

Despite the widespread unemployment which followed, particularly amongst blacks, the imposition of trade sanctions proved to be an effective weapon in the breaking down of apartheid. The outlawed ANC attracted an international following of sympathisers who, in particular, campaigned for the release of Nelson Mandela. During this period, Chief Mangasuto Buthelezi of the Zulu Inkatha Freedom Party and Desmond Tutu, Archbishop of Cape Town, kept the issue of apartheid in the world headlines through frequent overseas visits. P W Botha began to make some limited reforms but in 1989, after a stroke, he resigned and was succeeded by F W de Klerk.

From his inauguration in September 1989, President de Klerk surprised many, not least the members of his own party, with dramatic changes in policies that saw the collapse of the barriers which the National Party had established over the previous forty-three years. President de Klerk promised to create a new South Africa within five years and his immediate actions reaffirmed his words. Key ANC leaders were released from their life prison sentences and rumours abounded of frequent meetings between de Klerk and Mandela.

The following February, in his opening of parliament speech, de Klerk stunned political observers by lifting the ban on thirty political organisations, including the ANC and PAC and, a few days later released Nelson Mandela from jail.

This heralded the beginning of a working relationship between de Klerk and Mandela, and they jointly pledged to work together to end violence in South Africa and achieve a political settlement. This led to the ANC denouncing the armed struggle and the National Party opening its membership to all races. Most political prisoners were released and exiles slowly began to return to the country.

Top: President Nelson Mandela who became the first democratically-elected and black president of South Africa in 1994.
Above: In 1992 President F W de Klerk was awarded a joint Nobel Peace Prize with Nelson Mandela for their commitment towards a new South Africa.

In September 1991, the National Peace Accord was signed by twenty-nine political and trade union organisations, followed in December by the Convention for a Democratic South Africa (CODESA).

In March 1992, almost seventy percent of white South Africa voted 'Yes' in support of President de Klerk's reforms in the referendum. However, the massacre in June of forty-two blacks at Biopatong halted talks between the ANC and the government for almost six months.

Later the same year, Nelson Mandela and President de Klerk were awarded a joint Nobel Peace Prize for their continued commitment towards a new South Africa.

Once the multi-party talks were back on track again, a new constitution was agreed upon and a date set for the first democratic election the next year.

In April 1993, Chris Hani, the leader of the South African communist party, was assassinated by a right-wing activist. His supporters reacted violently by marching in protest, resulting in many shops in the centre of Cape Town being damaged and looted. Talks at the World Trade Centre took on a new dimension, as it became apparent that urgent compromises had to be made. As a result of the discussions, the ANC agreed to share power with minority parties and the National Party agreed to relinquish all its power.

In the run up to the election, some groups remained committed to white supremacy. A small, but powerful breakaway group, the *Afrikaaner Weerstandsbeweging* (AWB) were determined to fight the process. This conservative extreme right-wing group upheld a whites-only society based on the original Boer republics.

The hatred between the ANC and Inkatha Freedom Party, along with the refusal of Inkatha and the AWB to meet around the negotiating table, proved to be a stumbling block in the attempts at conciliation. Violence escalated to an unprecedented level and seemed to be the main obstacle to the creation of a new nation.

On 7 December 1993, multi-racial transitional authorities took over the running of South Africa and ended three centuries of white rule. However, fears that the elections would incite further violent clashes throughout the country appeared well-founded when the AWB began a bombing campaign against the process of change and the Zulus continued in their determination to battle for autonomy.

Despite all these obstacles, the Zulu Inkatha party eventually joined the election process, and the following week the whole country lined up for the first time to vote together: blacks, whites, Indians, coloureds — along with all of South Africa's cross section of immigrants.

The ANC won with a landslide victory and on 10 May 1994, the whole world watched as Nelson Mandela was inaugurated as the first democratically-elected and black president of South Africa.

Presidents and representatives arrived from around the world to join the celebrations and in a spirit of reconciliation black South Africans sang the Afrikaans national anthem *Die Stem*, while white South Africans attempted *Nkosi Sikileli Afrika* (God bless Africa) — the new joint anthem.

Since the inauguration, all sanctions have been lifted and both the World Bank and the United Nations have thrown their support behind the new government. In June 1994, South Africa rejoined the Commonwealth and the country is now enjoying political and social freedom under a government committed to true democracy.

GEOGRAPHY

The Republic of South Africa covers an area of 1,219,080 square kilometres, about one eighth of the size of the USA, or five times the size of the United Kingdom. It is bordered by the waters of the Atlantic and Indian oceans, by the nations of Botswana, Namibia and Zimbabwe in the north and Mozambique in the east. South Africa also encloses the Kingdoms of Lesotho and Swaziland.

The republic is divided into nine provinces; Gauteng, Mpumalanga, Northern Transvaal, the North-West Province, KwaZulu-Natal, Free State, Eastern Cape, Western Cape and Northern Cape. There are three capital cities, Pretoria (administrative), Cape Town (legislative) and Bloemfontein (judicial).

The coastline stretches for almost 3,000 km (1,865 miles) from Ponta do Ouro on the Mozambique border to the Orange River in the west. Some of the major rivers of southern Africa including the Orange, its tributary the Vaal, and the Limpopo, traverse the country and drain most of the inland plateau.

The interior consists of the Veld — a semi-arid plateau with an average elevation of 1,200 metres (3,936 feet), sprinkled with isolated hills and low mountain ranges. This is surrounded by a mountainous rim and escarpment which is more pronounced in the east and south where it incorporates the country's highest mountain ranges, including the Drakensberg.

The climate varies throughout the country. The Cape has a Mediterranean climate with cool, wet winters and warm, dry summers while the north has hot, wet summers and dry winters. The eastern coast is sub-tropical with high humidity in the summer months, while the west is semi-desert with light, summer rains.

POPULATION/POLITICS AND ECONOMY

The latest figures estimate the population at just under forty million, but without the benefit of an electoral roll, along with the large numbers of squatters and illegal immigrants, it is difficult to obtain accurate statistics. The black population is made up of distinctive ethnic groups, each of which has its own language, social system and culture — as well as a distinctive traditional territory settled over the centuries (see History). The Zulu are generally associated with KwaZulu Natal; the Xhosa with the Eastern Cape; the Ndebele (the northern section of this tribe has joined the Sotho, but the South Ndebele still reside in the Transvaal); North Sotho and Venda live in the Northern Transvaal; the West Sotho (or Tswana speaking people) in the Northern Cape and North West Province; the South Sotho in Lesotho, the Free State and surrounding area; and the Tsonga in the Eastern Transvaal. The majority of the whites are descended from Dutch, French, British and German settlers who arrived between the seventeenth and nineteenth centuries. There has also been an influx of European immigrants including large numbers of Portuguese over the last few decades, many of whom fled the collapse of the Portuguese colonies in Angola and Mozambique. There is also a large Jewish community living in South Africa, particularly in Johannesburg.

More than eighty per cent of all coloureds in South Africa live in the Cape. The coloureds are made up of distinct sub-cultures — the Griquas, the Cape Coloureds and the Cape Malays. The largest group, the Cape Coloureds are descended from interbreeding between the Khoikhoi, the early white settlers, from slaves im-

Above: The Addo Elephant Park near Port Elizabeth supports of herd of nearly 200.

ported from the East, and later the Bantu. They reside mainly in the Western Cape. The Griquas, who number about 100,000, are primarily of Khoikhoi/European descent. They live mainly in the north-western and north-eastern Cape Province and are mostly Christian.

The Cape Malays are a mixture of Indians, Cingalese, Chinese, Indonesians and Malagasy. The Malays reside in the Malay Quarter of Cape Town where they have retained their Islamic traditions. The Asians in South Africa consist mainly of Indians who were brought into the country to work as indentured labourers on the Natal sugar plantations, and their numbers were later supplemented by Gujarati-speaking Muslims. Over eighty per cent of the Asian community still live in KwaZulu-Natal.

Between 1904 and 1906, about 60,000 Chinese labourers were indentured to work in the goldmines in Johannesburg. Although many were later repatriated, about 13,000 Chinese now reside in Johannesburg and Port Elizabeth. The population living in the nine provinces is divided as follows:

Above: The annual International Yacht Race in Cape Town.

Western Cape	3,676,335
Northern Cape	739,450
The Free State	2,749,583
Eastern Cape	6,416,965
KwaZulu-Natal	8,577,799
Mpumalanga	2,953,232
Northern Transvaal	5,772,583
Gauteng	6,946,953
North West	3,315,671

Conservation

South Africa is one of the forerunners in wildlife conservation. The national parks and game reserves are extremely well-organised and place a strong emphasis on anti-poaching laws. Animals are allowed to roam freely in their natural habitat, as the many tarred roads throughout the parks allow visitors the ability to view the animals in their own environment, without disturbing their indigenous feeding and breeding patterns.

South Africa is the only country on

the continent where the 'big five' (lion, elephant, rhino, leopard and buffalo) occur in sufficient numbers to justify the hunting of these magnificent creatures. For further information contact the Professional Hunter's Association of South Africa (PHASA). Telephone: (011) 706 7724.

The increase in the number of visitors, combined with the development of the tourist industry and its impact on local communities, is currently undergoing serious consideration. Many local people are being encouraged to support themselves through involvement in the industry.

Many companies, including the Conservation Corporation are considering the effects of tourism on the environment. Their operating ethics ensure the development of the wilderness areas and their continued sustainability, as well as the participation of local communicties in the benefits of ecotourism. Their reserves include Londolozi and Singita with a dazzling array of wildlife, Ngala which is renowned for its elephant and lion and Phinda Resource Reserve.

The National Parks Board is efficient and well-run and maintains specific conservation projects for different species of endangered creatures in certain parks i.e the Mountain Zebra National Park, near Cradock in the Eastern Cape Province. The majority of parks require game-viewing from a vehicle, although there are some trails specially organised by the National Parks Board, but these have limited spaces and require advance booking.

Arts, Culture and Entertainment

Because of the years of cultural isolation from the rest of the world, South African art has received very little exposure overseas. Many tourist centres throughout the country issue maps of arts and crafts routes which guide visitors to the artists' homes or studios where they display their work. This offers an excellent opportunity to purchase unusual and creative gifts at reasonable prices. The craftwork available includes pottery, weaving, beading, sculpture, wood carving as well as numerous fine and traditional paintings. There are also many theatres, opera houses and large cinema complexes as well as drive-in theatres.

Sports and Pastimes

Sport has always played an integral part in the life of most South Africans — particularly since their return into the world sporting arena. South African teams are considered amongst the best — especially in the field of cricket and rugby. The climate and the wide-open spaces lend themselves perfectly to the variety of sports and adventure activities available. The most popular sports include soccer, rugby, cricket, golf, fishing, boxing and hunting.

With its long coastline, South Africa is ideal for surfing and Jeffrey's Bay is considered to be one of the world's top surfing spots. Other watersports, including white-water rafting, provide exciting opportunities for the more adventurous, while scuba diving is very popular along the coast — particularly on the reef off Sodwana Bay which is considered one of the best in the world.

There are an abundance of hiking and walking trails throughout the country ranging from one hour to eight days, as well as some excellent mountain climbing in areas like the Drakensberg.

South Africans like the outdoor life and even the most sedentary person can be found making a *braai* (barbecue) in the garden. *Braais* can be enjoyed anywhere — at sports events, by the river or even by the side of the road. They are definitely a way of life and not just a way of eating. An opportunity to attend a *braai* should not be missed as it is a good way to experience South African hospitality at its best. It is customary to bring your own meat and drink but don't be in a hurry to eat — the essence of the *braai* is the talking and drinking while the wood burns.

FOOD AND DRINK

With so many cultural influences, South Africa can boast a variety of national and regional dishes. Traditional foods include *Boerewors*, a long curl of spiced sausage, *Potjiekos*, a meat and vegetable casserole usually *braaied* (barbecued) in a special three-legged pot. In the Karoo area, ostrich steak and lamb are very popular, while around the Cape, dishes have a strong Malay influence such as *bobotie* (rice casserole covered with meat and egg sauce), and Natal has its own spicy Indian heritage. South African's also enjoy the Voortrekker speciality of *biltong*. It is served as a snack and is made out of venison or beef cut into strips. The strips of meat are marinaded overnight in layers of salt, pepper and vinegar and then hung in the cool until the strips are dried.

Meat in South Africa is excellent quality and usually comes in large portions. It is possible to enjoy various game roasts including springbok, crocodile and impala as well as regular cuts of beef and lamb.

Fresh fish and seafood are found in abundance around South Africa's coastline and fresh fish is available in most restaurants. It is often flavoured with a variety of tasty spices to create mouthwatering Malay-style dishes.

Restaurants cater for every taste and combine the many ethnic qualities which have existed in the country for hundreds of years with the fresh ingredients produced here including fruits, vegetables and spices.

For fast food enthusiasts, *Wimpy* and *Kentucky* franchises are usually clean and good value, as are the drive-in restaurants which serve a wide range of food. *Mike's Kitchen* and *Spur* are both nationwide franchises and offer good value steaks, burgers and salad bars.

South Africa has a large selection of wineries and there are many excellent locally-produced wines to suit every budget. South African wine is now acclaimed as one of the finest 'New World' wines and continues to win increasing respect in the export market. The temperate conditions of the Cape, with its fertile soils and dry summers, make this a perfect area for cultivating vines. Ports and sherries are also being produced here. Visitors can enjoy tours through the wine regions stopping at traditional farmhouses where they can sample the fresh food and wines of each estate.

HOW TO USE THE GUIDE

With over a million kilometres of spectacular scenery and attractions, it can be a bewildering prospect for first time visitors to South Africa, to know where to begin and how to use their time effectively. Anybody here for only a short period should not try to cover the whole country.

The following four chapters offer various itineraries which cover South Africa's main attractions, including a contrast of cities, spectacular coastlines, hiking trails, game-viewing and places of historical interest.

This guide recommends logical overnight stops to ensure that in areas where there is a lot to see, the distance covered will be minimal. At other times, it will require virtually a whole day of driving to reach the next destination.

The North and Wester

Provinces

1

This itinerary begins in the capital city of Pretoria, in the most economically important and smallest province of South Africa — Gauteng, meaning gold in Sotho. It leads through the Venda region — the land of legend — up to Northern Transvaal near the Zimbabwe border. From here, visitors may head south through the Kruger National Park to witness a magnificent spectacle of wildlife all living in their natural habitat. From here, the mountains, gorges, waterfalls and fascinating towns, like the former gold rush town of Pilgrim's Rest, are all within easy reach. The route continues on a beautiful drive through mountain forest, across a tiny border post into the Kingdom of Swaziland. Stay in one of the country's majestic game parks or a luxury hotel in the Ezulwini valley. The journey returns to South Africa into the province of KwaZulu-Natal — home of the Zulu warriors — and its many beautiful, unspoiled beaches and nature reserves. Travel via the major cities of the province — Durban and Pietermaritzburg to the battlefields of the Boer wars or visit the dramatic Drakensberg mountains before returning to Johannesburg, South Africa's major city.

By following this route visitors will enjoy an excellent cross section of the many attractions for which South Africa is noted. The itinerary can also be easily broken at Nelspruit by returning to Johannesburg on the N2, if time is limited.

After landing at **Johannesburg International Airport** transfer directly to Pretoria, 30km (19 miles) away, following the signs on the R24 freeway. Unlike Johannesburg, its noisy and bustling neighbour, Pretoria is a spacious and elegant city. In spring, its thousands of trees and beautiful gardens burst into bloom and the city becomes a blaze of colour, giving it the name 'Jacaranda City'. The ultra-modern buildings, with their strong European influence, blend well with the old buildings from the nineteenth century when Pretoria was the capital of the Transvaal Republic.

PRETORIA

Pretoria is still the administrative capital of South Africa, but has recently been ousted by Johannesburg as the capital of the Gauteng province, (formerly the PVW — Pretoria, Vereniging, Witwatersrand). Many major institutions and establishments have their headquarters here and it is the capital of research, sport, the military, education and home to most foreign embassies.

The Voortrekkers who had moved up from the Cape on their Great Trek began farming along the Apies River at the foothills of the Magaliesburg mountain range around 1837. However, it was in 1855 that the city was officially founded by Martinus Wessel Pretorius who named it after his father, Andries Pretorius, a Boer hero at the Battle of Blood River.

In the 1850s, the city was eventually chosen as the central seat of government for the bands of Voortrekkers scattered across the Transvaal, and in 1855 it became the headquarters of Paul Kruger's *Suid Afrikaansche Republiek.*

In 1910, when the Union of South Africa was formed, it became the administrative capital of South Africa.

Pretoria enjoys an excellent climate with warm, sunny winter days and crisp, cold nights. The rest of the year is hot, but because of the low humidity, is quite comfortable. The best time to visit is during the springtime (October and November), when the jacaranda trees which line the streets are in full bloom. In the third week of October, Pretorians stage a one-week Jacaranda festival which includes rock concerts, shows and flea markets.

The building which dominates the skyline as one enters the city is the **University of South Africa** (UNISA), one of the largest correspondence universities in the world.

Head directly to the **Tourist Rendezvous Travel Centre** at the **Sammy Marks Centre** where friendly staff will work out travel itineraries, book accommodation to suit any budget, and provide a wealth of useful information. The centre also houses the South African Tourism Board (Satour), the Pretoria Publicity Association, a National Parks Board reservations office, a travel agent, a curio shop and a ticket kiosk. There are a large number of three- and four-star hotels in Pretoria and the Tourist Rendezvous Centre can provide full details on available accommodation including guest houses and small hotels. The Hotel Formule 1 chain has budget price rooms that accommodate up to three people.

There are plenty of restaurants within Pretoria which cater for all tastes and budgets. As a guideline, the city centre and the eastern suburbs have a large concentration of expensive restaurants, while Esselyn Street in the nearby suburb of Sunnyside offers a wide range of more reasonably-priced restaurants. There are a number of the national franchises of Spur and Mike's Kitchen in the cheaper price range and Poor Boys is a family-style restaurant.

From the Sammy Marks Centre, walk down Church Street towards **Church Square**, which is overlooked by a large statue of Paul Kruger. Church Square is the heart of Pretoria and is surrounded by fascinating architecture. The northern side of the square is built in the style of the Place de la Concorde in Paris, while the southern side is similar to London's Trafalgar Square. It is the place which residents use as a lunchtime meeting place. Among the buildings which surround the square are the old **South African Republic Raadzaal** (Council Chambers) and **The Palace of Justice.** Both buildings are of historical interest and are similar in architectural design. The Palace of Justice today houses the Transvaal division of the Supreme Court and the Raadzaal can be visited by appointment.

All the main streets are accessible from Church Square, but most of the streets in Pretoria are long so plan routes carefully. Public transport is easily available as there are numerous public bus routes. Taxis, as well as three-wheeled vehicles known as city bugs are easily found.

In nearby Pretorius Street is the **Police Museum** which houses a display of gruesome exhibits, including instruments used in crimes.

On **Strijdom Square** there is a striking memorial to South Africa's fifth Prime Minister, Advocate J G Strijdom depicting a group of horses in a storm. Nearby is the **State Theatre**.

Head up Paul Kruger Street in the direction of the railway station and into Skinner Street. The **Museum of Science** is located here and features exhibits of space and technology. Also in Skinner Street, the **Staats Model School** is housed in the library and is best-known as the place from which the young Winston Churchill, then working as a war correspondent, escaped in 1899 following his capture one month earlier near Estcourt.

The **Transvaal Museum of Natural History**, also located in Paul Kruger Street, houses an extensive collection of mammals, birds and fossils. **City Hall**, with its massive clock tower containing thirty-two bells, is located opposite. The building is bordered by lovely gardens with enchanting fountains and murals.

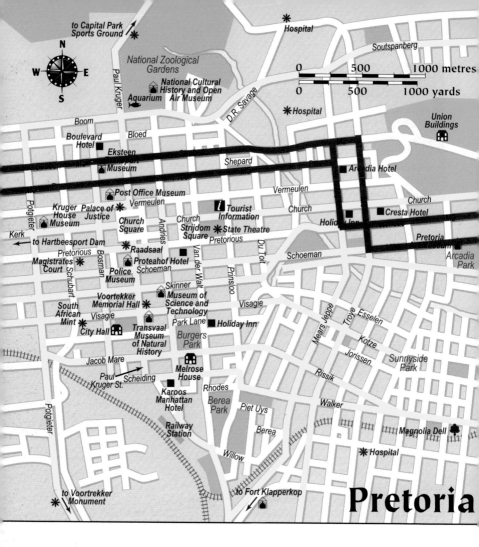

to Capital Park
Sports Ground

N
W   E
S

National Zoological
Gardens

Paul Kruger

National Cultural
History and Open
Air Museum

Aquarium

D.R. Savage

Hospital

Soutspanberg

0   500   1000 metres
0   500   1000 yards

*Hospital

Union
Buildings

Boom

Boulevard
Hotel   Bloed

Eksteen

Museum   Shepard

Arcadia Hotel

Potgieter

Post Office Museum

Vermeulen

Kruger   Palace of
House   Justice
Museum   Church
Square

Church
Square

Church
Strijdom
Square

Tourist
Information
State Theatre
Pretorious

Vermeulen

Church

Church

Holiday Inn

Cresta Hotel

Pretoria

Kerk
to Hartbeespoort Dam

Pretorious
Magistrates
Court

Bosman

Schubart

Raadsaal

Proteahof Hotel
Police
Museum

Schoeman

Skinner

Van der Walt

Schoeman

Prinsloo

Arcadia
Park

Voortrekker
Memorial Hall

South
African
Mint   Visagie

City Hall

Museum of
Science and
Technology

Park Lane

Transvaal
Museum
of Natural
History

Burgers
Park

Visagie

Holiday Inn

Mears

Jeppe

Troye

Esselen

Kotze

Jorissen

Sunnyside
Park

Jacob Mare

Paul
Kruger St.   Scheiding

Melrose
House

Rhodes

Rissik

Walker

Karoos
Manhattan
Hotel

Berea
Park

Piet Uys

Magnolia Dell

Potgieter

Railway
Station

Berea

Willow

to Voortrekker
Monument

to Fort Klapperkop

*Hospital

Pretoria

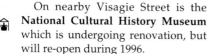

On nearby Visagie Street is the
National Cultural History Museum
which is undergoing renovation, but
will re-open during 1996.

   Melrose House is one of the oldest
buildings in Pretoria situated on Jacob
Maré Street. It was built in 1886 and it
was here that the Treaty of Vereeniging
was signed in 1902, signalling the end
of the Anglo-Boer War. It is a beautiful
Victorian building containing period
furniture, stained glass windows and
an excellent doll collection.

   Another landmark is the **Railway
Station** which was designed by re-

Opposite top: The majestic Voortrekker
Monument on the outskirts of Pretoria.
Opposite: Jacaranda blooms adorn the
skyline of Pretoria.

---

nowned South African architect, Sir
Herbert Baker. Return to Church
Square and head down Church Street
to **Paul Kruger's House**, now a
museum and national monument. It
is a modest bungalow which has
been restored and contains many
possessions that belonged to the man
who was president of the former South
African republic from 1883 to 1900.

From here, it is a short walk to the old cemetery on the corner of D F Malan Street where **Hero's Acre** is the resting place for many South African leaders including Paul Kruger, Commandant General Andries Pretorius, Advocate J G Strijdom and the 'architect' of apartheid, Dr H F Verwoerd, who was assassinated in 1966.

The **National Zoological Gardens** in Boom Street houses the largest collection of animals in South Africa with over 140 mammals and 320 bird species. A cable-car ride to the top of the hill affords excellent views over surrounding parklands, and from the summit the walk down leads past the enclosures. The night tours are worth joining, but need advance booking.

One of the finest collections of South African art can be found in the **Pretoria Art Museum** in the nearby **Arcadia Park**. It houses the famous Michaelis collection along with many works by South Africa's best-known artists.

The **Union Buildings** are a familiar landmark to all South Africans and were the setting for the inauguration of President Nelson Mandela after the 1994 democratic elections. The building was designed by Sir Herbert Baker, and on completion in 1913 became the South African seat of government. The magnificent gardens stretch down to the city and feature a statue of General Louis Botha, (first Prime Minister of South Africa), the Pretoria War memorial and the Delville Wood Memorial. The Tourist Office can provide details on tours of the Union buildings.

No trip to Pretoria would be complete without visiting the **Voortrekker Monument** and **Museum**. The Afrikaner government which came to power in 1948 quickly started work on this massive granite monument to celebrate their victory after a century-long struggle for nationwide power. The friezes in the **Hall of Heroes** recount the story of the Great Trek and the 'Day of the Vow' when the Voortrekkers achieved an incredible victory over the Zulus after making a vow to God. Each year, at noon on 16 December, a beam of sunlight shines through an aperture in the upper dome onto the cenotaph where the words *Ons vir jou, Suid Afrika* (We for thee, South Africa) are inscribed. Every aspect of the monument is dedicated to the courage of the Voortrekkers and for all Afrikaners, it is a shrine to their memory.

There are many beautiful parks and gardens to visit in and around Pretoria including the **National Botanical Gardens** located 10km (6 miles) east of the city on the Brummeria Road. It is a lovely place to picnic or walk and enjoy the varied species of indigenous trees and shrubs cultivated here.

The **Austin Robert's Bird Sanctuary** is a fenced sanctuary housing an excellent collection of indigenous birds all living in a natural environment. The sanctuary overlooks a dam which also attracts a variety of waterbirds. The **Wonderboom Nature Reserve** is named after a 1,000-year-old wild fig tree which grows within the reserve with branches that extend over 55m (180ft).

As most of the overseas embassies are situated in Pretoria a diverse and interesting selection of places to eat have sprung up in or near the city centre. Sunnyside, a few kilometres from the centre, has a wide variety of good restaurants.

There is a bustling flea market every Saturday at the State Theatre and every Sunday at **Sunnypark**, where a selection of arts and crafts are sold. The Art in the Park exhibition is held on the last Saturday of each month at Magnolia Dell.

AROUND PRETORIA

A trip to the **Sammy Marks Museum** and the **Pioneer Open-Air Museum** is a 46km (29 mile) round-trip travelling eastwards along Church Street in the direction of Silverton. The Pioneer Open-Air Museum is situated in an old thatched farmhouse and is the original home of David Botha, one of the early pioneers. There are interesting demonstrations of bread-baking in an outdoor oven, soap-making, coffee-roasting and corn-stamping. Eight kilometres (5 miles) further along is the Sammy Marks Museum (Zwartkoppies Hall), named after Samuel Marks, another of South Africa's renowned early pioneers. He was born in Lithuania and emigrated to South Africa in 1868 to become one of the country's greatest entrepreneurs, playing an important role in the development of the ZAR. The museum houses most of the original Victorian furniture belonging to the Marks family.

The nearest coastline is over 700km (435 miles) away, so many Pretorians escape at weekends and holidays to the Hartebeespoort Dam. It is situated 35km (22 miles) west of the city and is a popular recreational area. The dam is surrounded by dramatic scenery and the drive from Pretoria offers many beautiful views. There are excellent watersport facilities, walking trails, an aquarium, snake park and nature reserve on its banks. On one side of the dam is the Oom Tan Malie se Winkel, an old-fashioned trading post selling home-made chutneys, biltong and souvenirs. The grounds are open daily from sunrise to sunset and they are noted for the Sunday *braai* lunch cooked here. The Hartebeespoort cableway offers excellent views of the area from the highest point of the Magaliesburg mountain range.

The nearby **De Wildt Cheetah Research Centre** offers tours Saturday and Sunday at 9am and 1.30pm and on Thursday at 10am. The tours last approximately two hours and incorporate a game drive in an open vehicle and feeding of various endangered species including cheetah. It is essential to make advance reservations and only children over the age of six are allowed on the tours.

One of the daily tours of the **Premier Diamond Mine** is well worth the visit. It is situated 50km (31 miles) from Pretoria and is the site where the famous Cullinan diamond was found. As the Cape was under British rule at the time of its discovery, the diamond was presented to King Edward VII. It took two years to cut the 3,106 carat diamond into nine major stones including the 530 carat Great Star of Africa and the Lesser Star of Africa, both of which are set in the British Crown Jewels.

The Crocodile River Arts and Crafts Ramble is a self-guided driving tour of the artists colony along the banks of the Crocodile River. The artists open their homes, studios and workshops to visitors and offer a good selection of pottery, paintings, jewellery, furniture and sculptures for sale. The artists will also give practical demonstrations of their craft and provide visitors with soft drinks and lively conversation. The route is officially open on the first weekend of each month, but many will let you view by appointment at other times. It makes for an interesting day visit and there are many restaurants to be found, as well as places to stay overnight. A route map is available from the Tourist Information Office.

The **Old Doornkloof Farm** at **Irene**, 16km (10 miles) south of Pretoria, was the home of former Prime Minister Jan Smuts. The modest house, constructed from timber and galvanised iron, has been declared a national monument. It contains much of the original furniture

29

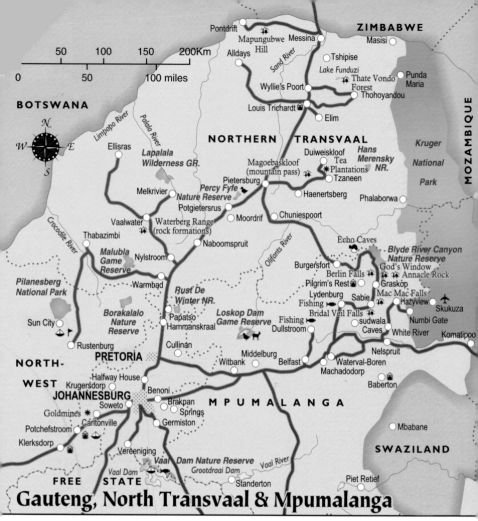

Gauteng, North Transvaal & Mpumalanga

Map labels:

ZIMBABWE

Pontdrift
Mapungubwe Hill
Messina
Masisi
Alldays
Tshipise
Sand River
Lake Funduzi
Thate Vondo Forest
Punda Maria
Wyllie's Poort
Thohoyandou
Louis Trichardt
Elim

BOTSWANA

Limpopo River
Palala River

NORTHERN TRANSVAAL

Kruger National Park

MOZAMBIQUE

Ellisras
Lapalala Wilderness GR.
Magoebaskloof (mountain pass)
Duiweiskloof
Hans Merensky NR.
Tea Plantations
Tzaneen
Pietersburg
Melkrivier
Percy Fyfe Nature Reserve
Haenertsberg
Phalaborwa
Potgietersrus
Moordrif
Chuniespoort
Vaalwater
Waterberg Range (rock formations)
Thabazimbi
Naboomspruit
Echo Caves
Crocodile River
Malubla Game Reserve
Nylstroom
Olifants River
Burgersfort
Blyde River Canyon Nature Reserve
God's Window
Annacle Rock
Pilanesberg National Park
Warmbad
Berlin Falls
Pilgrim's Rest
Graskop
Mac Mac Falls
Rust De Winter NR.
Lydenburg
Sabie
Hazyview
Skukuza
Fishing
Bridal Veil Falls
Sun City
Borakalalo Nature Reserve
Papatso
Hammanskraal
Loskop Dam Game Reserve
Fishing
Dullstroom
sudwala Caves
White River
Numbi Gate
Komatipoo
Rustenburg
Cullinan
Nelspruit
PRETORIA
Middelburg
Witbank
Belfast
Waterval-Boren
Machadodorp
Halfway House
NORTH-WEST
Krugersdorp
Baberton
JOHANNESBURG
Benoni
Brakpan
MPUMALANGA
Goldmines
Soweto
Springs
Carltonville
Germiston
Potchefstroom
Mbabane
Klerksdorp
SWAZILAND
Vereeniging
Vaal Dam Nature Reserve
Grootdraai Dam
Vaal River
Vaal Dam
Standerton
Piet Retief
FREE STATE

Scale: 0 50 100 150 200Km / 0 50 100 miles

---

and artifacts. The grounds offer excellent picnic and *braai* facilities as well as tea rooms and a campsite.

Tswaing (meaning 'place of salt') **Enviro Museum** is 40km (25 miles) north-west of Pretoria. One of the best-preserved meteorite craters in the world has been converted here into the first museum of its kind in South Africa. The crater contains a unique saline lake which leaves soda and salt deposits when it evaporates. The museum aims to educate visitors about the impact of meteorites on the earth and its environment. Numerous research projects are carried out within the museum.

Pretoria to Tzaneen
362km (225 miles)

It is advisable to purchase anti-malaria tablets at a pharmacy before leaving Pretoria. They are widely available and effective immediately. Malaria is still present in some areas of the Lowveld, but it is not particularly prevalent nowadays. Some rivers have bilharzia which, along with the crocodiles, make them unsafe for swimming.

Leave Pretoria on the N1, the Great North Road, which runs up to the Zimbabwe border. This was principally the same route taken by the

Above: Tea is one of the agricultural products which grow in abundance in the area around Tzaneen.

early Voortrekkers on the Great Trek north and several town names and monuments are indicative of the clashes between the early pioneers and tribes people.

After 100km (62 miles), the road passes the town of **Warmbad** (Warm Baths), renowned for its mineral springs. The hot springs have been developed into a holiday resort and recreational complex with indoor and outdoor mineral pools, squash, tennis and a wave pool. This is an excellent place to relax and enjoy the reputed healing powers of the mineral baths. Accommodation is available in both the spa and in the town.

Nylstroom (Nile Stream) is the next town and was named by the Voortrekkers, who discovered the nearby river in full flood and believed it to be the unknown source of the River Nile. Further along the road is **Naboomspruit**, another area of health spas built up around mineral springs. Follow the sign to 'mineral baths' and the road leads past one spa after another.

The next town of **Potgietersrus** was named after the Afrikaner Commandant General Piet Potgieter. On the northern outskirts of town is the **Nature Reserve and Game Breeding Centre** which specialises in the propagation of rare species from all over the world, including the West African pygmy hippo and the South American llama.

From Potgietersrus follow the N1 to **Pietersburg**, capital of Northern Transvaal. This pretty town with wide tree lined streets is located on top of the Pietersburg plateau and has an invigorating climate with cool nights.

The Satour office can provide information on the surrounding areas and
there are many places of historical
interest to visit in the area.

The **Bakone Malapa Museum** is
situated 9km (5 miles) south of
Pietersburg on the Chuniespoort/
Burgersfort road. There is a traditional
kraal located here where tribesmen
demonstrate age-old skills and visitors
can also see examples of ancient rock
paintings. The information centre is
well-stocked with details on local
history.

Return to Pietersburg and take the
R71 towards **Tzaneen**, home of the
University of the North — the largest
African university in the country. The
Zion Christian Church has the largest
African following of all churches in
South Africa and is a spectacular sight
at Easter when worshippers descend
on the area.

The area was opened up in the 1860s
when the discovery of gold in the
mountains brought fortune hunters
from around the world in search of
wealth. The sub-tropical climate with
high summer rainfall is ideally suited
for the abundant fruit plantations
which grow here. Mists are common
which brought about its name of the
'land of silver mists'. The small town of
Haenertsburg is famed for its trout
streams and the Cherry Blossom and
Azalea Festival which is held in the
spring. This spectacular route through
the **Magoebaskloof Mountain Pass**
starts on the edge of the northern
escarpment and drops 600m (1,968ft)
down to the Letaba valley, in less than
5km (3 miles). The road passes through
a splendid indigenous forest region
with a hiking trail that leads to the
northern slopes of the mountain. The
nearby **Debegeni Falls** cascade 80m
(262ft) into a deep pot-like pool which
is safe for swimming. Care should be
taken however as the rocks can be
slippery.

The R71 road winds through extensive tea plantations until it reaches
Tzaneen situated at the foot of the
Drakensberg mountains on the south
bank of the Letaba River. The name is
derived from the phrase 'round basket'
as its excellent year-round climate
guarantees a high agricultural yield
from this fertile area. Fruit (including
avocados, mangos, bananas and pawpaw), vegetables, nuts and coffee are the
main produce of the area. Tours through
tea plantations can be arranged.

The area offers some charming
accommodation, including the award-
winning Coach House Hotel with its
English country hotel atmosphere
and incredible views towards the
Drakensberg escarpment. There is an
excellent *a la carte* restaurant serving a
wide range of local dishes. The nearby
King's Warden Hotel is situated in
picturesque gardens and has a limited
number of luxury rooms.

The Magoebaskloof Holiday Resort
is situated on the R71 Pietersburg road
between Magoebaskloof and Tzaneen.
The resort offers self-catering accommodation in rondavels as well as an *a la
carte* restaurant serving tasty dishes.

A visit to the picturesque little
village of **Duiwelskloof** ('Devil's
Valley') is worthwhile, especially
during the summer when the streets
are a blaze of colour from the
bougainvillea and frangipani trees.
There are various enjoyable forest
drives, most notably to the cycad forest
in the **Modjadji Nature Reserve**,
which has the world's largest
collection of these ancient plants.

Tzaneen to Thohoyandou
210km (131 miles)

Take the R36 north of Tzaneen and
continue to just beyond Soekmekaar,
where there is a left turn to Ga-
Ramokgopa. After a few kilometres
there is a column on the left side of

the road marking the point where the road crosses the **Tropic of Capricorn**.

The town of **Louis Trichardt** was named after a Voortrekker leader who farmed the area in 1837. It was from here that Trichardt began his ill-fated journey to Lourenço Marques (now Maputo) in Mozambique where half his followers died within days of arrival from a disease they contracted along the way. There are various monuments to the memory of this pioneer and his harsh trek northward by ox-wagon.

The region is extremely fertile and produces plentiful quantities of exotic and citrus fruits, avocados and tea.

The nearby **Schoemansdal White Pioneer Settlement** on the R522 provides a fascinating insight into the interaction between the different communities in the region and their dependence on nature for their survival. There are demonstrations every day except Monday.

Take the busy R524 west from Louis Trichardt towards **Thohoyandou**. This is the Venda region which, until 1994, was a self-governing homeland for the Vhavenda people. Although it is today considered part of the Northern Transvaal, the administrative change has not altered the Vhavenda people's cultural identity, and it is still referred to as Venda.

This land of rugged beauty and legend, just south of the Limpopo River, has an abundance of tumbling waterfalls and streams earning it the name 'Land of a Hundred Streams'. The area is dominated by the Soutspanberg mountains, which bisect the entire country in a series of mountain ridges, up to the savannah plains of the arid Malonga Flats in the north. Centuries ago, the peaceful BaNgona tribe settled in the area, followed by the Vhatavhatsinde who were regarded as powerful medicine men and hailed from north of the Limpopo. In the early eighteenth century, the Vhasenzi and Vhalemba people arrived from what is now Zimbabwe and Chief Dimbanyika established his *kraal* in the mountains of the Soutpansberg at Dzata, ruins of which can still be seen today.

Eventually these different tribes united under Chief Thohoyandou, (meaning 'the head of the elephant') and the nation of Venda was born. Thohoyandou was a powerful chief who mysteriously disappeared whilst attempting to enlist supporters to prevent his brothers' attempt to overthrow him. His importance to the people of Venda remains to this day, and they believe that one day he will return and the nation will be restored to its former glory.

Today the majority of the population in the area is made up of the MaKhwinde and Vhatavhatsinde. The Balemba people form a small group of the population and are believed to be descended from Judaic-Arab traders. They are renowned for their skilful metal work.

Although the area was opened up in the 1860s when gold was discovered in the mountains, it remains extremely underdeveloped, although the level of highway construction work indicates it will not remain this way for long.

The Vhavenda are hospitable and friendly people. However, it is recommended when visiting their sacred places to be respectful of the fact that virtually every aspect of their life is affected by age-old legends and superstitions. This folklore also affects the decoration of their homes, arts, crafts and tribal dancing, which make it a fascinating area for tourists, particularly those with an interest in art.

Dancing is an integral part of the Vhavenda life and is best witnessed at the initiation ceremonies for young girls held between June and August each year. It is called the *domba*, (the python dance) and the significance of its name lies in the rhythm of the dance and the belief that the python is the God of Fertility. The boys are initiated at the *murundu*, an initiation hut built by the elders of the *kraal*. After they have been circumcised they must squat in an icy river for six consecutive nights to relieve their pain and wash away their boyhood.

Thohoyandou is a bustling lively town and many tourists are attracted to the hotel and casino here — the Venda Sun.

Visit the Ditike Craft House where arts and crafts, including traditional cooking pots are sold. The pots were originally used for storing food or liquids and are made without the use of a potter's wheel. The decoration is applied by engraving interesting geometric designs with graphite. This art is slowly dying out making these pots collectors' items. There are also traditional baskets, mats and wood sculptures on sale. The Venda Tourism Office is located here and will provide maps of the area as well as organise tours and accommodation. At the small **State Museum** there is a display of traditional Venda Huts and a replica of a chief's home.

The main attraction in the area is the **Thathe Vondo Forest** which has both exotic plantations and indigenous forests. It is traversed by attractive rivers and sparkling waterfalls and contains the **Holy Forest**, which according to local people is the resting ground of ancestral chiefs. Legend tells that the area is protected by a lion spirit who is believed to be the reincarnation of one of these great chiefs. Although tourists are permitted to drive, it is forbidden to walk through the forest for fear of disturbing spirits at rest there.

Lake Funduzi is the centrepiece of Vhavenda mysticism. It is surrounded by mountains and is reputed to have been formed when a landslide blocked the course of the Mutale River. It is believed that a Python God lives in the lake, which is fabled to be a remnant of the water which covered the earth before creation.

Beer and food are left annually on a sacred stone for the Python God. It is only possible to visit the lake with prior permission from the chief and priestess of the lake, although it can be seen from the winding road which runs through the hills.

Thohoyandou to Kruger National Park
277km (172 miles)

Take the R524 to the Punda Maria Gate of the **Kruger National Park** — one of the most famous national parks in the world and the second largest game reserve in Africa. Occupying nearly two million hectares, the park is roughly the same size as Wales. It is 350km (217 miles) in length and stretches up to 60km (37 miles) in width. The park is naturally bordered by the Limpopo River in the north, the Crocodile River in the south and the Lebombo Mountains which separate it from Mozambique.

Kruger supports the widest variety of wildlife of all the parks of Africa and has become the role model for other reserves on the continent. Five rivers cross the park which is home to 147 species of mammal, 507 species of bird and 49 species of fish. The Park has large numbers of the 'big five' — lion, leopard, rhino (both black and white) elephant and buffalo.

Opposite top: Leopard are commonly seen in Kruger National Park.
Opposite: Burchell's zebra in Kruger National Park.

President Paul Kruger, after whom the park is named, first initiated the idea of wildlife conservation in the 1850s. Various laws were passed during the late 1800s attempting to restrict hunting in the game reserves and prevent the potential devastation of the game population.

The National Parks Board was instituted to run the park in 1926 when it was first opened to the public, and today they operate strict control over the numbers of visitors particularly in the high season. Accommodation, even camping, can sometimes be impossible during this time and it is always advisable to make advance reservations.

No open safari vehicles are allowed in the park and it is forbidden to get out of a car in unprotected areas. The gates open at sunrise and close at sunset and visitors should allow adequate time to either leave the park before sunset, or be within the grounds of their camp as heavy fines are imposed on latecomers.

The speed limit is 50 kph (31 mph) on tarred roads and 40 kph (25 mph) on gravel so one should not attempt to tour the park in one day. It is also recommended to drive slowly in order not to miss sightings of the animals. It can sometimes be useful to glance through the visitor's book at each rest camp, where visitors note what they have seen and where. The wardens and guides at the camps are also very helpful and can advise on the areas that animals favour at certain times of the day.

Accommodation varies throughout the park from basic campsites to fully self-contained chalets. It is advisable to book all accommodation in advance, particularly at weekends and during peak periods. There are a number of wilderness trails and visitors can join walking safaris which last up to three days and are led by experienced guides. The National Parks Board can provide information on these trails and reservations should be made well in advance as they are very popular.

Apart from the National Parks Board accommodation, there are a number of private game reserves situated close to the western boundary of the Park. All these reserves offer luxurious accommodation and provide game drives for their guests led by experienced guides in open safari vehicles.

The climate is subtropical with summer rains between October and March when the park is green and lush. It is also extremely hot, and long drives in vehicles not equipped with air-conditioning, are unwise. Winter is very dry and warm and the best time to visit the Kruger National Park as the bush is less dense which makes game spotting easier.

From Punda Maria, follow the main road south through the northern part of the park. This is the quietest part of Kruger and there is abundant growth of the low Mopani shrub. This makes it perfect elephant country and is where nearly two-thirds of the Park's elephant herds live.

The **Olifants camp** has one of the best settings of all the park's rest camps as it is situated beside the Lebombo mountains and offers magnificent views to the Olifants River below.

The camp is located in the central area of the park and its grassy vegetation attracts large herds of grazers including wildebeest, buffalo, antelope and zebra, as well as lion and cheetah. There is a scenic drive along the two rivers in the area, where elephant, kudu, zebra and impala are usually easily spotted. The river obviously attracts the animals which makes game viewing here very rewarding when they venture down to the water during the day to either drink or graze.

Olifants to Satara camp
54km (34 miles)

It is worth leaving Olifants early to enjoy a good game drive en-route to **Satara camp**. Satara is a perfect place to be based for visitors wishing to explore some of the southern regions of the park. There are large concentrations of game in this area and the three dams and six waterholes make it a good place for viewing. Some of the rare species found here include white and black rhino, nyala and wild and sabled dog. The camp has an education centre and holds regular slide shows and discussions on conservation issues, followed by a question time with the rangers.

There are a number of excellent rest camps in the south of the park, including the main administration centre of **Skukuza**, where there are several museums, a library, shops, a bank, a post office, a church and a football pitch. The Visitor's Centre provides information on the fascinating history of the park, along with charts of the various species of animals found here.

Satara to Blyde River Canyon
191km (119 miles)

It is best to leave the park at dawn in order to enjoy a final game drive on the way to the gate. Leave at Orpen Gate and follow the R531. The escarpment which runs through the area divides the highveld and lowveld and there is an immediate contrast between the arid vegetation of the Kruger National Park and the lush vistas of the highveld. In season, the roadside fruit stalls are laden with colourful produce from the area including avocados, mangoes, bananas, oranges and lemons.

In the highveld the air is crisp, clear and invigorating and the verdant landscape is dotted with cascading waterfalls plunging over the edge of the escarpment.

Follow the R531 and the R36. There are incredible views over the lowveld where the road climbs up the mountain to the **J G Strijdom Tunnel**. The road leads through the **Abel Erasmus Pass** which rises 800m (2,624ft) within 24km (15 miles), snaking its way around steep curves and bends.

Take the R532 and turn left towards the Blyde River Canyon. There is a signpost to the **Echo Caves** which are perhaps not worth the detour as the Sudwala Caves are far more spectacular. Accommodation is available at the Aventura Blyderivierspoort resort perched on the edge of the canyon, or 50km (31 miles) further on in **Graskop**. The Graskop Hotel in the main street is reasonably-priced for bed and breakfast and the Hardidar Restaurant in the hotel is recommended by locals. The Blyde Lodge in Louis Trichardt Street offers good value hotel and self-catering accommodation and there is an *a la carte* restaurant on the premises. Harry's Pancake Place in Louis Trichardt Street serves delicious pancakes and is a popular place to eat

The **Blyde River Canyon** starts at the confluence of the Blyde and Treur rivers. It is a gigantic gorge, 600m (1,968ft) in depth and 26km (16 miles) long. The road hugs the canyon and offers spectacular views. The best lookout is to follow the signs to the **Three Rondavels**, the name given to the natural rock towers which stand sentinel over the gorge, a few kilometres from the adventure resort in the direction of Graskop. The view across the lowveld is stunning, especially at sunset, when the rocks are painted in magical hues of reds and gold by the setting sun. There are a number of both short and long hiking trails and it is best to seek advice either from the

Above: The town of Pilgrim's Rest which has been recreated as a living museum. Opposite top: The spectacular Blyde River Canyon is over 600m (1,968ft) in depth. Opposite: From the lookout, visitors are afforded fabulous views of the Three Rondavels — the natural rock towers which tower above the gorge.

resort, or from the information centre close to Bourke's Luck potholes. Take the R532 in the direction of Graskop 56km (22 miles). **Bourke's Luck Potholes** are situated where the Blyde and Treur rivers meet, and were named after a digger who found large amounts of gold in the potholes. The action of the pebble-laden water has created cavities or 'potholes' in the rocks and a series of bridges and walkways allow visitors to walk around and view these.

The rivers were named after a party of Voortrekkers who ventured forth in search of better land. When they failed to return, their wives and children named the bank from where they departed Treur (meaning sorrow). Finally, when they saw their menfolk returning on the opposite river bank,

they named this side Blyde (meaning joyful).

Follow the signpost to the **Berlin Falls** where the river plunges 80m (262ft) into a deep pool. The **Lisbon Falls Waterfall** is situated a little further along the R532. On a clear day it is possible to see as far as neighbouring Mozambique from the lookout point of **God's Window** — 8km (5 miles) before Graskop, and clearly signposted left off the main road. The lookout affords magnificent views over the lowveld 1,000m (3,280ft) below. Visitors can follow a guided walk through the rainforest.

Graskop is primarily a forestry town perched on the edge of the Drakensberg escarpment. On the outskirts of the town there is an indigenous forest named 'Fairyland'.

Seventeen km (10 miles) along the R533 from Graskop, down a beautiful winding road, is the early gold rush town of **Pilgrim's Rest**. The town was purchased in 1974 by the Transvaal Administration who recreated the entire village as a living museum. All the buildings have been lovingly restored as testimony to the country's heritage of gold mining.

Gold was first discovered in 1873 in the stream near the town, by a digger known as 'Wheelbarrow' Patterson because he kept all his belongings in a wheelbarrow. He kept his find a secret until a few weeks later another prospector William Trafford found the gold. Trafford named the town Pilgrim's Rest, as he believed the gold would finally enable him to rest after his life-long search for riches. The town then experienced one of the greatest gold rushes on record, as thousands of adventurers flocked to the valley to seek their fortune. By 1881, the river gold was exhausted and the fortune hunters moved to new areas. There is an Information Office located in the museum building opposite the Royal Hotel.

The town's cemetery is worth a visit to see a number of interesting epitaphs on the headstones. The **'Robber's Grave'** marks the grave of a prospector who stole a claim and it faces north, instead of the traditional south as a mark of disrespect. The walk up to the cemetery is via a steep pathway from the front of the church.

There are curio shops and craft stalls, including some good tea rooms situated along the main road. There are also some interesting gifts to be purchased here, although they can be expensive.

Head back towards Graskop turning right onto the R532. The road leads through lush grasslands to the **Mac Mac Falls** named after the number of Scottish and Irish prospectors who

flocked to the area in the 1870s in search of gold. A path down the escarpment leads to a viewpoint at the side of the falls where one can watch the sparkling waters tumble over the edge of the cliff into a densely-wooded chasm. There is a picnic area with beautiful pools where swimming is permitted.

Continue along the R532 to the pretty town of **Sabie**. Set in the foothills of the Drakensberg, Sabie is renowned for its timber industry. The magnificent pine plantations which surround the town make up the largest man-made forest in the world and supply half the country's timber. The **Cultural Historical Forestry Museum** 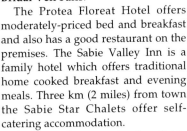 is well-laid out and has various exhibits on the wood and paper industry in South Africa. Travelling west from Sabie, the road leads to the **Lone Creek Waterfall**, and after a ten-minute walk into the forest, to the **Bridal Veil Falls**.

The Protea Floreat Hotel offers moderately-priced bed and breakfast and also has a good restaurant on the premises. The Sabie Valley Inn is a family hotel which offers traditional home cooked breakfast and evening meals. Three km (2 miles) from town the Sabie Star Chalets offer self-catering accommodation.

An interesting excursion from Sabie is to the imposing **Sudwala Caves**. Follow the R532, R37 and then the R539 from where the caves are signposted. The caves were once the sanctuary of a Swazi tribe led by Captain Sudwala. They include fabulous stalagmites and stalactites tinted in shades of reds and yellow by the iron and manganese oxides. A magnificent sight is the **P R Owen Cavern** — a vast natural underground amphitheatre often used for concerts. It is unknown how far the caves extend into the mountains and a strange phenomenon is the undiscovered source of cool air which provides ventilation and maintains the caves at an even temperature of 20°C.

Knowledgeable guides conduct regular tours around the caves which last for approximately one hour. A five-hour tour into the deeper caves and **Crystal Chamber** can be arranged with prior notice.

Next door to the Sudwala Caves is **Dinosaur Park** where life-size models of prehistoric reptiles are situated in attractive gardens. The park has been particularly popular since the making of *Jurassic Park*.

Sabie to Ezelmui Valley, Swaziland 290km (180 miles)

Take the R537 from Sabie to Nelspruit via the pretty farming town of White River. **Nelspruit**, the capital of Mpumalanga, is a charming picturesque town with wide tree-lined streets situated on the banks of the Crocodile River. This is a rich agricultural area producing exotic fruits including avocados, mangoes, pawpaw, grenadillas (passion fruit), litchies and macadamia nuts. On display in the library gardens is the anchor of the *Dorothea*, a British cargo ship which sank in 1898 with a cargo of over one million rand worth of gold bullion, which was never recovered. The **Lowveld Botanic Gardens** are located on the White River Road and can be a welcome respite from the heat on summer days. There are a host of brightly-coloured indigenous plants on display and walks within the gardens, including one leading to the **Crocodile River Falls**.

Leave Nelspruit on the road which runs through the scenic **Crocodile Valley**. At certain times of the year the air is heavy with the heady scent of orange blossom from the orchards in the area.

At the turn-off towards Matsulu, there is a small market selling fresh fruit at bargain prices.

Continue on the road in the direction of **Komatipoort** followed by the R38 towards Barberton. The road leads through banana plantations and there are several mines in the area.

The peaceful town of **Barberton**, which nestles at the foot of the Makhonjwa mountains, was the centre of a gold rush in 1884 when brothers Fred and Harry Barber, along with their cousin, stumbled upon gold quartz. Almost overnight, a prospecting camp was established and the town which subsequently developed lured prospectors from all over the world.

When the Sheba Reef was discovered the following year, the suburb of Eureka City grew up, and by the end of 1886 the area boasted 200 bars and two stock exchanges. The gold deposits were soon exhausted and in 1888, the discovery of gold on the Witwatersrand marked the end of this gold boom. The ghost town of Eureka City and the ruins of the Sheba Mine remain to this day and make an interesting excursion.

Barberton is the last town before the Swaziland border, so it is essential to ensure that all your re-entry visas and papers into South Africa are in order. Leave Barberton on the R40 towards Bulembu which is initially tarred, but becomes a dirt road after a few miles. The views across the **Saddleback Pass** are incredible as the road winds over the imposing mountain range.

For most of the drive, a cableway is visible which is used to carry asbestos between Barberton and the mine at Havelock.

The small border post at **Bulembu** is the entry point into Swaziland, one of only three remaining kingdoms on the African continent, along with Lesotho and Morocco. The border is open from 8am to 4pm daily.

SWAZILAND

Swaziland is an extremely stable country, largely because it is composed of a homogenous population who share a common language, culture and a strong loyalty to their King and country. Economically, it is not particularly sound and relies heavily upon the income of its migrant workers in South Africa. However, tourism is gaining in economic importance as Swaziland has started to attract holidaymakers from afar, as well as becoming a popular weekend playground for South Africans keen to try their luck in the gambling resorts.

Swaziland is approximately the same size as Wales and is split into four regions, each of which is divided by altitude. It is bordered by South Africa on the north, south and west and by Mozambique in the east. The Swazi people are a welcoming, friendly nation keen to talk to visitors and exchange views and opinions on most subjects.

The origins of the Swazi people can be traced back to the 1600s and the arrival of the Nguni people from the great lakes of central and east Africa. Under the leadership of Dlamini II, forefather of today's royal clan, they settled along the Pongola River where it bisects the Lubombo Mountains. On his death, his grandson, Sobhuza I expanded their colonies to the north and west absorbing the Sotho, Tsonga and Nguni chiefdoms. The ever-present threat from the Zulus forced Sobhuza to move north and establish his headquarters at Ezulwini. He colonised the north as far as the Sabie River, bringing together many immigrants fleeing from the Zulus.

Sobhuza had the foresight to marry two of his daughters to the Zulu King Shaka, thereby bringing a period of peace to his nation. Legend tells that before his death he had a prophetic dream about 'the arrival of white people with hair like cattletails, carrying a book and money pieces'. He told his people to accept the white people and the book, but to refuse the money. True to his vision, British missionaries arrived in Swaziland in 1840 and nurtured a strong Catholic following. At this time the country was ruled by Msazi, after whom the name Swaziland originates. On his death he was acceded by his son, Mbandzeni, who sold two-thirds of the country for personal gain, in the form of concessions to prospectors after gold was discovered in 1879. There followed a period of chaos until the Boers took control of the administration of Swaziland in 1895.

Swaziland first became a British Protectorate after the Anglo-Boer War, and it was not until 1968 that it regained its independence under King Sobhuza II. The King's death in 1982 marked the end of the longest reigning monarch in the world and, in accordance with local custom, the country entered a seventy-two-day period of mourning. The struggle to find a successor was complicated as he had fathered over 600 children.

During this period, the Queen Regent reigned until the arrival of eighteen year-old, English-educated, Prince Makhosetive. He was crowned King Mswati III in 1986 and still rules as executive head of state and spiritual leader of his people. The Royal family are considered a fundamental part of Swazi life.

The Swazi people maintain age-old traditions and family life is considered extremely important. Families are usually large, and elders are treated with great respect. An integral part of Swazi culture is the role played by the *sangomas* and *inyangas*. Despite colonialist attempts to discredit the *inyanga* as witch doctors, about eighty percent of the population still consult them today. The *inyanga* is a respected member of the community and enjoys a high social position. His main function is divination, for which he uses bones, and the way they fall after being thrown, determine the interpretation. The *sangoma* is generally a woman and is a traditional healer.

Being a people devoted to tribal ceremonies, there are many which occur throughout the year including the *Tinkomo Temadluti* which honours the nation's ancestors. This is held every year in the first week of April and includes the entertaining spectacle of the *Sibhaca* dance. It is possible to attend this ceremony and enquiries should be made through the Tourist Board in Mbabane. It is essential to observe Swazi custom which restricts photography or recording certain parts of the ceremony. Anybody wishing to take photographs should submit applications in writing to the Government Information Service, PO Box 338, Mbabane.

Crafts are also an important part of Swazi culture, and throughout the country there are numerous stalls and centres displaying colourful goods, including baskets and mats, made by the traditional method of grass weaving. Swazi candles which come in all shapes and sizes are popular gifts.

From the border post the road leads through the town of **Bulembu** and its colourful miners houses built on terraces. Follow the signs to **Piggs Peak** which is about 22km (13 miles) on a mostly gravel road. The town was named after William Pigg, an early French prospector, who discovered a gold reef here. The land in the area has been bought by Swaziland Plantations and timber is now the major industry.

Tintsaba Crafts is a craft centre located at the Highlands Hotel which encourages rural craft development on a non-profit making basis. There are some unusual handicrafts to be found here, including the traditional 'Swazi loveletter' made from wildebeest tail threaded with beads. These are made by Swazi girls and handed to their chosen male to be worn at his waist. There are bushmen rock paintings protected by fencing at the **Nsangwini Shelter**.

The **Malolotja Nature Reserve** is situated about 35km (22 miles) in the direction of Mbabane on the King Mswati II Highway. It contains two of Swaziland's highest mountains and most spectacular waterfalls, including the **Malolotja Falls** which plunge 95m (312ft) into the waters below. There are a number of hiking trails which range from strenuous climbs to easy walks, as well as game drives. Apart from its abundant birdlife, one of the major attractions of the park are the luxuriant fields of wildflowers in the vicinity. Accommodation is available.

Continue on the main highway to Mbabane through the **Komati River Valley**. Along the side of the road are ramshackle craft stalls constructed from wood and stone, selling well-made arts and crafts. This is an excellent place to buy stone-carved animals as the prices are a fraction of those charged in South Africa.

The land here is overgrazed because of the Swazi belief that cattle symbolise wealth, and so few are slaughtered.

Entering **Mbabane**, the capital of Swaziland, follow the signs to the Tourist Office past **Swazi Plaza**, the main pedestrian precinct. There are some excellent shops here, including the African Fantasy Shop, a treasure-trove for those seeking unusual souvenirs.

The Swazi market is full of beautiful carvings, unusual pottery, baskets and mats. Whilst this is not the cheapest place in the country to shop, there is a wide variety of goods on sale, and it is worth negotiating prices. The fruit market is located next door, although it is usually cheaper and more interesting to buy from the roadside sellers throughout the kingdom. Alistair Miller Street is a good place for restaurants and there is quite a strong Portuguese flavour in the cuisine from the influence of neighbouring Mozambique.

Despite western influence, Swazi customs and tribal rituals are still part of their everyday life. It is not unusual to see a Swazi dressed in the *mahiya*, the colourful national costume, complete with spears and shield walking through the capital.

Most Swazi men and boys have a passion for the nation's favourite game — soccer. On Saturdays, makeshift pitches around the country are packed with supporters urging on their team.

Leaving Mbabane, the road is a notorious black spot where irresponsible drivers have caused accidents by trying to overtake on the steep bends and curves. The road leads through the **Ezulwini valley**, known locally as the 'Valley of Heaven', and passes through many of the kingdom's main tourist attractions.

The road is dotted with fine handicraft stalls and curio sellers. Beware of the vendors who sometimes jump into the road in an attempt to get cars to stop.

It is worth visiting the Art Industries Centre where a handful of independent workshops sell beads, earrings, pottery, traditional masks and leatherwork. At the back of the shops one can usually find the potters and craftsmen at work.

The Tea Road is 10km (6 miles) from Mbabane, just before the turning to the Timbali Caravan Park. Rich tea plantations once grew on these hills which undulate through beautiful scenery offering spectacular views over the valley and the royal area of Lobamba, across to the Mdzimba mountain

range. The road is gravel and steep in places, so drive carefully especially in the summer months when rain makes the road very slippery .

The Swazi Spa is an excellent resort for those looking for a relaxing break. It has a hot mineral spa bath and a jacuzzi (affectionately known as the 'Cuddle Puddle'), as well as a fully-equipped gymnasium.

The Royal Swazi Sun is further along and its casino lures many South Africans at weekends. There are two other Sun International hotels in the valley which offer a wide range of facilities for tourists. There are also numerous campsites and resorts in the area catering for all price ranges.

Accommodation is also available at the **Mlilwane Wildlife Sanctuary**, Swaziland's wildlife success story. In the 1940s the area was home to abundant wildlife, but hunting and modern farming methods virtually decimated the game population. Swaziland's renowned conservationist, Ted Reilly, was determined to protect the remaining herds and sought government support to proclaim a number of areas as game reserves. When his efforts failed, he turned his entire family farm into a wildlife sanctuary. During the 1960s, he gradually reintroduced animals into the area, and today, the herds in the park are so vast that they are able to donate game to stock other reserves around the kingdom. It is a beautiful park with many species of wildlife including hippo, giraffe, crocodile, warthog and impala. At 3pm every day, visitors can watch the animals being fed from behind the safety of a stone wall. The Hippo Haunt restaurant has an unusual menu featuring a variety of game, including warthog and impala. The rest area is one of the finest in the kingdom with thatched huts and camping facilities centred around a dam. There are numerous facilities including horse riding trails through the reserve, as well as night game tours which require advance booking.

Due to recent radical conservation measures, the kingdom can now boast six major game and nature reserves which provides sanctuary to many endangered species, including the white and black rhino and elephant. Poaching is an incessant problem because of the easy access across Swaziland's borders from neighbouring countries like Mozambique. The game reserves work relentlessly to protect their animals, and snares and observation towers are a feature of some parks.

The nearby **Mantenga Falls** are stunning and are one of the most photographed attractions in the kingdom. At the nearby Swazi Ethnic Village and Copperland, crafts produced by handicapped people are sold. Mantenga Craft is further along on the right and the main shop is primarily used by tour buses. Although the products are fixed in price, they can be expensive. It is worth stopping, however, to see the potter's workshop and watch these craftsmen at work.

The **Houses of Parliament** are at nearby Lombana and while this imposing building may only be photographed from the outside, tours may be arranged at times when parliament is not sitting. Men are required to wear a jacket and tie, and women smart dresses (no trousers) in order to be allowed into the public gallery to listen to debates. Enquire at the museum next door.

The **National Museum** has a comprehensive display of Swazi culture and traditions which provide an excellent insight into the heritage of these people. Another interesting aspect is the photographic display of significant historical events and visitors to the kingdom. There is a traditional Swazi homestead outside the museum consisting of four beehive huts. A guide takes visitors through each one explaining their use and the hierarchy of the family.

The King's residence, the **Embo State Palace** is nearby, but it is not open to the public and it is forbidden to photograph the building.

The **Somholo Stadium** is used for soccer matches and rock concerts — Eric Clapton and Joan Armatrading are two of the international artists who have performed there in recent years. The Stadium is also host to the annual independence celebrations and the reed dance ceremonies.

At certain times, the King will call the people of the nation to the Royal Kraal to advise and discuss issues affecting the kingdom. Clothed in full traditional dress, the King and his ministers, the Liqoqo, face the sacred hills, while the people of the nation face the King and are permitted to voice their opinions on certain topics. Resolutions made as a result of this ceremony are legalised in parliament.

The **Tishweshwe Cottage Crafts** runs a group of colourfully-decorated thatched cottages at **Malkerns**. A project was incepted approximately fourteen years ago to encourage local people in the art of weaving, stone carving, wood sculpture, needlework and pottery. It has grown rapidly and today promotes the individual talent and crafts produced in the cottages. In addition, the shop displays handicrafts from all over southern Africa.

The Malandelas Farmhouse and Restaurant is next to Tishweshwe Crafts and the fare consists of all home-grown produce. It is definitely worth stopping here to enjoy either a snack or a delicious, nourishing lunch.

The **Swazi Candles factory** where these unique candles are produced is also nearby. They make the perfect souvenir with their brightly-coloured wax layers often shaped into such animals as frogs, elephant and rhino. Visitors are welcome to visit the farmhouse to watch the candles being made, and prices here are a fraction those in South Africa.

Ezulwini Valley to Mkuze, South Africa 237km (147 miles)

Continue onto **Manzini**, formerly the capital and now the main industrial town of Swaziland. Its original name until 1960 was Bremersdorp, after the one-time owner of the hotel and trading store, Albert Bremer. He ran a flourishing business during the concession rush of the late nineteenth century, during which time it attracted adventurers and horse thieves and became synonymous with violence. The capital moved to Mbabane when the town was destroyed, after which the name was changed to Manzini meaning 'in the water'. Today, it is a bustling city, known as the 'hub' of the nation because of its location. Unfortunately, there have been recent reports of violence, especially around weekends and pay days.

Swaziland's main airport is situated 8km (5 miles) from Manzini and there are daily international and regional flights originating from here.

Leave Manzini on the MR 8 towards Big Bend/Lavumisa — where a new highway is under construction and the road is excellent. Shortly after Big Bend it passes the Swaziland Sugar Association and the drive continues through sugar plantations along a straight road. Sugar is the country's largest foreign exchange earner and its most important cash crop.

Leave Swaziland at the **Lavumisa/ Godlela border post** (open 7am-10pm) and return to South Africa in the KwaZulu-Natal province. The area from here to **Empangeni** was formerly

known as Zululand and has the largest concentration of game parks and private game ranches in the country nestling amidst majestic scenery. The KwaZulu-Natal province has its own separate parks board — the Natal Parks Board.

Over the centuries, much blood has been shed in battles over the control of this province. It was finally incorporated into Natal in 1897 after the Zulu nation was defeated. KwaZulu was later formed into a self-governing African state within Natal with Chief Buthelezi as its leader. Its seat of government is in **Ulundi**.

Since the restructuring of South Africa in 1994, the areas of KwaZulu and Natal have been combined and the two former capitals of Ulundi and Pietermaritzburg respectively share provincial capital status.

Follow the N2 along the coast and the signs to **Mkuze Game Reserve** in the Ubombo Mountains, between the natural boundary of the Mkuze River. The reserve covers over 30,000 hectares (74,100 acres) and is situated in a tree-covered plain characterised by fever trees and fossil remains. It has a large black rhino population, as well as giraffe, leopard, crocodile and various antelope species. There are three strategically-placed hides at **Bube**, **Msinga** and **Malibali** which make observation and photography easier. Supervised bush trails operate from April to the end of October. There are 400 bird species, particularly in the vicinity of the **Nsumu Pan** which also boasts large herds of hippo and Nile crocodile. At the Natal Parks Board rest camps there is a wide range of accommodation including bungalows, rustic huts and camping.

Opposite top: Cheetah family at rest.
Opposite: The Umfolozi Game Reserve contains the largest herd of white rhino in Africa.

Mkuze to Hluhluwe/Umfolozi
98km (61 miles)

From Mkuze return to the N2 heading in the direction of the beautiful and isolated **Sodwana Bay**. Although it will add a further 200km (124 miles) along a gravel road to the journey, it is a must for anyone interested in fishing or scuba diving. It is advisable to make arrangements before travel as accommodation is limited.

Sodwana Bay National Park is a haven for fishermen and diving enthusiasts. The park is situated amidst forested dunes, white sandy beaches and boasts offshore coral reefs comparable to the Great Barrier Reef in Australia. There are daily excursions in December and January to view the breeding ground of the rare loggerhead and leatherback turtles. These graceful marine creatures were saved from extinction by the worthwhile efforts of the KwaZulu Division of Nature Conservation and the people of Tongaland.

After returning to the N2 follow the signs to the **Hluhluwe Game Reserve**. Hluhluwe was established in 1897 and is one of the oldest game reserves in Africa. It surrounds the deep valley of the Hluhluwe River and neighbours the Umfolozi Game Reserve. It is one of the most scenic reserves in the country and is famous for black and white rhino, as well as lion, buffalo, giraffe, leopard, cheetah, hippo, crocodile and elephant. The best areas for game viewing is either the northern section or the extreme south, but there are no guarantees. There are some beautiful places to picnic and watch the monkeys and birds. There is a site museum displaying the traditional cultures and heritage of the Zulu people, as well as lectures and slide shows.

Boat trips on the Hluhluwe River can be arranged.

The **Umfolozi Game Reserve** is the largest game reserves in Natal covering an area of almost 48,000 hectares (118,560 acres). The rugged terrain is enclosed by the White Umfolozi and Black Umfolozi rivers and contains the largest herd of white rhino in Africa. Their name, however is deceptive as they are not white and it derives from the Dutch word meaning square-lipped which is the feature that distinguishes them from the black rhino. Umfolozi is a very successful breeding ground for white rhino and today they are exported to parks all over South Africa and various countries overseas. Other wildlife includes buffalo, cheetah, leopard, hyaena, various species of antelope, crocodile and over 300 bird species. There are several viewing points close to waterholes and rivers to allow for optimum game viewing .

There is a wide variety of accommodation available at the rest camps ranging from rustic huts, camping facilities and chalets. There are also cooks available who will prepare and cook any food brought along by visitors to the camp.

A unique aspect of the reserve is that half the camp has been declared a wilderness area where no cars are permitted. There is, however, some excellent game viewing on foot, and three-day trails under the supervision of a ranger can be arranged.

Hluhluwe to St Lucia
80km (50 miles)

Leave the park on the R618 towards Mtubatuba, and take the R620 following signs to **St Lucia Reserve**. The lake is the centre of the reserve and is a rapidly-expanding holiday resort mainly geared to fishing — especially grunter, mullet, bream and salmon. The St Lucia conservation area stretches 5km (3 miles) northwards from the estuary.

The game reserve is made up of the lake and 37,000 hectares (91,390 acres) of scrub, grassland and swamp forest. Sand dunes separate the lake from the Indian Ocean and there is a prolific birdlife including pelicans, fish eagles and saddlebills. There are also over 400 hippos here, as well as reedbuck, bushbuck, impala and bushpig. There are several self-guided trails through the reserve of varying lengths or those which are led by a park ranger.

Fishermen should exercise caution as there are numerous crocodiles at the river mouths, and in the lake, between February and May after the breeding season when they are hungry and at their most aggressive.

The Natal Parks Board run an excellent guided boat trip along the estuary mouth during which there are often sightings of hippos. The trips should be booked in advance as they are very popular. Self-drive boats can also be hired at the fishing resort.

It is not advisable to turn up at the weekend expecting to easily find accommodation. Bed and breakfast in the area can be arranged and there are three Natal Parks Board camp-sites. The Boma Hotel provides four-star facilities and the Sea Sands operate charming self-catering chalets set in large grounds close to the beach.

There are many restaurants along Main Road including Roberto's Restaurant which serves excellent steaks and an exquisite seafood platter. The Quarterdeck restaurant also offers a variety of steak and seafood dishes.

The **Natal Parks Board Crocodile Research Centre** is open to the public and the best time to visit is on Saturday afternoons when the crocodiles are fed around 3pm. It is fascinating to watch them move slowly into position as they anticipate feeding.

St Lucia to Nkwalini Valley 169km (105 miles)

Return to Mtubatuba and take the N2 heading south towards Durban. Follow the signs to **Richard's Bay**, which served as a port for landing provisions and soldiers during the Zulu war of 1879. The naval presence here played a large part in averting an invasion by the Zulus after the Battle of Isandhlwana.

The deep-water port was opened in 1976, largely because of an urgent need for a facility to handle the export of minerals mined here. It now has the largest coal terminal in the world and exports almost fifty million tonnes a year. There is also an airport with connections around the country.

A section of the lagoon is isolated from the harbour and serves as wildlife sanctuary, where guided tours can be arranged via the Publicity Association. There is also a museum and the only safe-bathing beach in the area.

On the other side of the N2 is the turning to **Empangeni**, the principal centre of the sugar industry in the region and the town where the in-famous Zulu King Shaka grew up. Continue along the N2 toll road to the Mtunzini turn off. Situated near the Umlalazi River, **Mtunzini** is a quaint little village whose name means 'place of shade' after the rare Raffia palms found here. The **Umlalazi Nature Reserve**, run by the Natal Parks Board covers 908 hectares (2,243 acres) of coastal dune and swampland and there is a mangrove trail which can be walked at low tide.

Just before the entrance to the reserve, follow a dirt road on the right to the **Raffia Palm Grove** which has been declared a national monument. The Raffia palm originates from the seeds of trees planted by early Portuguese missionaries. Visitors can see several examples as they walk over

Above: Zulu women demonstrate the traditional methods of basket-weaving.
Opposite top: The fish-eagle is a regular visitor to the St Lucia Game Reserve.
Opposite: Crocodiles are found in abundance at river mouths around the St Lucia Game Reserve between February and May.

a mangrove swamp along a palm-enclosed boardwalk. They may also be rewarded with a sighting of the extremely rare palmnut vulture of which there are only six breeding pairs left in South Africa.

Leave Mtunzini, crossing over the highway and turn right after a few kilometres onto the N68 towards **Eshowe**. The town is situated on a hill amidst the Dlinza Forest and was established as the retreat of Zulu King Cethswayo in 1860. Nearby, there is a monument which marks the site of Shaka's principal *kraal*, which he named kwaBulawayo. The Eshowe

Publicity Office in Osbourne Road will provide information on the history of the area and places to visit.

The **Zululand Historical Museum** at **Fort Nongquai** was originally built to house the Zululand police force. It is now a museum displaying relics from the struggle for control of Zululand and the relationship between the Zulus and the British. There is also a prehistoric room with exhibits of shark finds from the lake at St Lucia which date back twenty million years.

Continuing through the Nkwalini Valley, visitors can enjoy various aspects of Zulu culture and traditions.

There are two 'living museums' open to the public which recreate life in a *kraal*. The largest is **Shakaland** which is home to a number of Zulus and was used as the film sets for the making of *Shaka Zulu*, *John Ross* and *Ipi Tombi*.

Here visitors can experience the rituals of tribal life in the nineteenth century. There are two daily tours at 11am and 12.30pm each lasting two hours which include *ngoma* dancing and lunch. Visitors are accommodated either in a hotel or one of 120 beehive huts and overnight guests can enjoy demonstrations of spear-making, Zulu-dancing, beer-making, stick-fighting, and dancing around the fire to drums.

Nearby the **Kwaphekitunga** *Kraal* on Stewarts Farm on the Eshowe to Empangeni road offers a cross-cultural experience in a genuine Zulu home. Tours and overnight stays should be booked in advance.

Nkwalini Valley to Durban 157km (97 miles)

Five kilometres (3 miles) off the N2 heading south on a signposted dirt road is the national monument of **Fort Pearson** which was built by the British in 1878 to protect its northern borders. Nearby is the **Ultimatum Tree**, under which an ultimatum was read to Zulu King Cetshwayo's representative on 11 December 1818 which resulted in the Anglo-Zulu war. These relics, are situated on the south bank of the Tugela River. Tugela, which means 'something that startles' in Zulu, was named because of the incredible flow of its waters which were often impassable during high tides.

A leaflet is available with information on the area where some of the bloodiest battles in African history occurred.

There are a number of lovely resorts along the coastline north of Durban and the area is not as overcrowded as the popular south coast. Part of this coastline is known as the **Dolphin Coast** because it is one of the best places in South Africa for sightings of bottlenose dolphins, particularly during the calving season.

To enjoy a more scenic route, leave the N2 at **Ballito** in order to travel along the coastal road. This fast-growing tourist resort began life as a township in 1954 and was developed into a resort in 1966. It maintains a charming village atmosphere, despite the increased timeshare developments which have been constructed in recent years. There are good facilities here, including two shopping centres.

Boulder Bay and **Compensation Beach** are excellent spots for surfing and for the price of a licence visitors can pick their own mussels off rocks as well as collect oysters and crayfish.

This is cane country and the vast stretches of extensive green sugar plantations produce over two million tonnes of sugar a year. The area abounds with a variety of tropical fruits including litchies, mangoes, avocados, pawpaws, guavas and bananas.

It was also the area where Zulu King Shaka lived and built his principal *kraal* on the site which became the city of **Stanger**.

On the other side of the N2 is the town of **Tongaat** where the Tongaat Hullett Sugar group have their headquarters. Free tours of the mill are conducted between May and November when the cane is crushed.

It is also where the **Juggernthi Puri temple** (a copy of the Puri temple in India) is located and which claims to be the tallest and oldest Hindu temple in South Africa.

The town itself is very pretty with many houses designed in the Cape Dutch style, and the local market is modelled on the Groot Constantia winery in Cape Town. There are also a number of fascinating oriental stores in the market.

Further along the R102 is **Verulam**, the third oldest town in Natal. It has a distinctly Indian flavour which dates back to the days of the indentured Hindu labourers imported in 1860 to work in the sugar industry. In 1967 it was the first town in South Africa to be handed over to the Indian community. Authentic spices are blended here and the local market is a colourful, bustling place. The **Shiri Gopalal Hindu temple** was opened by Mahatma Ghandi in 1913.

The coastal road continues through Umdloti with its beautiful sandy beach — one of the safest on the north coast for swimming. There is also a lovely natural rock pool.

Umhlanga is 17km (11 miles) from Durban. The town offers excellent facilities for holidaymakers with restaurants, shops, fine accom- modation and a lively night life. It is a fashionable place to live and holiday in one of the several exclusive suburbs including that of La Lucia. The Oyster Box Hotel offers luxury accom- modation and serves excellent cuisine.

The **Umhlanga Lagoon Reserve**, a rich area of forest and lagoon has an abundant bird life and many indigenous species can be spotted here. The Umhlanga Publicity Association is situated at the muni- cipal library. (See Chapter Three for Durban).

Durban to Pietermaritzburg
80km (50 miles)

Leave Durban on the N3 toll road north towards Pietermaritzburg. The city lies in a beautiful spot surrounded by green hills, 677m (421ft) above sea level. It is the capital of the former province of Natal, and shares status as joint capital of KwaZulu-Natal with Ulundi.

PIETERMARITZBURG

The origins of **Pietermaritzburg** date back to 1838 when Voortrekkers from the Cape settled in the Umsindusi valley. The land was largely un- inhabited, except for the vast herds of eland, wildebeest and springbok, as most of the tribes had fled south escaping the advancing Zulu warriors. The Voortrekkers named the town after their two leaders, Piet Retief and Gert Maritz, and it became the seat of their government until 1843 when the land was annexed by the British.

The British influence is clearly evident from the rows of redbrick Victorian houses and buildings in and around the city.

In 1853, the district of Natal was created a Diocese of the Church of England with the controversial John Colenso as its first bishop. Bishop Colenso was friendly with the Zulus and created an uproar by refusing to force them to practice monogamy and divorce their additional wives. He wrote articles challenging the literal truth of the scriptures and was charged with heresy and excommunicated. He fought the charges and was finally reconfirmed back in office by the British Privy Council. The enigmatic Bishop wrote the first Zulu dictionary and reading literature. His tomb is in front of the altar at **St Peter's Church** in Church Street which was originally his cathedral.

'Maritzburg', as it is often known, has thirty-one national monuments — hence its nickname of 'Heritage City'. It is also renowned for its profusion of trees and flowers, public parks and gardens. Part of the University of Natal's faculties are located here which contribute to the young and lively spirit of the city. The Publicity Association is located beside City Hall and provides a booklet of detailed

Above: The origins of the elegant city of Pietermaritzburg date back to 1838. The Voortrekkers named the town after their two leaders, Piet Retief and Gert Maritz, and it became the seat of their government until 1843.

walks through the historical city centre, as well as an audio visual centre for visitors.

City Hall, at the centre of the historic centre of the city, is the largest redbrick building south of the Equator. The original City Hall was destroyed by fire in 1898.

The **Tatham Art Gallery**, on the opposite side of the road, is housed in the renovated **Old Supreme Court** and is a fine example of colonial architecture. The gallery includes several examples of nineteenth and early twentieth-century French and English paintings, as well as an ormolu clock which is rung on the hour and half hour by medieval figures.

There are a number of statues on Commercial Road, including one of Mahatma Gandhi which was erected in 1993 to commemorate the day, a century earlier, when he was removed from a first-class train carriage for being an Indian. This incident led to him developing a political strategy of passive resistance.

The nearby statue of Queen Victoria is a replica of the marble statue in Sydney, Australia. It stands outside the home of Natal's first newspaper, *The Natal Witness*, which appeared on 21 February 1846. Its editor was imprisoned for contempt of court, although he continued working and many of his features bore the dateline *Pietermaritzburg Gaol*.

The **Natal Museum** in Loop Street

has excellent displays of African mammals, birds, reptiles and fish as well as a good overview of the history of Natal. The Imperial Hotel, opposite the museum, has an original hitching post and the brass plaque outside commemorates the visits of Louis Napoleon, Imperial Prince of France, who was later killed during the Zulu War of 1879.

Nearby Longmarket Street is the location for the old **Natal Parliament Building** which housed the Assembly from 1900. Today it contains fascinating relics from colonial days.

The **Church of the Vow**, on the corner of Church and Boshoff Streets, was built by the Voortrekkers after their victory over the Zulus at the Battle of Blood River in 1838. It is a simple building which now houses the **Voortrekker Museum**. Outside the museum are the statues of Piet Retief and Gert Maritz, the Voortrekker leaders after whom the city was named.

The central shopping area is a pedestrian area and an excellent place to browse through colourful ethnic stores displaying a variety of goods including saris, spices and ornaments. The Craft Market in Hawkins Arcade sells a good selection of handicrafts.

There are hotels and guest houses which cater for every taste and the local Tourist Office can provide full details on all accommodation in the area. There are over fifty places to eat in the city which include Greek, Italian, Portuguese and Chinese speciality restaurants.

Alexandra Park at the Scottsville end of Commercial Street, is a pretty park and a fitting testimony to the city's abundance of colourful trees and flowers. A flea market is held here on the first Sunday of every month.

The **Botanic Gardens** are noted for their fine azaleas and long avenue of plane trees. The **Exotic Garden** con-

tributes to the annual Azalea Festival which is held every August. There is a good tearoom alongside the ornate bandstand and the onion-domed Pavilion.

The annual flower show takes place every September when residential gardens are open for viewing to the general public.

The **Queen Elizabeth Park** is north of the city and is home of the headquarters of the Natal Park Board. The park features a nature reserve and offers a variety of peaceful walks. Near the entrance to the park is **World's View**, a 305-metre (1001 feet) observation point which offers spectacular views over the city and surrounding areas. The original Voortrekker road from Durban to the interior, via Pietermaritzburg, passed beside this spot.

The **Garden of Remembrance** is situated on Leinster Road just beyond Alexandra Park. It is primarily a tribute to the fallen from the two world wars, as well as being the home of the **Weeping Cross of Delville**. The cross was made from one of the few remaining tree stumps in Delville Wood, after a major battle in World War I. It was shipped to South Africa after the war and is said to 'weep' just before or after the anniversary of the battle on 14 July. According to legend, it will stop 'weeping' on the death of the last surviving soldier from the battle.

The **Comrades Marathon House Museum** is located in a restored Victorian house and tells the story of the Comrades Marathon which is held annually between Pietermaritzburg and Durban 96km (60 miles) away. It is a good time to visit as the marathon generates a very festive atmosphere. The Hansa Dusi canoe marathon from Pietermaritzburg to Durban each January is also quite a spectacle when 1,500 canoers participate in this sporting event.

Zulus and the Voortrekkers

Piet Retief and his party of Voortrekkers, escaping British rule in the Cape, arrived in Natal in 1838 and attempted to conclude peaceful negotiations with the Zulu King, Dingaan for permission to settle on land south of the Tugela River. A treaty was signed after Retief's men successfully returned cattle stolen by another tribe, in exchange for the land. However, Dingaan immediately reneged on the deal and ordered their murder. Other Voortrekker parties responded angrily to the murders and set out to avenge their deaths. On 16 December 1838, despite their small numbers, 640 Voortrekkers defeated 15,000 Zulus in what became known as The Battle of Blood River. In the battle only three Voortrekkers were wounded, while over 3,000 Zulus died.

This day is still commemorated by a public holiday — until recently known as the Day of the Vow — because prior to the battle, the Voortrekkers vowed to God that if he granted victory, they would remember the day forever. Since the elections the name has been altered to the Day of Reconciliation. The Voortrekker Monument in Pretoria and the Church of the Vow in Pietermaritzburg were both erected in memory of this momentous day in history.

Zulus and the British

In 1878, Zulu King Cetshwayo reinstituted the brilliant military tactics of his predecessor, the brutal King Shaka. He repeatedly ignored warnings from the British to uphold peace and eventually the British troops attacked. During this battle at Isandhlwana in 1879, the Zulus virtually eliminated the entire force of 1,500 British soldiers. This was one of the most disastrous military losses in the history of Britain's colonial battles. Two days later, an attack on a small number of British soldiers at Rorke's Drift was repelled by the 'heroic 100' who had previously fled Isandhlwana. They repelled a force of 4,000 Zulus, ultimately preventing a large-scale Zulu invasion in Natal. The Zulu stronghold was finally crushed seven months later when British troops attacked Cethswayo's royal residence at Ulundi and defeated 20,000 Zulus. Cetshwayo was banished to England and the might of the Zulu army crumbled when Zululand was divided into thirteen chiefdoms.

The Spioenkop reserve, on the shore of the Spioenkop dam, is where one of the fiercest battles of the Anglo-Boer War took place. At the outbreak of the war in 1899, Ladysmith hit the world headlines when it was besieged by the Boers. The siege lasted 118 days during which time all supplies, including water, were cut off. Over 300 British died, mainly due to sickness and disease, before additional troops arrived.

The **Scottsville Race Course** is one of the main courses in South Africa and hosts a number of events throughout the year.

There are regular flights from Johannesburg, coach services between Durban and Johannesburg, and the daily Trans-Orange Express train between Cape Town and Durban also stops here.

The **Natal Lion Park** is situated 11km (7 miles) south of Pietermaritzburg off the N3. The entrance fee includes a visit to the zoo next door.

Arts and crafts routes are becoming increasingly popular through the country and the Natal Midlands region is no exception. The **Midlands Meander** cover the studios and workshops of many artists in the area and also incorporates many of the enchanting country inns and hotels in the area. The Publicity Association has a map of the route.

Pietermaritzburg to Ladysmith 182 km (113 miles)

Leave Pietermaritzburg on the N3 and take the turning towards **Howick**, following the signs to the **Howick Falls**. Here, the Mgeni River plunges 100m (328ft) into a stunning gorge which can be viewed from the town of Howick or the **Mgeni Valley Nature Reserve**. A grave, marked by a pile of stones at the foot of the waterfall, belongs to the son of one of the first settlers of Howick who was swept over the falls during a flood.

The Howick district reputedly has one of the healthiest climates in the world and is an area rich in agricultural wealth.

The Midmar Public Resort in the Mgeni Valley offers camping and chalet facilities and is a popular spot for watersports. It is home to the annual Midmar Mile swimming race in February each year.

From here, take the road to **Mooi River** ('beautiful river'), a town built on the banks of the river which meanders through a lush and fertile valley. The village hosts one of the largest stock sales in the area on the first Wednesday of each month.

Continue north along the N3, taking the R600 left to **Spioenkop Reserve** to explore some of the northern KwaZulu-Natal battlefields.

Some of the most dramatic battles in South African history took place in KwaZulu-Natal and the area is rich in historical and military importance. There are thirty-six preserved battlefields which reflect the years of turbulence and bloodshed. In response to an increased interest in the area, an official Northern KwaZulu-Natal Battlefields Route was created in 1990, covering all the major battlefields.

There are numerous museums to visit and the information offices in major towns can advise where to go, as well as provide background information on the historical significance of each area. They can also arrange for local historians to take visitors on personal tours. The **Talana Museum** in Dundee provides taped commentaries — with sound effects — to guide visitors through the exhibits.

At the Spioenkop Reserve there is a walking trail over the hill, which leads past memorials and significant observation points, and overlooks a vista of spectacular scenery. There is also a museum which provides information on battles which took place in the area. The National Parks Board trail guide follows a numbered route which explains the course of various battles and the outcome.

Accommodation is available at the Natal Parks Board Ntenjwa Camp which is situated beside the dam. Canoes can be hired and horse and pony treks are available.

From here take the R600 and the N11

Above: The memorial at the site of the Battle of Blood River.

Below: Memorial to the Zulu warriors who fought in the Battle of Rorke's Drift.

"IN PROUD MEMORY OF THE BRAVE ZULU WARRIORS WHO FELL AT THE BATTLE OF RORKE'S DRIFT 22 JANUARY 1879 SOME OF WHOM LIE BURIED HERE."

"SIYAZIQHENYA UKUKHUMBULA AMABUTHO ANGAMAQHAWE AKWAZULU ASALA ENKUNDLENI ESHIYANE NGOMHLAKA 22 KU JANUARY 1879 AMANYE AWO ALELE LAPHA."

"IN EERVOLLE HERINNERING AAN DIE DAPPER ZOELOEKRYGERS WAT GESNEUWEL HET BY DIE SLAG VAN RORKESDRIF 22 JANUARIE 1879 SOMMIGE WAARVAN HIER BEGRAWE LÊ."

into **Ladysmith**. The town was named after Lady Juana, wife of the popular governor of the Cape, Sir Harry Smith. It is one of the nicer towns in the area with its redbrick Victorian buildings. It makes a convenient base for trips to the Drakensberg mountains.

The **Siege Museum** and neighbouring **Town Hall** both contain interesting displays and artifacts from the Anglo-Boer War. The Information Office is located in the museum and can arrange guided tours on request. One of the Boer 'Long Tom' cannons, which was so successful in the town's siege, sits outside the museum complex.

Mahatma Ghandi worked as a stretcher bearer throughout the siege and a statue was erected here in his honour by the local Hindu community. There is a memorial to the 3,000 British soldiers who died in the siege and a relief model of the town at **All Saint's Church**.

The Royal Hotel has three different restaurants on its premises and there are also two in the Crown Hotel. The Ladysmith Motel offers the cheapest accommodation in town, apart from a number of bed and breakfast establishments.

The Tourist Office can provide full details on places to stay.

Ladysmith to Dundee 73km (52 miles)

Leave Ladysmith on the N11 heading north and take the R68 turning towards the town of **Dundee**. It is an important coal mining town and is home to the **Talana Museum** situated on the outskirts of the town.

The battle at Talana was the first of the Anglo-Boer War and this is the only museum built on the site of a battlefield with preserved buildings dating from the period. Several of the most significant battlefields are close

by. There is a Publicity Association Office and an Information Office in the museum who can provide details of places to stay.

The Miner's Restaurant in the museum serves meals from 10am-3.30pm and on Friday evenings when it is open for dinner. The Buffalo Steakhouse and Edwards Restaurant are the most popular restaurants in town.

The site of the **Battle of Blood River** is situated off the R33 in the direction of Vryheid. The memorial consists of a bronze replica of the Voortrekkers *laager* which was attacked on 16 December 1838.

In the centre of the *laager* is a plaque of the vow made to God by the Boers to remember the day forever if He granted them victory in battle.

Dundee to Vryheid (via Ulundi) 345 km (214 miles)

Take the R33 towards Vryheid and turn right onto the R68 following the signs to **Rorke's Drift.** In January 1879, 24,000 Zulus attacked the main British camp at Isandhlwana killing over 1,000 British soldiers. The survivors fled to Rorke's Drift where the 'heroic 100' British soldiers held out against the might of 4,0000 Zulu warriors until they finally withdrew. Eleven Victoria crosses were awarded to those who fought in battle — the most ever given in British history.

There is an arts centre here displaying an interesting selection of Zulu crafts. Fifteen kilometres (9 miles) further along is the site of **Fugitive's Drift**. The Fugitive's Drift Lodge is nearby and offers comfortable accommodation.

Return to the R68, turn right and follow the signs to the **Isandhlwana** battlefield. On 30 January 1819, a Zulu army of 25,000 under King Cetshwayo virtually eliminated the entire British regiment of 1,500. There is a small museum overlooking the battlefield displaying a relief model, shields, badges and uniforms from both sides. The stones along the side of the road mark the graves of men killed in the fighting.

Return to the R68, passing through **Babanango**, and the turning to **Umginginhlovu** in the Emakbosini Valley, the site of the former royal town of the Zulu King. It was at KwaMatiwane that Voortrekker Piet Retief and his men were murdered. The huts of the royal quarters have been restored and there are some interesting archaeological artifacts in the museum. There is a cenotaph and memorial to Piet Retief and his men on the gravel road leading to the *kraal*.

Return to the R68 and take turn off the R66 to Ulundi, the scene of the final defeat of the Zulus in 1897 when the British attacked and burned the Royal *kraal* to the ground, crushing the might of King Cetshwayo and the Zulu nation. The Royal *kraal* has now been meticulously reconstructed by archaeologists as a cultural and historical showpiece and the site museum portrays life during Cetshwayo's reign. The cultural museum exhibits the history and arts of the Zulu people and visitors can stay overnight in traditional 'beehive' huts.

Ulundi was the capital of the independent homeland of KwaZulu which was incorporated into the KwaZulu-Natal province in 1994. The New Legislative Assembly building can be visited by arrangement and the colourful tapestries which hang in the lobby depict the history of the Zulu people.

Ulundi is home to both Chief Mangosuthu Buthelezi, who was elected the Minister of Home Affairs in the first elections in 1994, and also to the current Zulu King, Goodwill Zwelithini.

From here return to the R66 taking the R34 to Vryheid. When the Boers took over the land and established the 'New Republic', **Vryheid** (meaning 'free city') was established as the capital. It was incorporated into the Transvaal Republic before being annexed to Natal at the end of the Anglo-Boer War. The town lies in a valley at the foot of the Zungwini mountains and today is an important coal mining and farming centre.

The **Dutch Reformed Church**, **Church Square** and the **police station** are all national monuments. The **Old Raadzaal** (council chamber) was erected in 1884 as the parliament building of the new state and there is an old fort and gaol located behind it.

The Knabbelhuisie is the oldest home industry in South Africa producing an impressive range of arts and crafts and home baking. There is a popular tea garden next door to the Knabbelhuisie.

The Stilwater Protea Hotel has comfortable rooms at reasonable prices. There is a carvery in their restaurant during the week, as well as full *a la carte* and vegetarian dishes. There is a Spur family restaurant in Utrecht Street and Sergio's Italian restaurant in Landdros Street which serves good pasta and regional dishes.

Vryheid to Johannesburg 403km (250 miles)

Take the R33 from Vryheid towards Dundee, the R34 to Utrecht and left turn to Newcastle. **Newcastle** was the fourth town to be established in Natal and was the scene of many battles between the British and the Boers. In 1889, it became the main stronghold from which the Boers held northern Natal and besieged Ladysmith and Dundee.

There is a festival every March when national and ethnic com-

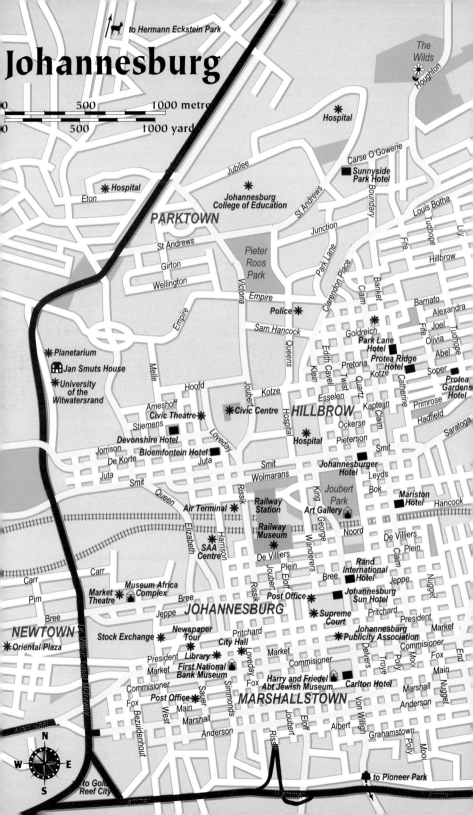

Above: The sun's golden rays illuminate the skyline of Johannesburg at sunset.

munities display their traditions and culture with dance shows and food dishes. The Newcastle Publicity Association is located at the **Town Hall** in Scott Street.

✳ Forty km (25 miles) north of Newcastle, off the main N11, is **Majuba**, where a major battle of the first Anglo-Boer War was fought in February 1881. The British forces were determined to break through Boer lines by seizing Majuba Hill, but were defeated during a bloody battle. At the foot of the hill is O'Neill's Cottage, which improvised as a hospital during the fighting, and where the peace treaty which ended the first Anglo-Boer War was signed.

Continue to Volksrust, taking the R23 left and join the N3 toll road at **Heidelberg** heading in the direction of Johannesburg.

JOHANNESBURG

The city is considered to be the gateway to southern Africa with a wide network of flights across the whole of Africa and to many cities worldwide. Johannesburg is known locally as *Egoli*, meaning 'city of gold' as it was the discovery of the goldfields just over a century ago which funded the rapid development of this city.

Although this is not the capital, many people from southern Africa gravitate here in the hope of making their fortune, and it is also where most large organizations base their headquarters. This has led to a fascinating mix of different cultures, traditions and lifestyles amongst the city's inhabitants.

In 1886, when Australian prospector, George Harrison found gold on the farm Langlaagte, it heralded the start of the greatest gold rush in history. Ironically Harrison gave away his claim and later died in poverty in the Eastern Transvaal.

The city was named after two mining officials, Johannes Joubert and Johann Rissik, who chose the site for the gold diggers town. The discovery of the seemingly inexhaustible seam around the Witwatersrand ('the ridge of white waters') area led to the city attracting fortune hunters from all over the world. By 1889, Johannesburg was already established as the largest town in South Africa with its own stock exchange. Men outnumbered women by three to one, as hotels, brothels, and liquor stores sprang up throughout this shanty city. Various entrepreneurs including Cecil Rhodes, Charles Rudd and Julius Werener came to the fore and were named the 'rand lords'. They poured money into the area which made it expand even faster — particularly with the extension of the rail link between the Transvaal and the Cape. Since the discovery of this precious metal, almost 40,000 tonnes of gold has been mined on the rand.

Johannesburg is now the capital of the Gauteng province and the hub of South and southern Africa. This diamond-shaped province, with Johannesburg at its centre, is for many their first glimpse of South Africa. It is a sprawling city of skyscrapers which spreads out across almost 4,800 hectares (12,000 acres).

Johannesburg can often appear very dreary in the middle of winter when the dry season has drained every ounce of colour from the landscape. However, in the summer the landscape burgeons forth into numerous shades of green and the trees burst into vibrant purples, yellows and reds.

Despite its lack of aesthetic appeal compared with Cape Town, Johannesburg has an ambience of its own. There is an eclectic quality to the city which attracts many people hoping to make their fortune in either the mining, commercial or financial industries.

Johannesburg produces about forty percent of South Africa's GDP alone and has a strong infrastructure. It is situated 1,760m (5,773ft) above sea level and has around nine hours of sunshine with an average temperature of 22°c. Summers are hot and sunny with dramatic late afternoon thunderstorms which often disappear as quickly as they appeared. Winter days are bright and sunny with cold, crisp nights. Rain is a very rare occurrence during the winter and causes the arid, burnt appearance to the landscape during these months. The dryness of winter causes tremendous static electricity in the air.

There is very little to see in the city centre as it is primarily a commercial centre, although it boasts twenty-two museums, thirty art galleries and over twenty markets. Whether travelling on business or as a tourist, it is advisable to stay at one of the hotels in the suburbs and only venture into town during the day. Beware, as thieves and muggers tend to lie in wait for people carrying cameras or hand baggage, and anybody who appears unsure of their surroundings.

The network of freeways which snake across the city can be confusing and visitors should check their route carefully before setting out, to avoid ending up on a road heading in the direction of Durban instead of the city centre. There is a good public bus service within Johannesburg, but it is often quicker to walk around the centre. The bus station is located at Vanderbijl Square on the corner of Main and Rissik Streets. The black kombi buses are everywhere and are a cheap and efficient way to reach suburban points. Taxis do not cruise the streets so it is necessary to telephone and book in advance.

The **Carlton Centre** is the main shopping complex in the city centre and from the top floor, the 202-metre (663 feet) **Carlton Panorama** observation deck affords incredible views across the city. The vast complex houses a luxury hotel, offices, shops and a variety of restaurants.

From the Carlton Centre walk along Commissioner Street and turn left into Kruis Street. The offices of the Johannesburg Publicity Association and Satour are on the corner of Kruis and Market Street. Continuing west along Market Street, one encounters the **First National Bank Museum** (formerly the Barclays Bank Museum). It documents the financial development of the mining industry, and houses a fascinating collection of old banking equipment, furniture, money, photographs and documents.

City Hall is also located in Market Street and visitors are permitted to look around the hall and the old council chambers.

Opposite City Hall is the **Post Office** which has been declared a national monument and the fountain standing behind it features eighteen leaping bronze impala.

Market Square is across from the First National Bank Museum and the offices of the *Star* Newspaper are located opposite. The *Star* is one of the country's largest daily newspapers and has a long and fascinating history. Visitors may tour the building by prior arrangement.

The **Stock Exchange** in Diagonal Street is the financial centre of South Africa and is located in an impressive modern building. Visitors may observe the trading from the public gallery, as well as enjoy conducted tours by knowledgeable guides who explain the workings of the Stock Exchange. The **Hall of South African Achievement** is next to the Visitors Gallery and records the country's achievements over the years.

There are a collection of herbalists and traditional healers in Diagonal Street where visitors can purchase some of the unusual ingredients used in traditional African medicine. The African Herbalist shop is the most intriguing, with its dark interior and daunting exterior. Visitors may consult the on-site *sangoma* on any sickness or infirmity.

A few blocks away, the **Market Theatre Complex** in the Newton Cultural Precinct has evolved for the city's up-and-coming art world and is currently being revamped. The Market Theatre produces some of the city's best shows, and is also a very popular to place to meet and eat — particularly at Kippie's, the theatre's jazz club. An ethnic flea market is held outside the theatre each Saturday.

The old Market building in the complex houses the **Museum Africa** which opened in 1994. The building was originally Johannesburg's fruit and vegetable market until it closed in the mid-seventies. There are a number of displays and exhibits which portray the country's development right up to the present day. It also houses the **Bensusan Museum of Photography** which features displays of leading edge developments in photography, video and multimedia, and the **Museum of South African Rock Art**.

The Museum Africa houses a large ethnological gallery which illustrates the lifestyles of the various tribes of southern Africa in a series of photographs and paintings. It also details the role of the Europeans in the country's history dating back to van Riebeeck's day. The Johannesburg Room which portrays the growth of

the city from 1866 to the present day is worth a visit.

The nearby **Oriental Plaza** shopping complex between Bree Street and Main Road in Fordsburg is a lively centre for the bargain hunter. It is a unique blend of east and west and sells a wide selection of colourful Indian clothing and spices.

Return along Bree Street towards the city centre turning left into Eloff Street. At the far end is the **South African Railway Museum** which is located in the old concourse of the Johannesburg station complex. It contains a collection of relics from South Africa's early days of public transport, including locomotives and rolling stock, dating from the first steam trains in southern Africa.

Across the railway bridge in **Braamfontein** is the **University of Witwatersrand**, known locally as the WITS. It is the largest university in South Africa and tours are conducted every Wednesday morning. Tours include a visit to **Jan Smuts House**, a memorial to South Africa's famous general, located in the campus. There is an authentic reproduction of the study from his home Doornkloof, which includes many original pieces.

The original **Diaz Cross** planted by Bartholomew Diaz at Qwaai Hoek, Algoa Bay stands at the entrance to the university library. The **Johannesburg Planetarium** is on the east side of Yale Road next to the university entrance. There are multi-visual sky shows which explore the marvels of astronomy and the science of the universe.

The **Standard Bank Foundation** Collection of African Art is housed in the **Gertrude Posel Gallery** at WITS and is the largest public collection of its kind in South Africa, featuring masks, beadwork, head dresses and Ndebele fertility dolls.

Nearby, **Joubert Park** is bounded by Klein, Wolmarans and Twist Streets

Above: The Chamber of Mines can arrange fascinating visits to the working face of a gold mine.
Opposite top: The building which houses Museum Africa was originally the city's fruit and vegetable market.
Opposite: The attractive Wilds gardens.

and dates back to 1887. It is the city's best known recreation area and contains a conservatory, floral clock, giant chess board and an art gallery. The **Johannesburg Art Gallery** features excellent paintings by nineteenth-century European artists including Renoir, Cezanne and Picasso, as well as some fine examples by South African artists. Take particular care with cameras, handbags and day-packs as theft is rife outside the gallery.

The adjoining suburb of **Hillbrow** is now a sleazy area with late night shops, nightclubs and restaurants with seating spilling out onto the pavements. Once a cosmopolitan spot with it has degenerated ... unsafe area where ... on the increase, so take ... gardens known as the **Wilds** situated five minutes from Hillbrow and a number of indigenous plants are cultivated in special plant houses within its grounds.

The centre of town is no longer the place to shop. Most suburbs have their own large shopping malls and there are a number of hypermarket complexes dotted throughout Gauteng.

Sandton, a fast-growing city has an elegant shopping mall which incorporates two five-star hotels and fine restaurants. Here, the Sandton Sun Hotel offers visitors a choice of excellent cuisine in either the Portuguese Villa Moura restaurant or the elegant Chapters restaurant. The hotel is now linked by an aerial walkway to the luxurious Sandton Towers Hotel. A visit to Sandton is a must for visitors wishing to shop in a modern and safe environment.

Rosebank has also become a popular place for visitors to reside and shop and is slightly closer to the city centre. The Hardrock Cafe here is very popular and the Mall has a weekend market with entertainment.

Several flea markets have established themselves as permanent shopping areas, and one of the best and most central is **Flea Market World** which is located at **Bruma Lake**. It is well organised with a small arena where tribal dancers and magicians perform regular shows. It is a bustling, vibrant place at the weekend and is open daily until 7pm, except Monday.

There is no shortage of restaurants in Johannesburg, although they are generally located in the suburbs rather than the city centre. However, Rockey Street is quite popular and attracts a young and trendy crowd. There are vegetarian cafes, cafe theatres and late night coffee bars.

Gold Reef City has a number of theme bars and restaurants and is a nice place to spend the evening. Melville is one of the liveliest suburbs and home to the popular Roxy's Rhythm Bar which usually features some excellent jazz musicians.

Around Johannesburg

Visitors interested in walking trails should take the Braamfontein Spruit trail which follows the stream through central Johannesburg, Randburg and Sandton to join the Klein Juskei River beyond the Sandton boundary.

Four kilometres (2 miles) to the north is the **Herman Eckstein Park** which covers over 100 hectares (247 acres) and features the **Johannesburg Zoo**. The zoological gardens is home to over 3,000 different mammals, birds and reptiles, as well as the first white lions born in captivity. The night tours are highly recommended and are conducted by a zoo guide who gives lectures at various cages. Reservations for the night tours must be made through Computicket.

Zoo Lake, opposite the zoological gardens, is a delightful place for a picnic or lunch in the restaurant overlooking the lake. There is a swimming pool and bowling green, and arts and craft exhibitions and markets are held here at weekends.

For those interested in art and crafts, the **Johannesburg Studio Route** is open to the public on the last Sunday of every month between 10am and 5pm. Artists and craftsmen in the city and its environs open up their studios to visitors, and a map of the route is available from the Publicity Office.

Pioneer Park is one of the largest parks in the city and is popular for its multi coloured musical fountains which are synchronised to popular tunes. It is a novel evening out and shows take place every evening except

Monday between September to March.

As this is the 'city of gold' visitors often wish to visit a gold mine during their stay. The **Chamber of Mines** can arrange trips to the working face of a mine to watch pure molten gold being poured into molds and experience all the workings of a gold mine. Transport, food and refreshments are included in this fascinating insight into the underground life of the city. The tours are very popular so reservations should be made well in advance.

A trip to **Gold Reef City** is a recreational alternative to a real mine and is one of Johannesburg's main tourist attractions. It is 6km (4 miles) from the centre on the M1 heading south towards Bloemfontein. Take exit 12 and follow the signs to this reconstruction of a pioneer town from the gold rush days which has been built on the site of the Crown mine.

There is a Victorian fun fair, an old brewery, apothecary, Chinese laundry and newspaper office as well as numerous bars and restaurants. For an additional charge visitors can take a trip down a mine shaft to explore the workings of a disused gold mine, as well as watch gold being poured into a bullion bar. The mine dancers who perform twice daily during the week and three times a day at weekends are excellent and demonstrate the style of dance which labourers developed as a means of release from their punishing work schedule.

There are guided tours throughout the complex, including the museum which displays artefacts from the early gold mining industry.

The African township of **Soweto** — an abbreviation of South Western Townships — is 25km (15 miles) to the south-west of Johannesburg. It is South Africa's second largest city which grew up when the blacks from rural communities were drawn by the city lights in search of employment after World War II. It is a vast residential area with over a million inhabitants who were forced to make their homes here when the Group Areas Act was still in force. Although parts of Soweto have been improved in recent years, many of the residents live in appalling conditions without even basic amenities. Some of these homes are now interspersed with the homes of successful residents who do not wish to leave the area.

It is extremely inadvisable to visit Soweto without a guide. Go with one of the tour companies like *Jimmy's Face to Face Tours*. Jimmy, a charismatic, entrepreneurial character from Soweto has earned himself a good reputation for his tours which use black kombi buses to transport tourists without attracting too much attention. Visitors see an institution for the handicapped and a cultural village as part of the tour.

A visit to the **Lion Park** on the Krugersdorp Road, 23km (14 miles) north of Johannesburg on the old Pretoria Road is major tourist attraction. The park is a sanctuary for many zebra, impala, wildebeest and springbok and has a huge collection of lions. There is a restaurant, *braai* area and swimming pool, as well as an excellent curio shop.

The **Transvaal Snake Park** at Halfway House, Midrand on the old Johannesburg to Pretoria Road is the largest reptile park in South Africa. There are organised tours with interesting lectures on these fearsome reptiles, as well as the opportunity to watch snakes being milked for their venom, which is subsequently used to produce snakebite serum.

Heia Safari Ranch is a well organised ranch where visitors can enjoy a game drive. On Sundays, Mzumba African dancers perform ethnic dances which is followed by a *braai*.

Above: Gold Reef City is a reconstruction of a pioneer gold rush town.
Opposite: The Arts Alive Festival each September hosts a variety of colourful events performed by artists and musicians.

The **Sterkfontein Caves** are 55km (34 miles) from Johannesburg near Krugersdorp. The caves consist of six chambers with fantastic rock formations and a large underground lake reputed to have special healing powers. It was here in 1947 that anthropologist Dr. Robert Brown found the 'Mrs Pless' skull which is estimated to be over one million years old from an ancient species of apeman.

The Crocodile River Arts and Crafts Ramble features the artists whose studios are located along the scenic Crocodile River. This route is also accessible from Pretoria. On the first weekend of each month, visitors are welcomed into these workshops where they can view and purchase the crafts. A route map is available from the Publicity Office in Johannesburg,

along with details of an Antique Route in the area.

The Lexington PGA Golf tournament is held each January and the Rand Show which takes place at Easter is the third-largest combined industrial and agricultural show in the world.

In April, the Johannesburg Pops Festival features popular classical music performed by orchestras, choirs and soloists. The International Eisteddford of South Africa is held each September/October during which time musicians and dancers from all over the world compete. The city also hosts the Art Alive Festival each September which features presentations and exhibitions around the city by members of the musical and arts world.

PLACES TO VISIT IN JOHANNESBURG

Africana Museum
Bree and Wolhuter Streets, Newtown
☎ (011) 833 5624

Braamfontein Spruit Trail
Johannesburg Hiking Club
☎ (011) 52 8311

Carlton Panorama
50th floor, Carlton Centre
Commissioner Street
Open daily: 9am-11pm
☎ (011) 331 6608

Civic Theatre
Loveday Street, Braamfontein
☎ (011) 403 3408

Chamber of Mines
Gold mine tours
By appointment only
☎ (011) 498 7100

First National Bank Museum
90 Market Street
Open Monday-Saturday: 9am-4pm
☎ (011) 836 5887

Gertrude Posel Gallery
Senate House Concourse
University of Witwatersrand
Open Tuesday-Thursday: 10am-5pm
Saturday: 2pm-5pm

Gold Reef City
M1 freeway south, follow signs
Open daily from 9.30am
☎ (011) 496 1600

Harry & Fiedal Art Jewish Museum
4th floor, Sheffield House
Corner of Kruis and Main streets
Open Monday-Thursday: 9am-4.30pm
Friday: 9am-4pm

Heia Safari Ranch
DF Malan exit, Swartkop
Open daily: 8am-10pm
☎ (011) 659 0605

Jan Smuts House at University
Open Monday-Friday: 8.30am-5pm
☎ (011) 716 3793

Johannesburg Art Gallery
Klein Street, Joubert Park
Tours: Wednesday & Saturday only
Open Tuesday-Sunday: 10am-5pm
☎ (011) 725 3180

Johannesburg Studio Route
Last Sunday of month: 10am-5pm
☎ (011) 646 1170

Johannesburg Stock Exchange
Diagonal Street, Newtown
Tours Monday-Friday: 11am
☎ (011) 833 6580

Kyalami Motor Racing Circuit
Midrand
☎ (011) 337 2727

Lion Park
Krugersdorp Road, Near Honeydew
Open daily: 8am-4.30pm
☎ (011) 460 1814

Market Theatre
Newtown
☎ (011) 832 1641

Magaliesburg Steam Train
Sundays twice a month only
☎ (011) 888 1l54

Museum Africa
121 Bree Street
Newtown
Open Tuesday-Sunday: 9am-5pm
☎ (011) 833 5624

Phumangela Zulu Kraal
DF Malan Drive
Open: Monday-Saturday appt only
☎ (011) 659 0605

Pioneer Park
Evening shows daily except Monday
September to March: 7.30pm-9pm
April to June: 6.30pm-8pm

The Planetarium
Yale Road, Braamfontein
Show times: Friday: 8pm
Saturday: 3pm & 8pm, Sunday: 4pm
☎ (011) 716 3199

Railway Museum
Railway Station
Eloff Street
Open Monday-Friday: 7.30am-4pm
☎ (011) 773 9118

Star Newspaper
47 Sauer Street
Tours Monday-Friday: 9.30am
(except Wednesday)
☎ (011) 633 2724

Soweto Tours
Jimmy's Face to Face Tours
☎ (011) 331 6209

Sterkfontein Caves
55km (34 miles) from Johannesburg
Open Tuesday-Sunday: 9am-4pm
☎ (011) 956 6342

Transvaal Snake Park
Halfway House
Old Jo'burg/Pretoria Road, Midrand
☎ (011) 805 3116

University of Witwatersrand
Milner Park
☎ (011) 716 3472

Zoological Gardens
Jan Smuts Avenue
Open daily: 8.30am-5.30pm
☎ (011) 646 2000

PLACES TO VISIT IN PRETORIA

Church Square Tours
Simon van der Stel Foundation
Monday & Thursday
Advance booking required
☎ (012) 463226

Kruger Museum
Church Street
Open Monday-Saturday: 8.30am-1pm
Sunday & holidays: 11am-4pm
☎ (012) 326 9172

Melrose House
275 Jacob Maré Street
Open Tuesday-Saturday: 10am-5pm
Thu: 10am-12noon
Sunday: 12noon-5pm
☎ (012) 322 2805

Museum of Science & Technology
Skinner Street
Open Monday-Saturday: 8am-4pm
Sunday: 2pm-5pm
☎ (012) 322 6404

**National Cultural History and
Open-Air Museum**
Visagie Street
Closed until 1996

National Zoological Gardens
Open daily: 8am-5pm
☎ (012) 28 3265

Police Museum
Compol Building
Pretorius Street
Open Monday-Friday: 8am-3.30pm
Saturday: 8.30am-12.30pm
☎ (012) 211678 ext. 268

Pretoria Art Museum
Arcadia Park
Open Tuesday-Saturday: 10am-5pm
Sunday: 1pm-6pm
☎ (012) 3441807

Sammy Marks Museum
N4 freeway to Witbank
Exit 11
Open Tuesday-Friday: 9am-4pm
Saturday & Sunday: 10am-4pm
☎ (012) 803 6158

State Theatre
Pretoria
☎ (012) 322 1665

Stats Model School
Library Building
Corner of Van der Walt and Skinner
Streets

South African Republic Raadzaal
Church Square
Advance booking required
☎ (012) 2019111

Transvaal Museum of Natural History
Paul Kruger Street
Open Monday-Saturday: 9am-5pm
Sunday: 11am-5pm
☎ (012) 322 7632

Voortrekker Monument and Museum
Off Eeusees Road
Open daily: 9am-4.45pm
☎ (012) 323 0682

PLACES TO VISIT AROUND PRETORIA

Jan Smuts House — Doornkloof
Jan Smuts Avenue, Irene
Open Monday-Friday: 9.30am-4.30pm
Saturday & Sunday: 9.30am-5pm
☎ (012) 667 1176

Pioneer Open Air Museum
Pretoria Road
Silverton
Open daily: 8.30am-4pm
☎ (012) 803 6086

Premier Diamond Mine
Cullinan
Tours weekdays 9am
☎ (01213) 92911

Tswaing (Soutpan) Eco-museum
c/o Cultural History Museum
Postbus 28088
Sunnyside 0132
Open Monday-Friday: 8am-4pm
Advance booking required
☎ (01214) 987302

OTHER PLACES TO VISIT

Blood River
R33 to Vryheid 25km (15 miles)
Open daily: 8am-5pm
☎ (03424) 695

Dundee

Talana Museum
Talana Hill
Open Monday-Friday : 8am-4pm
Saturday: 10am-4pm
Sunday: 12noon-4pm
☎ (0341) 22654

Eshowe

Zululand Historical Museum
Fort Nongquai

Graskop

Bourke's Luck Potholes
R532 to Graskop
Open daily: 8.30am-5pm
☎ (01315) 81215

Isandhlwana
R33 to Vryheid, Nqutu Road
80km (50 miles) from Dundee
Open daily: 8am-4pm
☎ (0358) 791223

Ladysmith

Siege Museum
Open Monday-Friday: 8am-4.20pm
Saturday: 8am-12noon
Sunday: 10am-11.30am
☎ (0361) 22231

Louis Trichardt

Schoemansdal White Pioneer Settlement
On 522 towards Vivo
Open daily: 8am-4pm
☎ (01551) 4237

Maidstone

Tongaat Hulett Mills and Estates
Tours Tuesday, Wednesday & Thursday
(May to November only)
☎ (0322) 24551 ext. 125

Ondini

KwaZulu Cultural Museum
Open daily: 9am-4pm

Pietersburg

Bakone Malapa North Sotho Kraal and Museum
Chuniespoort/Burgersfort Road
Open Monday: 8.30am-1.30pm
Tuesday-Saturday: 8.30-5.30pm
Sunday: 1.30pm-3.30pm
☎ (0152) 295 2867

Pietermaritzburg

Natal Museum
237 Loop Street
Open Monday-Saturday: 9am-4.30pm
Sunday: 2pm-5pm
☎ (0331) 451404

Tatham Art Gallery
60 Commercial Road
Open Monday-Friday: 10am-5pm
☎ (0331) 421804

Comrades Marathon House
18 Connaught Street, Scottsville
Open Monday-Friday: 10am-3.30pm
☎ (0331) 943511

Rorke's Drift/Fugitive's Drift
Open daily except Sunday
☎ (03425) 627

Sabie

Sabie Forestry Museum
Opposite Spar Centre
Open Monday-Friday: 9am-4pm,
Saturday: 9am-1pm
☎ (01315) 43492

St Lucia

Crocodile Research Centre
Open daily: 8am-4.30pm
☎ (035) 5901342

Sudwala

Sudwala Caves and Prehistoric Park
Open daily: 8.30am-4.30pm
☎ (01311) 54152

Thoyanandou

State Museum
Punda Maria Road
Open Monday-Friday: 8am-4.30pm
☎ (0159) 21461

Tzaneen

Middlekop Tea Estate
Tours: Tuesday-Friday: 9am, 10.15am,
11.15am, 2pm and 3pm
Saturday: 10am except last one of month
☎ (01523) 53241

Ulundi

KwaZulu Monuments Council
PO Box 523
Ulundi 3838
Open daily: 7am-6pm
☎ (0358) 791223

Umgungunhlovu

Vryheid Road
24 km (15 miles) from Ulundi
☎ (0345) 2254

SWAZILAND

Ezulwini Valley

Swazi Ethnic Village and Copperland
Open daily

Lobamba

National Museum
Open Monday-Friday: 9am-3.45pm
Saturday & Sunday: 10am-3.45pm
☎ (268) 61151/61178

Malkerns

Tishweshwe Craft
Open daily
☎ (268) 83336

Swazi Candles
Open daily
☎ (268) 83219

Mantenga

Mantenga Craft
☎ (268) 61136

Mbabane

Houses of Parliament
Telephone in advance
☎ (268) 61286/7/8/9

Piggs Peak

Tintsaba Crafts at Highlands Inn
Open daily: 9am-5pm
☎ (268) 71260

National and Provincial Parks

Alexandra Park
off Commercial Road
Pietermaritzburg
Open daily

Austin Roberts Bird Sanctuary
Boshoff Street
Waterkloof
☎ (012) 344 3850

Garden of Remembrance
Leinster Road
Pietermaritzburg

Hluhluwe/Umfolosi
Natal Parks Board
☎ (0331) 471981

Kruger National Park
Open daily: 6.00am-5.30pm
(longer in summer)

Lowveld Botanical Gardens
White River Road, Nelspruit
Open daily: 8am-5pm
☎ (01311) 25531

Mkuze
Natal Parks Board
☎ (0331) 471981

Natal Lion Park
Umlaas Road off N2
Open daily: sunrise to sunset
☎ (0325) 51411

Natal National Botanical Gardens
2 Swartkop Road
Prestbury
Monday-Friday: 8am-5.30pm
☎ (0331) 443585

National Botanical Gardens
Brummeria Road
Pretoria
Open daily: 8am-5pm
☎ (012) 861165

Queen Elizabeth Park
R103 to Howick
Natal Parks Board
☎ (0331) 471981

Spioenkop Reserve
Natal Parks Board
☎ (0331) 471981

St Lucia
Natal Parks Board
☎ (0331) 471981

Umlalazi Nature Reserve
Natal Parks Board
☎ (0331) 471981

Wonderboom Nature Reserve
Open Monday-Thu: 10am-5pm
Friday-Sunday: 9am-5pm
☎ (012) 543 0918

Swaziland

Malolotja Nature Reserve
Lobamba
☎ (268) 61179/43060

Mlilwane Wildlife
Sanctuary
☎ (268) 61037/61591

Tourist Associations and Publicity Offices

Dundee

Publicity Association
Gladstone Street
☎ (0341) 22139

Graskop

Information Centre
Louis Trichardt Street
☎ (01315) 71316

Hluhluwe

Publicity Office
Main Street
☎ (035) 5620353

Johannesburg

Publicity Association
Market and Kruis Streets
Open Monday-Friday & Saturday am
☎ (011) 336 4961/2/3/4

Satour
International Arrivals Hall
Johannesburg International Airport
☎ (011) 970 1669

Tourist Rendezvous Travel Centre
Rotunda Building
Leyds Street, Braamfontein
Johannesburg
☎ (011) 337 6650

Ladysmith

Tourism Office
Murchison Street
☎ (0361) 22992

Nelspruit

Satour
Shop 5, Promenade Centre
Louis Trichardt Street
☎ (01311) 551 988/9

Newcastle

Publicity Association
Town Hall, Scott Street
☎ (03431) 53318

Pietersburg

Satour
Corner Vorster and Landdros Maré
Streets
☎ (0152) 295 3025

Pietermaritzburg

Publicity Association
177 Commercial Road
☎ (0331) 451348

Pilgrim's Rest

Museum Building
Main Street
☎ (01315) 81211

Pretoria

Tourist Rendezvous Travel Centre
Sammy Marks Centre
Vermeulen & Prinsloo Streets
Daily: 9am-7pm
☎ (012) 323 1222

Sabie

'Sondela'
Main Road
Weekdays only
☎ (01315) 43492

St Lucia

Information Office
Corner McKenzie & Katonkel Streets
☎ (035) 5901143

Tzaneen

Information Office
Library Building
Agatha Road
☎ (015238) 3071411

Ulundi

Publicity Office
Princess Mogogo
Opposite Holiday Inn
☎ (0358) 791223

Venda Tourism Office
Ditike Craft House
Louis Trichardt/Kruger National Park Road
Thoyanandou
☎ (0159) 41577

Vryheid

Publicity Office
Corner of Market and High Streets
☎ (0381) 812133

Tourist Office
Embassy House
Morris Street
Mbabane
☎ (268) 42531/44556

Kwa Zulu Natal, Easter
and Lesotho

Cape, Free State

This itinerary begins in Durban in KwaZulu-Natal, and travels along the popular holiday coastline of the south coast, through the rugged beauty of the Wild Coast, to the settler country around Grahamstown and East London. The route continues onto the city of Bloemfontein in the Free State, followed by the Kingdom of Lesotho, before re-entering the Free State near the Golden Gate Highlands National Park. It returns to Durban via the majestic Drakensberg mountains of KwaZulu-Natal, and the pretty town of Pietermaritzburg.

DURBAN

On a voyage from Portugal to India, the Portuguese explorer Vasco Da Gama first sighted the Durban coastline on Christmas day in 1497. He christened it Natal — Portuguese for Christmas — and named the harbour, Rio de Natal ('river of the nativity').

It was not until three centuries later, whilst on a private trading survey of the eastern seaboard, that Lieutenant Francis George Farewell and Royal Navy Lieutenant James Saunders King discovered this protected bay. Farewell returned to Cape Town to organise the necessary support to establish a trading settlement, and soon returned with two parties, one under the command of Henry Francis Fynn. Farewell and Fynn met with the Zulu Chief Shaka in 1824 and signed a document giving Farewell all the land around Port Natal, from the Umdloti River in the north to the Umbogintwine River in the south.

Eleven years later the settlement was named D'urban in honour of the governor of Cape, Sir Benjamin d'Urban. In 1838, the Voortrekkers arrived in Natal, and the small community of Britons living in Port Natal came under the protection of the short-lived Voortrekker-run Natalia Republic.

However in May 1842, British troops were sent from the Cape to seize control of this land. The Voortrekkers besieged the British garrison in the Old Fort and it was only after the heroic 950km (590 miles) horseback ride by Dick King to Grahamstown that the British received reinforcements. The British had withstood the siege for thirty-four days and were finally relieved on 26 June 1842. Two years later, Natal was proclaimed a British colony and annexed to the Cape of Good Hope.

Labourers were indentured from India in the 1860s by British land-owners who were unable to persuade the proud Zulus to carry out the menial labour of cutting cane. It was expected that at the end of their ten-year term they would return home but most opted to stay and work as tradesmen. Today their culture is firmly established in their bazaars, temples and many businesses which are a feature of Durban. The city is an eclectic mix of old and new and west mixed with a strong flavour of the east.

The face of **Durban** has changed considerably over the last few years, particularly along the beachfront which has undergone extensive re-development. It is considered to be one of the fastest growing cities in the world. Durban attracts visitors all-year-round primarily because of its sub-tropical climate; although it can be unbearably humid in the summer months, especially between January and March.

Travel around Durban is easy — there are *tuk-tuks*, bicycle hire, a number of bus services and taxis. Durban International Airport is situated 10km (6 miles) from the city centre and serves both the major centres of South Africa, as well as international destinations. Durban is connected by intercity rail services to all major cities and there is a local train route along the south coast to Port Shepstone. Telephone 011-773-5878 for further information.

The brightly-decorated rickshaws pulled by traditionally-dressed Zulus are a more unconventional means of travel and can be picked up from Marine Parade. Prices should be agreed beforehand, along with a fee for photography, as the drivers will also charge for snapshots. *Tuk tuks* operate throughout the city and can be hailed anywhere in the street — but agree the fare first.

The **Tourist Junction Travel Centre** is located in the old station on the corner of Commercial Street and Soldiers Way. The local Publicity Association and Satour offices are both here and can provide a wealth of information on local sights. It is an interesting building with a curious roof that was originally designed to cope with sub-zero temperatures in Canada. However, the manufacturers confused the orders and the roof was mistakenly sent to Durban.

The beachfront at **Marine Parade** features a host of shops, restaurants, craft sellers, stalls, sun-worshippers and people strolling along soaking up the atmosphere. The **Seaworld Oceanarium** has an impressive collection of marine life including dolphins, seals, sharks, turtles and penguins. There is daily fish feeding at 11am and 3pm and divers handfeed sharks on Monday, Wednesday and Friday at 12.30pm. The entrance fee helps to support the marine projects of the Oceanographic Research Institute.

Continuing up the promenade past **North Beach** one reaches the **Amphitheatre Gardens** which have an open-air auditorium and fountains. It is an ideal setting for the lively flea market held here every Sunday where a variety of stalls sell handicrafts,

plants, clothes and food. Further along is **Minitown** which features an relief model of the city in the form of a reconstruction of the city's buildings, harbour and airport. The **Snake Park**, on Snell Parade which runs past Minitown, exhibits a wide collection of indigenous and exotic snakes, as well as crocodiles, tortoises and terrapins. Crocodiles are fed publicly at 2pm on Sundays and snake feeding is on Saturday and Sunday at 2pm.

While most people visit Durban to enjoy the beach and night life, the city's history and culture are an integral part of the atmosphere. All national monuments around the city are marked by a small plaque on the pavement.

The Greater Durban Marketing Authority runs a number of walking tours around town including the **Durban Architectural Meander**, which incorporates some of the older and historically significant buildings; the **Feel of Durban Walkabout**; **the Durban Oriental Walkabout**; and the **Durban Historical Walkabout**. The tours usually conclude with coffee at the Roma Revolving Restaurant at **John Ross House** on the Victoria Embankment. Located on the thirtieth floor, it has a splendid view of the city, harbour and surrounding area. Outside the building is a statue of John Ross who, when as a child in 1827, walked from Durban to Maputo to collect urgent medical supplies.

On the embankment opposite is the beautiful baroque-style **Da Gama clock** which commemorates the day in 1497 when Vasco Da Gama discovered the area. There is also a statue of Dick King in memory of his horseback ride from Durban to the garrison of Grahamstown in 1842 to bring the British Army reserves to the Old Fort in Durban.

City Hall is a near perfect replica of Belfast City Hall and is home to two of the city's museums. The **Durban**

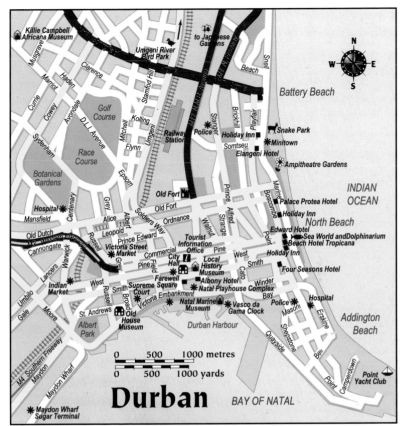

Killie Campbell Africana Museum
Umgeni River Bird Park
to Japanese Gardens
Battery Beach
Beach
Musgrave
Marriot
Currie
Covey
Haden
Clarence
Avondale
Sydenham
Marriott
Golf Course
Kolling
Mitchell
D.L.I. Avenue
Umgeni
Flynn
Race Course
Epsom
Stamford Hill
Stanger
Brickhill
Playfair
Snell
Railway Station
Police
Holiday Inn
Somtseu
Elangeni Hotel
Snake Park
Minitown
Ampitheatre Gardens
Botanical Gardens
Hospital
Mansfield
Centenary
Grey
Old Dutch
Cannongate
Old Fort
Old Fort
Alice
Leopold
Albert
Prince Edward
Victoria Street Market
Commercial
Russell
Grey
Pine
Field
Ordnance
Walnut
Strange
Prince Alfred
Boscombe
Point
Marine
Palace Protea Hotel
Holiday Inn
Edward Hotel
INDIAN OCEAN
North Beach
Sea World and Dolphinarium
Beach Hotel Tropicana
Warwick
Lancers
Indian Market
West
Umbilo
Gale
Moore
Smith
Russell
Broad
Tourist Information Office
City Hall
Local History Museum
Pine
Farewell
Supreme Court
Victoria Embankment
St. Andrews
Albert Park
Old House Museum
Natal Marine Museum
West
Smith
Cato
Winder
Smith
Albony Hotel
Natal Playhouse Complex
Vasco da Gama Clock
Durban Harbour
Holiday Inn
Four Seasons Hotel
Police
Hospital
Masoni
Bay
Quayside
Sheepstone
Bell
Addington Beach
Erskine
Point
Camperdown
Point Yacht Club
Maydon Wharf
Southern Freeway
Maydon
M4
Maydon Wharf Sugar Terminal

0   500   1000 metres
0   500   1000 yards

Durban
BAY OF NATAL

N W E S

M13 MR102 NMR Avenue
Soldiers Way

Opposite top: Bird's-eye view of Durban — considered to be one of the fastest growing cities in the world.

Opposite: Colourful celebrations Chinese-style during the International Day festivities.

Right: The Indian culture is firmly established in Durban and is one of the influences which makes the city an eclectic mix of east and west.

Museum is situated on the first floor and contains natural history displays (including a unique insect arcade), a bird hall and geological collection. The Art Museum on the second floor is worth a visit to view the collection of European and contemporary South African work. The concert hall inside the City Hall is extremely impressive with its high ceilings and polished wooden floors.

Opposite City Hall is **Francis Farewell Square**, a popular spot filled with life-size statues of local historical figures. The **Post Office**, across West Street, was originally Durban's first Town Hall and a bronze plaque on the front steps commemorates the spot where, on 23 December 1899, Winston Churchill made his historic speech after his escape as a prisoner of war of the Boer forces. The old post box is one of the oldest in the country and all letters posted here are specially franked.

The **Natal Playhouse** is a five-venue complex, including a Tudor-style theatre and a Moorish-style colosseum. Lunchtime concerts, dance, drama and jazz are amongst some of the arts performed here. There are tours of the complex on Tuesday, Thursday and Saturday at 10am.

The **Local History Museum** is located in the **Old Court House** which adjoins City Hall on Aliwal Street. It is a colonial-style museum exhibiting period costumes and relics from Durban and Natal history. Further along on Old Fort Road is the **Old Fort** where the British garrison was entrenched against the attacking forces of the Boers in 1842. **Warriors Gate** is a shrine and has a war museum containing relics from early Natal and battlefields all over the world.

Durban harbour is South Africa's largest and busiest port and cargo ships from around the world dock or sail from here twentyy-four hours a day. There is a good view from the ferry which runs from the Point to the Bluff on the opposite side of the harbour. However, it is mainly a service for the crews and fishermen.

There is a massive sugar terminal at **Maydon's Wharf** which houses up to half a million tonnes of sugar and where guided tours are run at 8.30am, 9.45am, 10am, 11.45am, 1.30pm, 2.00pm and 3.45pm daily. The **Natal Maritime Museum** is located by the pleasure terminal on **Albert Embankment** in a well-preserved steam tug.

Durban is a shopper's paradise — from the colourful Indian area around Grey Street to the new sophisticated shopping malls of the Workshop and the Wheel. Visitors can barter in the Indian market, shop cheaply in the host of factory shops, or browse in the flea markets for unusual items. The Indian market around Grey Street is an exotic centre which hums with activity throughout the day. One can buy virtually anything including saris, jewellery, carvings, spices and interesting foods. Many of the shops sell intricately-woven saris and are happy to demonstrate the art of wearing them.

The **Victoria Street Market** is housed in a colourful complex where there is both a fresh fish and a meat market. Visitors can purchase one of the 'secret' curry spice recipes available in the spice section, or make their own selection from the sacks on sale. There is also a stand selling *muti*, the 'medicine' prescribed by the witch doctors.

The **Emmanuel Cathedral** is opposite the market and its exquisite Stations of the Cross are carved from wood donated by Empress Eugiene of France in memory of her son, Louis Napoleon who died during the Anglo-Zulu War.

The **Hindu Temple** in nearby

Somtseu Road is the oldest in South Africa and is open daily. It is advisable to obtain advance permission to visit. The **Jumah Mosque** on the corner of Grey and Queen Streets is the largest mosque in the southern hemisphere and offers free guided tours.

West Street is the main shopping street of the city with air-conditioned smart boutiques and stores. Inside the shell of the railway workshop of old **Durban Station**, is the **Workshop** shopping mall. It has a charming atmosphere and contains a number of interesting speciality shops.

A bustling fleamarket is held every Sunday in the nearby South Plaza Market which sells an interesting mix of antiques, *bric-a-brac*, clothes and fruit. There is often live music, as well as fortune telling here. The **Wheel Shopping Centre** in Gillespie Street has a large Ferris wheel displayed on the outside and is one of Durban's newest shopping centres. It features an amazing collection of shops, restaurants and cinemas. The **African Art Centre** in Guildhall Arcade off Gardiner Street has an interesting collection of genuine African art and crafts and was opened to promote the artistic heritage of the African people.

Every conceivable taste is catered for in Durban. For a few rand the 'bunny chow' provides a large serving of tasty curry in either a quarter, half or full loaf of bread. It will satisfy even the heartiest of appetites but is a messy business unless there is an expert on hand to demonstrate the correct way to handle it. The traditional Indian curry has definitely been adapted to South African taste and there are many good Asian restaurants in the city.

There are a number of excellent restaurants located along the **Golden Mile** — the 6km (4 mile) stretch of beachfront which includes Marine Parade. Visitors can make their selection from the five-star hotel restaurants including the Elangani and Maharini to the smaller establishments which display their daily fare on blackboards outside. There are a number of Holiday Inn Garden Court hotels throughout the city, all of which are reasonably priced. TrafalgarTimeshare offer excellent rates on a wide variety of self-catering accommodation when the accommodation is not being used by its owners.

Sport plays a large part in Durban life and the city hosts several interesting events including the **Comrades Marathon** each June which alternatively begins or ends in Durban or Pietermaritzburg, 90km (56 miles) away. The Gunston 500 Surfing championships every July are a large international event and now form part of the Ocean Africa Water Sports Festival. The Rothman's July is the South African equivalent of Royal Ascot where high fashion is as hotly contested as gambling on the horses. One of Durban's most famous sons is golfer Gary Player and Durban has no shortage of excellent golf courses. The Champion of Champions Zulu dancing contest also takes place in July.

Around the end of June visitors can witness the bizarre Sardine run, when a huge shoal of sardines migrate up the coast followed by big game fish. The area becomes a fisherman's paradise and people can be seen standing in the waters scooping up the fish by the dozen.

Overleaf: The building of Durban City Hall includes a concert hall, a library, an art gallery and a museum.

Page 87 (*top*): The Golden Mile which stretches for 6km (4 miles) along the Durban beachfront abounds with various forms of family entertainment.

Page 87 (*below*): Twinkling lights of the elegant hotels along Marine Parade as dusk falls over the city.

AROUND DURBAN

The **Killie Campbell Africana Museum**, on the corner of Essenwood and Marriott Roads, was the home of Dr Killie Campbell, and is now maintained as a museum filled with Zulu arts and crafts and an Africana library. There are regular guided tours by appointment.

Near Greyville, the **Botanical Gardens** contain numerous indigenous and tropical plants and an orchid house. **Beachwood Mangroves Nature Reserve** north of Durban is one of the area's last remaining mangrove swamps. The **Bluff Nature Reserve** is an excellent bird-watching centre consisting of forest, grassland and wetland which is open from sunrise to sunset. The **Umgeni River Bird Park**, one of the world's top three bird parks, can be accessed from Marine Parade via the Umgeni River Bridge. Indigenous and exotic species of birds from south-east Asia and Australia are all housed in an enchanting setting.

The **Kenneth Stainbank Nature Reserve** is about twenty minutes from the centre in **Yellowwood Park**. The reserve features rhino, giraffe, zebra and several types of antelope.

The **Natal Sharks Board** offers tours of its headquarters at Umhlanga Rocks Drive. There is an audio-visual show followed by a lecture. This is the only tour of its kind in South Africa and a must for anybody wishing to advance their knowledge on these fearsome ocean predators.

An excellent drive from the city is to the breathtaking **Valley of a Thousand Hills** — a massive rift valley through which the sparkling waters of the Umgeni River meanders. The valley is dotted with endless green hills and there are several craft shops and places en route to stop for lunch or tea. Continuing on route 103, visitors will encounter **Phezulu**, a Zulu *kraal* where various aspects of Zulu lifestyle including tribal dancing, medicine and beadmaking are on display.

The **Assagay Safari Park** overlooks the valley and houses a Zulu village, crocodiles, snakes and a museum.

Durban to Shelley Beach
125 km (78 miles)

Take the N2 from Durban, following the signs to the airport and then head south towards Amanzimtoti. From here to Port Edward the area is referred to by most South Africans simply as '*the* south coast'. It is an extremely popular holiday destination, particularly during December and January, as many people from around the country have holiday homes here. A subtropical forest runs along the coast and the road leads past palm-fringed beaches, sparkling lagoons, secluded coves and river estuaries. Further inland, the hills are covered in sugar plantations and the aroma emanating from the mills of burning sugar becomes increasingly heady as the road leads through the small villages which are far removed from the glamorous coastal life.

This coastline is renowned amongst the international surfing community and there is also excellent safe swimming, fishing and golfing. The emphasis here is on relaxation and recreation. The sub-tropical climate attracts visitors throughout the year and there are plenty of places to stay ranging from luxurious to reasonably-priced rooms.

The accommodation along the south coast ranges from five-star hotels with world-class golf courses to small campsites beside the beach, chalets, time-share apartments and moderately-priced accommodation. Although it can be expensive to stay here during the peak season, there are some excellent bargains on offer during the quieter months.

Pawpaws, litchies, avocados, mangoes and pineapples grow in abundance and are sold in large quantities at extremely reasonable prices.

The last few years has seen extensive development of the coastline which has resulted in widespread destruction of the land. However new regulations are now in force to prevent the construction of any ecologically unsound buildings and major efforts are being made to restore parts of the area.

On the first Sunday of each month artists and craftsmen open up their studios and homes to visitors for both demonstrations, exhibitions and sale of their work. The Wildabout Arts and Crafts trail map gives details of the route and is available from the Publicity Office.

The first resort, 27km (17 miles) south of Durban, is **Amanzimtoti** or 'Toti', as it is known by locals. It was originally named by the Zulu King Shaka who tasted the water from the nearby river and declared '. . . so, the water is sweet'.

Its high-rise buildings appear quite out of character with the rest of the coast, but nevertheless Amanzimtoti is a popular destination. The **Ilanda Wilds Nature Reserve** is worth a visit and there are some self-guided walking trails along the river. The two main beaches, Inyoni Rocks and Pipeline are protected by shark nets and have swimming pools, and Chain Rock is excellent for surfing. Visitors can hire paddle boats from the boathouse on the lagoon for a river trip upstream.

The next town of **Kingsburgh** was named after Dick King who passed through on his heroic ride from Durban to Grahamstown in 1842 to bring the British Army reserves to Natal. Kingsburgh incorporates five beaches which run into each other, Doonside, Warner, Winkle Spruit, Illovo and Karridene. Warner, Winkle Spruit and Illovo are all protected by shark nets and Illovo is one of South Africa's few nudist beaches. There is windsurfing and water-skiing on the lagoon and walking trails through the woods.

Back on the N2 before **Umkomaas**, is the Umnini Craft Stall located at the Shell Ultra City, where stalls are laden with handiwork of the Amatuli crafts people. Across the main road towards the beach is the Umgababa Craft Market where fruit and vegetables are sold at very reasonable prices.

The **Aliwal Shoal**, 4km (2 miles) from Umkomaas is one of the best scuba-diving spots in southern Africa. The Aliwal Cove is a hotel and dive resort catering for visitors wanting to explore the reef and experience a wide variety of marine life including the ragged-tooth shark.

Continue along the R102 to the white, sandy beach of **Clansthal**, which incorporates **Greenpoint**, an internationally-renowned surfing spot. Further along is **Scottburgh**, which is built on a prominent headland overlooking the azure waters of the Indian Ocean. The rugged coastline features pools, rocky inlets and stretches of beautiful beaches. The main beach of Scott Bay is protected by shark nets and there is a tidal pool. The beach can become quite busy and there is a lively atmosphere in the summer months. Nearby at **Crocworld**, there are twelve pools containing Nile crocodiles and American alligators, and visitors can view these formidable creatures at close range. Feeding times are 11am and 3pm. For those with the heart, or the appetite, there are crocodile steaks on offer at the Crocodilian Restaurant here. There is also Zulu dancing every Sunday and Wednesday.

Pennington is more exclusive than the rest of the south coast and is probably best-known for Selborne Lodge where the golf course is considered to rival Augusta in the USA. From here, the road leads through **Ifafa Beach**, where a lovely lagoon offers good bathing, swimming and boating. **Hibberdene** marks the beginning of the Hibiscus coast, although the town is not particularly interesting. It is better to continue further south on the N2 to **Umzumbe Beach**, an idyllic and tranquil spot. Approximately 10km (6 miles) west of **Umzumbe** along the D453, and a 500m (1,640ft) walk up a well-worn pathway to the top of the ridge, there is a relic from King Shaka's attack upon the Hlongwa cannibals. Shaka carried out an ancient ritual of atonement with his ancestral spirits to ensure their success in battle. Followed by every man in the *impi*, Shaka would lead a stone-throwing procession, and it is those stones that are seen here. The huge pile of pebbles is considered good luck by the Zulus.

Banana Beach is halfway between Hibberdene and Port Shepstone and the budget resort of Club Tropicana is located here.

Port Shepstone is the oldest town on the south coast. It was founded in 1882 by 200 Norwegian immigrants who settled here with the intention of creating a successful fishing village. The town is the main coach terminus for the area, and although it has undergone some recent improvement, it generally lacks the charm of the other resorts along this coast.

Port Shepstone's greatest attraction is the **Banana Express** steam train which departs from here and is one of the highlights of the coastline. The old steam train rattles along the narrow-gauge track past the palm-fringed beaches, before heading inland through the banana plantations. Every

Thursday at 10am and Sunday at 11am (there is an increased service during the peak season) the train goes to Izotsha. At 10am each Wednesday and Sunday it leaves for **Paddock** where visitors, accompanied by an experienced ranger, can enjoy the Baboon View trail through the Oribi Gorge Nature Reserve.

By car, the 19km (12 mile) drive north from Port Shepstone, to the **Oribi Gorge Nature Reserve**, leads through some remarkable scenery where the Umzimkuluwana River has carved a gorge 24km (15 miles) long, 5km (3 miles) wide and 366m (1,201ft) deep. Some of the viewpoints include Echo Valley, Horseshoe Bend, Hanging Rock, Baboon's Castle and Oribi Heads. The reserve is home to over forty species of mammal including antelope and baboon.

Back on the coastal road the atmosphere becomes increasingly commercial as it passes the Shell Centre Shopping Centre at Shelley Beach, as well as several shops and restaurants. There are many good hotels and guest houses in the area.

Shelly Beach to Port Edward 46 km (28 miles)

A few kilometres further along the N2, the road passes through **St Michael's-on-Sea**, a small well-groomed residential resort on the banks of the Umhlanageni River. This is followed by **Uvongo**, whose name is derived from the Ivungi River which flows through the town and means 'low murmur' in Zulu. It refers to the sound of the waterfall which tumbles some 23m (75ft) into the lagoon near the sea. It is a quiet, sophisticated resort with one of the best beaches on the south coast. At the coastal lagoon, two sheer headlands of rugged rock protrude high above the bush on the southern side of the main bathing beach. The

Uvongo Bird Park offers sightings of several indigenous and exotic birds.

Margate takes its name from the Margate monster which reputedly washed up on the beach in the 1920s. It is the main entertainment centre of the south coast and is very popular with families and young people. It has one of the safest bathing beaches along the entire coast and the town is very busy during the summer. There is a variety of entertainment along the beach in summer months and a large airshow is held each May.

The tourist towns of Margate and **Ramsgate** virtually converge together, although Ramsgate is quieter and has a more nautical atmosphere.

The **Blue Lagoon** is popular for water-skiing and the teahouse on the lagoon is worth a visit. It is situated in a beautiful setting where visitors can sit outside on the veranda, or wander around the small arts and crafts centre. Originally a Chinese restaurant, there is a distinctly eastern feel to it, including a small wooden bridge which leads to the beach. The Nelson Pub in the Crayfish Inn is crammed with nautical memorabilia and they offer excellent value lunches.

Further along the coast, the spectacular 5km (3 mile) **Marina Beach** provides uninterrupted views of white sands and lush sub-tropical vegetation. There is an outcrop of rocks along the beach which are known as 'Plum Pudding'. Nearby, the exclusive resort of San Lameer is situated within a beautiful nature reserve and day visitors are welcome.

Port Edward is the most southerly

Above: (*left*) The lesser double-collared sunbird and (*right*) the red bishop are two of South Africa's dazzling and colourful bird species.

of all the coastal resorts and is situated 5km (3 miles) before the road crosses into the Eastern Cape province — formerly the self-governing homeland of the Transkei. The beach is good and from here one can see **Tragedy Hill** where, in 1881, a group of traders were captured by Dingaan's Zulus and massacred. Until recently the hill was littered with the bones of victims.

The nearby **Mtamvuna Nature Reserve** has fine examples of San rock art and it is one of the last breeding colonies of the Cape vulture.

The luxury Wild Coast Sun resort and casino is a short distance away and a must for visitors wishing to try their luck at the many tables and gaming machines. It is situated on a river estuary, and offers dazzling beaches, excellent watersports and a variety of sparkling shows and entertainment. The Mzamba Village market which is opposite the resort sells Transkeian crafts and there are performances of dance and folklore at the cultural centre.

Port Edward to Port St John 201 km (125 miles)

The 250km (155 miles) of Wild Coast from Port Edward in the north to the Kei River in the south is quite beautiful. Unfenced gravel roads wind their way from the main tarred N2 through rolling green hills dotted with traditional thatched rondavels, down to the rugged coastline of wide, sweeping beaches, shipwrecks, coves and rivers.

The emphasis is on the outdoors and hiking trails along this coastline are some of the best in southern Africa. The fishing is excellent and there are huge quantities of fresh fish and crayfish for sale on the beaches at extremely reasonable prices. Dolphins play in the waters along the coast, the scuba diving is first-rate and there are plenty of places for water-skiing and boating.

Until 1994 when all homelands rejoined South Africa's administration, this area was formerly the Transkei, the independent homeland of the Xhosa people. It was granted independence in 1976, but never really achieved economic autonomy. It relied heavily on subsidies from the South African government and from the migrant labourers working for South African organisations.

Because of the poverty which still exists today, many local children in the resort towns are eager to earn a few rand, and tourists rarely object to paying for their services as a guide along walking trails, or to the best fishing spots in the area. The locals are generally friendly, although there have been times in the past when it was considered unsafe to travel alone on the Transkei part of the N2.

The name Transkei, meaning 'land beyond the Kei', refers to the homeland of the descendants of various Xhosa tribes who moved south in the nineteenth century fleeing the Zulu King Shaka's *difaqane* ('state of continuous war'). They clashed with the Europeans as they moved northwards, which led to nine frontier wars and the eventual annexation of its territories to the Cape government in 1879.

The Xhosa are of Nguni stock, which also incorporates the tribes of the Pondo, Pondomiese, Tembu and Bomvana. Witchcraft and superstition play a large role in daily life as the Xhosa believe that the spirits of their ancestors determine their good fortune by how much respect is paid to them through sacrifices and offerings. Diviners, who are usually women, mediate between the living and the dead. Old people are also held in high esteem as they are believed to be living spirits and sacrifices are offered to them while they are alive.

A little over a century ago, their beliefs almost caused the destruction of the entire tribe. In 1856, a young girl named Nongqawuse claimed to be a prophetess. She announced that ancestral spirits has visited her and promised that if the Xhosa slaughtered all their cattle and destroyed their crops, their warrior ancestors would arise and help them drive the white man from their land, after which new crops and cattle would appear. In February 1857, the Xhosa did as she ordered which resulted in a massive famine, and despite aid from the Cape government, approximately 25,000 people died from starvation and many more became refugees.

This is one of the most exceptional and undeveloped stretch of coastline in the world where the sub-tropical vegetation and long golden beaches are interspersed only by sparkling rivers, dramatic gorges and beautiful lagoons. The area is renowned for its excellent game fishing, as well as scuba diving — particularly wreck diving — and for water-skiing on any one of the twenty rivers in the region.

Over 800 recorded species of fish have been found in these waters, and it is also shell-collectors paradise, where examples from the Indo-Pacific region have been found. There are also several species of exotic flowers which carpet the surrounding hills including red hot pokers, orchids, flame lilies and crane flowers.

The small family-style resorts dotted along the coastline are simple but comfortable, and excellent value. All resorts include three meals a day and most offer a seafood feast on a Saturday evening where crayfish, fresh oysters, prawns with fresh avocado, pears, bananas and pawpaw are served in abundance.

Most of the resorts offer free sporting facilities with the exception of golf for which there is a nominal fee.

There are good opportunities for camping here in the many nature reserves, as virtually 40,000 hectares (98,800 acres) of evergreen forest are preserved here in nature reserves and state forests. However, campers are advised to come well-prepared as the facilities at the camp sites are somewhat limited.

There is no coastal road because of the twenty rivers which bisect the coastline. Travelling between resorts therefore takes time as visitors have to return each time to the N2 and take the next gravel road back to the coast. As the popularity of this coastline rises, there is an increase in the number of tarred roads in the area. Watch out for the cattle that stray into the middle of the road and allow plenty of time for the journey.

The **Wild Coast** is famous for its hiking trails — the most popular and well trodden of which is the Port St Johns to Coffee Bay trail. The trails get booked up well in advance so it is not advisable to turn up on the day expecting to find space. A maximum of twelve people are allowed on each trail and reservations can be made up to eleven months in advance through the Department of Agriculture and Forestry in Umtata. They will also handle reservations for the hutted accommodation at Dwesa, Hluleka and Silaka Nature Reserves and issue permits for the campsites along the coast. The price of the trail includes basic accommodation but visitors must provide their own provisions and bedding.

The hike from Port St Johns to Coffee Bay takes six nights; the Mtamvuna to Msikaba trail takes three nights; Msikaba to Agate Terrace (at Port St Johns) takes seven nights; the Coffee Bay to Mbashe trail takes five nights and Dwesa (Nqaraba) to Kei River takes six nights.

Leave Port Edward on the R61

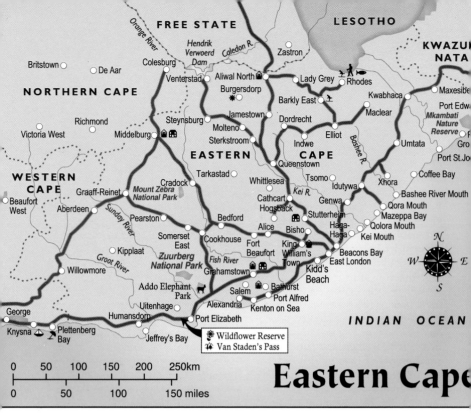

Below: The spectacular Hole in the Wall which has been eroded in the cliffs over the years by the constant pounding of the sea.

heading south and cross the bridge which marks the old border of the Transkei, now part of the Eastern Cape province. There is a stark change in the scenery as the sub-tropical beach vegetation changes into small undulating hills scattered with small, thatched round huts made of clay, broken down cars and cattle grazing by and on the road. At **Bizana** take the left turn and follow the signs to Lusikisiki/Port St Johns. Along this stretch of road the little homes vary in shape and size and are painted in colourful shades of blues, greens, pinks and yellows.

The road passes through Lusikisiki but here is little to stop for, so continue through town heading towards Port St Johns. The scenery along this route is incredible with endless, unspoilt stretches of forest. About 10km (6 miles) before Port St Johns there is a marvellous view of the two sandstone headlands of **Mount Thessiger** and **Mount Sullivan** which stand sentinel either side of Port St Johns. They were named after two men who hoisted the Union Jack here after the area ceded to Britain in 1870.

Follow the road left into **Port St Johns** — the largest resort along this coast, and certainly the one with the most beautiful setting. It was named after the Portuguese galleon, the *Sao Joao*, which was wrecked off the coast here in 1552. The town boasts three excellent beaches, a nature reserve and some of the best angling in South Africa. In July, there are frequent displays by porpoises which swim close to the coast and many locals will swim along with them. Relics of many shipwrecks may be seen around the town including the cannon retrieved from the wreck of the *Grosvenor*. There is also a small museum in town.

First Beach is most popular for fishing, while **Second Beach**, 5km (3 miles) from the town centre is more secluded and attractive for swimming

in the lagoon or sea. There are several small resorts beside the beach, lagoon and river with basic accommodation and camping for budget travellers. There is no decent hotel, but the Umngazi River Bungalows are about 30km (19 miles) further along the coast road, for those looking for a more comfortable place to stay. About halfway along the road to Second Beach from Port St Johns, there is a dirt track which twists around the grassy hilltop to a spectacular lookout point.

The road snakes up the headland beyond Second Beach to the **Silaka Nature Reserve** where there is a limited amount of self-catering accommodation that should be booked well in advance from the Department of Agriculture and Fisheries. There are numerous walking trails from **Third Beach** through to the giant trees of the evergreen forest where colourful orchids grow in abundance, and bushbuck roam wild. This is also a bird-watchers paradise.

Port St Johns to Coffee Bay
190 km (118 miles)

Take the R61 tarred road to the old capital of **Umtata** where it is possible to see the *Bunga*, or parliament from the days when the region was self-governed. The city is an eclectic mix of old colonial-style architecture standing between modern high-rise buildings, and its name originates from the name of the local Mthatha River. There is little point in stopping here except to make bookings through the TDC/Wild Coast Reservations for accommodation, or to arrange a permit at the Department of Agriculture and Forestry for one of the nature reserves. There is a small museum on York Street which contains information about the former Transkei homeland and its people.

Midway between Port St. Johns and

Umtata the road leads past the **Rock of Execution** which rises 240m (800ft) from the road and is where criminals were pushed from the top in pre-colonial times.

K D Matanzima Airport is located 17km (10 miles) from Umtata and has regular flights to many cities throughout South Africa. There is also a helicopter service from Umtata to Lusikisiki, the Mkambati Game Reserve and Mzamba, as well as weekly flights to resorts along the coast. There is no public transport from the airport, but cars may be hired through the Avis office there.

Leave Umtata on Alexandra Road past the small **Nduli Nature Reserve** on the right. The reserve is open daily and is home to fifty species of bird, antelope and wildebeest indigenous to the Transkei.

Further along, the road passes the **University of Transkei**, followed by the Ultra City service station where the Wonk'umntu Handicraft Centre is situated in a cluster of tribal huts. Visitors are encouraged to browse through the impressive range of traditional beadwork, jewellery, clothes and pots.

Take the left turning to Coffee Bay approximately 20km (12 miles) later through glorious scenic vistas and small villages of traditional tribal character where women dressed in the traditional Xhosa cloth and colourful jewellery work the land, or congregate beside the rivers with their laundry. The scene is very picturesque despite the severe examples of soil erosion along the way.

Coffee Bay is about 100km (62 miles) from Umtata and there is a spectacular view of the town nestling between the surrounding cliffs and hills from the outskirts of the settlement. According to local legend, Coffee Bay received its name after a large shipwrecked cargo of coffee beans was washed up at the mouth of the Nenga River.

It has a wide golden beach which is the best place to watch the stunning sub-tropical sunsets for which the bay is renowned. The Ocean View Hotel has recently been refurbished and is the only accommodation in town apart from a very basic campsite used by hikers. There are some excellent walks and spear-fishing in the area.

Accommodation is also available at **Hole in the Wall** which is 20km (12 miles) back along the road to Umtata and follow the signs. The resort takes its name from the spectacular hole which has been eroded in a cliff by the constant pounding of the waves. There are walks along the clifftops and along the coast, and for a small fee the local children will show visitors the best route to follow.

Coffee Bay to East London 285 km (177 miles)

Return to the N2 heading south along which there are a number of left turns to several other secluded resorts along the Wild Coast.

Wild Coast Reservations in Umtata or East London can recommend the ideal places to stay according to interest and budget.

At the mouth of the Bashee River, between Coffee Bay and Qolora Mouth, is the **Dwesa Nature Reserve**. Accommodation is either in a log cabin within the evergreen forest by the sea, or at the Haven Hotel which has a golf course, sports facilities and walking trails.

Qolora Mouth is a fisherman's paradise and each August and September, the pignose gunter run attracts anglers to the Kob Inn from all over southern Africa. There is a lovely sandy beach and lagoon with rowing boats, canoes and sailboards available. There are two hotels here — Seagulls which is situated on the beach and Trennerys which offers a grand view across the bay. There is scuba diving, windsurfing, canoeing, horseriding and a golf course. The remains of the *Jacaranda* shipwreck is 7km (4 miles) away and can be seen at low tide.

The Wavecrest Hotel is at the mouth of the Nxaxo River and is situated in a marvellous setting directly on the beach overlooking the estuaries of the Nxaxo and Ngwasi rivers. It is an ideal resort offering a wide variety of watersports. Professional divers make good money from the abalone caught here.

From Qolora Mouth to East London, the coastline has earned the name of 'the Romantic Coast' because of the charming resorts amidst virtually English-style scenery.

East London

At **East London**, the Buffalo River (known to the Hottentots as *Igaablab*) provides South Africa with its only river port of any significant size. The town was formally established in 1848 after the British annexed the area and the name East London was given to the harbour. During the frontier wars, the harbour was used for troop and equipment movement to avoid the long march overland through the several battles zones in surrounding areas.

There is an airport a few kilometres from the city centre at Willow Park, which has regular flights to cities within South Africa. Coach services between Port Elizabeth and Durban stop here and there is a train link to Johannesburg.

The **East London Metropolitan Tourism Association** is well-stocked with information on the area, and they share their offices with Satour. The **East London Museum** in Oxford Street has a comprehensive range of

natural history exhibits, including the first coelacanth fish ever to be caught in the world. This odd-looking fish with stumpy leg-like fins was believed to be extinct but was caught in the nearby Chaluma River in 1938. A second was caught off the Comoros in 1952. There is also a dodo egg which was brought from Mauritius in 1846 and is believed to be the only one left in the world. The nearby **Ann Bryant Art Gallery** is situated in lovely grounds and was named after a collector who bequeathed her Victorian-style house and collection of English artworks to the city. Paintings by contemporary South Africa artists are also on display.

In Fleet Street, the **Lock Street Jail** was originally the site of the first women's prison in South Africa. It has now been uniquely developed into a shopping centre, primarily serving cottage industries. Some old prison cells have been preserved and there is a collection of emotional letters and interesting accounts on display of life in prison.

The **Oriental Plaza** is located off Oxford Street and sells mainly oriental clothing, brassware, jewellery and spices, and visitors can barter in an eastern style for goods. There are a number of other plazas including Chamberlain Road and the Vincent Park Shopping Centre which offer excellent shopping.

Queen's Park covers 34 hectares (74 acres) on a hillside between the city centre and river. The gardens display a number of indigenous plants and exotic flowers, and incorporate the **Queen's Park Zoo**.

There are many excellent beaches within easy access of the city. **Orient Beach** is considered to be one of the safest beaches in South Africa and was named after a Russian sailing vessel that was wrecked off the coast here. Along the promenade there are brass plaques which mark six of the eighty-

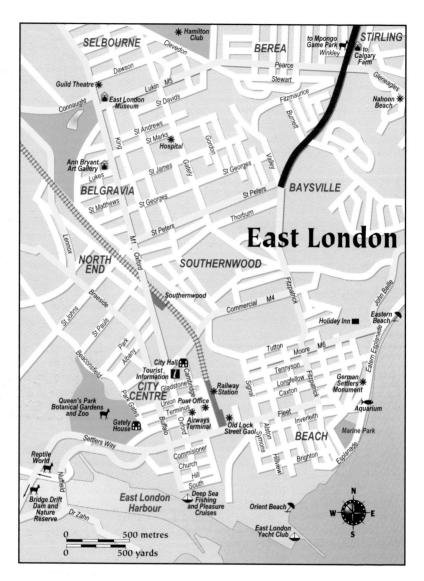

two shipwrecks along this coast. Scuba diving trips can be arranged to explore some of the wrecks in the area.

Eastern Beach is considered the best beach for surfing, although it was Nahoon Beach which once hosted the world surfing championships.

The King David Hotel is a three-star property which rates as one of the finest establishments in East London. It has three different restaurants which cater for breakfast, lunches and *a la carte* evening meals. The Holiday Inn situated on the beachfront is also good value, or alternatively Osner Resorts can arrange self-catering accommodation. The Movenpick Swiss restaurant on the beachfront is very popular, although prices can be high.

Above: The attractive town of Port Alfred has developed around the estuary of the Kowie River.

Around East London

Mpongo Game Park in the charming Mpongo River valley is 29km (18 miles) from East London. There are over forty species of wildlife including giraffe, zebra, rhino and elephant. The park offers excellent hiking and horse-trails as well as night safaris. The Huberta Restaurant is named after Huberta the hippo, whose wanderings have become legendary along the Eastern Cape coast and some of her antics are documented inside the restaurant.

The Calgary Wagon Museum has become quite popular and is 13km (8 miles) from East London. It features a collection of restored horse-drawn vehicles and a gypsy caravan.

East London to Grahamstown 205 km (127 miles)

Take the coastal road from East London in the direction of Port Alfred. This is the former Ciskei homeland which has now been officially incorporated into the Eastern Cape province. There is a strong Germanic influence throughout the area, notably in the names of towns like Hamburg and Berlin. In 1857, German immigrants landed here and named the town Port Kowie.

The main tribe of the area is the Xhosa, who congregated here in 1610. A century later part of the tribe migrated across the Great Kei River after a family feud for leadership divided the tribe.

At the time, the territory was largely occupied by Hottentots who resented the invasion, but after their chief was killed in battle, Hoho, the Hottentot queen agreed a deal for land. The Ciskei was granted independence in 1981 and was incorporated back into South Africa in 1994.

Port Alfred is situated on the coastal road halfway between East London and Port Elizabeth. It lies on the banks of the estuary of the beautiful Kowie River and the town is known by locals as 'Kowie'. A quiet seaside resort with golden beaches and a large marina, it is growing in popularity and some luxurious holiday homes have been built on a canal system in the estuary. The river provides the main source of entertainment for the area and is where the popular Kowie canoe trail and the 8km (5 mile) Kowie hiking trail starts. The huge sand dunes at **East Beach** provide a centre for sand skiing.

From Port Alfred, take the turning inland to Grahamstown via Bathurst. This area is known as settler country as its development began with the arrival of a few British settlers from the original 4,000 who had landed at Algoa Bay in 1820. They were mostly skilled workmen, such as masons and carpenters, who had been lured to South Africa as a result of the hardships they faced in Britain at the end of the Napoleonic Wars. They experienced further difficulties in their new homeland when faced with poor soil, drought, and the continuing battles with the Xhosa. Many of the settlers who were uneducated in farming techniques, and unprepared for the harsh African conditions, opted to move to Grahamstown and Bathurst after losing considerable land and livestock during the frontier wars. It was this drift towards the towns which established the Eastern Cape as a commercial area and saw the development of cities like Port Elizabeth and Grahamstown.

Bathurst was the centre from which the 1820 settlers were despatched to the lands allocated to them. It has a distinctly English atmosphere with a small village green and old-world Pig and Whistle pub. The people are a hardy breed who welcome visitors and enjoy recounting fascinating tales of their pioneering ancestors.

The **Toposcope Memorial** at nearby Thornridge, consists of fifty-seven bronze plaques detailing the history of each of the original settler parties. It marks the point from which the settlers were sent to their new homes.

St John's Anglican Church in Donkin Street is the oldest unaltered church in southern Africa and contains plaques bearing testimony to those who lost their lives during the many wars in the area. It was built with defence in mind and many settlers took refuge there during raids by the Xhosa.

Bathurst comes alive during the agricultural show which is held each April when the village is packed with visitors from the surrounding areas. It lasts for a week and there are colourful events and unusual displays. On the closing night of the fair, there is a huge spit *braai*.

Summerhill Farm offers a tractor ride around the pineapple farm. A video portraying the customs and traditions of the Xhosa people is shown and there is traditional dancing. The farm is immediately recognisable by the 16m (52ft) fibreglass pineapple outside which is a replica of the one in Queensland, Australia.

GRAHAMSTOWN

Continue along the R67 towards Grahamstown, considered by many as the cultural centre of the Eastern Cape. Grahamstown is known under many banners — 'City of the Saints', 'City of Schools' and 'Settler City' — all of which are appropriate names to reflect the many aspects of this fascinating city. It was founded in 1812 by Colonel John Graham who chose this site as his military outpost after he drove back 20,000 Xhosa from the Great Fish River frontier during the fourth Frontier War.

Grahamstown is a university city of wide tree-lined streets, beautiful gardens and countless churches. The city is centred around the triangular **Church Square** which is dominated by the **Cathedral of St Michael and St George**. It contains many fine examples of Anglican architecture along with dedications and memorials to those who died during the frontier wars.

During term time, the streets of the city are packed with school children and students from the numerous schools and **Rhodes University** — one of South Africa's leading academic institutions. The city has a distinct flavour of England's university town, Oxford.

The **Albany Museum** is the second oldest museum in South Africa and the complex now incorporates various other museums.

The **Natural History Museum** traces the history of early man, aspects of daily life and the customs of the people of Africa. The **History Museum** provides displays and information on settler history and Xhosa culture. The **Observatory Museum** is located in the home of jeweller, Henry Galpin, who had a strong leaning towards scientific matters. The interior of the house has been authentically restored and displays several objects dating back to the Victorian era. The most fascinating aspect of the house is the tower where Galpin built his camera *obscura*. Using a series of lenses and natural light, the camera will reproduce the activity from the surrounding streets on the table inside the tower. It also houses a display which recounts the discovery of the Hope diamond in 1867. The diamond was authenticated by Galpin and heralded the start of the diamond industry in South Africa.

The **1820 Settlers National Monument** on **Gunfire Hill** was completed in 1974 to commemorate the British pioneers who contributed to the development of South Africa. It is set in a floral reserve and its facilities include a conference centre, a theatre and a restaurant. It is the main site for the annual Grahamstown Arts Festival. **Fort Selwyn**, a preserved fort in its grounds, dates back to the 1830s, but is not open to the public.

Provost House and Prison was built in 1838 to accommodate deserters and other military offenders, and tours are carried out by prior arrangement. An feature of the prison is the round tower which allowed the warden to observe all the cells from one position.

The **Drostdy** was demolished in 1936, but the right wing survived and is now used as the main entrance to Rhodes University.

The post box on the corner of Worcester and Somerset Street is the oldest post box in South Africa and mail posted here is franked with a special post mark.

Grahamstown is a hive of activity during the Arts Festival at the end of June/early July. A variety of amateur performing arts including music, theatre and dance is offered with the aim of promoting a common South African culture. It is equivalent to the Edinburgh Festival on a smaller scale

Above: White rhino are one of the many species found in Shamwari Game Reserve.

and is already attracting a large international following. Accommodation is scarce during this period so advance booking is recommended.

Grahamstown has several bed and breakfast establishments and the Tourist Office on Church Square can provide details. The Cathcart Arms and Grand Hotel are both hotels providing accommodation in elegant colonial-style properties.

Sixty kilometres (37 miles) from Grahamstown is the Shamwari Game Reserve which is located on an 8,000 (19,760) acre reserve. This five-star reserve offers either luxury overnight accommodation in rustic, thatched lodges, or day excursions conducted by highly experienced rangers. The game includes elephant, black rhino, white rhino, lion, leopard, buffalo,

hippo and giraffe and guests are driven around in open vehicles through sloping valleys and over scenic hillsiddes.

Guided walks with armed rangers in search of rare species are available and there is a luxury train service to the reserve. Shamwari is endorsed by conservationists and one of the recently completed projects has been the reintroduction of the endangered black rhino.

There are many good restaurants in Grahamstown including La Galleria Italian restaurant which serves fresh home-made pasta in a variety of sauces. The Monkey Puzzle restaurant at the Botanical Gardens offers a range of unusual South African dishes, but for the less adventurous there is a Spur restaurant in the high street.

Above: Students enjoy the festivities at the Grahamstown Festival.

Grahamstown to Hogsback
121 km (75 miles)

Rejoin the R67 following the signs to **Fort Beaufort**. The road winds over hills and moorland and there are some magnificent uninterrupted views of the area. Turn right at the end of road into Fort Beaufort which is built on a bend in the Kat River, and was once considered the perfect location for a military defence on the frontier.

 It is an attractive town with a good military museum in Bell Street and an historical museum in Durban Street. The **Martello Tower** — one of only two in South Africa — the other being at Simonstown in Cape Town, is preserved as a national monument. It is a tall, circular building with a turret from which a machine-gun can be

swivelled in full rotation and was an extremely popular method of defence for the British military.

From here, take the road to the town of **Alice**, named after Queen Victoria's daughter when it was first set up in 1824 as a mission for the Xhosa living in the Tyume River valley. It has since become a commercial and farming centre and the town is noted for the **Fort Hare University** which was established in 1916 as the first university for black Africans in South Africa. It was named after the ruins of Fort Hare which is in the grounds of the university. The university also houses a museum displaying Xhosa history and culture, along with an art collection inspired by anthropologist Eddie de Jager, who questioned how black people reacted to years of

103

apartheid and repression. This is demonstrated through paintings by South Africans from a number of different tribes.

Follow the road left towards Hogsback shortly after leaving Alice. The mountains and scenery are dotted with green fertile valleys, rich woodlands and sparkling waterfalls. Beware of children who leap into the road trying to stop motorists and get them to buy one of their clay creations.

The road that winds up the mountain becomes a gravel track at the top as it enters the mountain village of **Hogsback**. It is claimed that the magic of the Hogsback mists inspired Tolkien to write *Lord of the Rings*. There are several walks through the enchanting forest where giant Shellwoods are surrounded by ferns and colourful wild flowers. The trails include the waterfalls of **Madonna and Child**, **Bridal Veil** and the fascinating **Kettlespout** where the water forces its way through a natural spout at the top of a cliff. The routes are defined by markers using the Hogsback Inn's emblem in either red green, yellow and blue and the corresponding, *Piggy Guide* is widely available here. There is an arts festival here in October when the local artists and craftsmen open their homes to visitors.

Hogsback enjoys warm sunny days and cool evenings, and snow is quite common between June and August. Many English flowers and shrubs, including the rhododendron bloom during the months of August and September, and the climate is ideal for growing blackberries, strawberries and raspberries.

St Patricks-on-the-Hill, is a non-denominational church and is one of the smallest in the country. The **Eastern Monarch** is a giant Yellowwood tree located twenty minutes from the main road through the forest. There are private cottages available for rent and a few mountain lodges and inns. It is also possible to camp in the forest on condition that the necessary permits have been obtained.

Hogsback to Bloemfontein
582 kilometres (371 miles)

Return to the main road and follow the signs to **King William's Town**. This is one of the oldest border towns which was originally established in 1826 as a mission station when the British governor moved the frontier to the Kei River in an attempt to expel the Xhosa from the territory. At the end of the seventh Frontier War, it was re-established as a military centre and today it is a bustling industrial town.

Its most interesting attraction is the **Kaffararian Museum** which houses a fascinating collection of African mammals. It contains the mounted figure of the legendary Huberta the hippo. In 1928, Huberta wandered throughout the entire countryside, turning up in many unexpected places, including Durban. Her travels covered over 1,000km (621 miles) until she came to a tragic end in April 1931 when she was accidentally shot by a farmer.

The Information Office is located in the Town Hall next door.

Nine kilometres (6 miles) south of town on the Buffalo River are the ruins of **Fort Murray** where the Xhosa 'prophets' Nongquawuse and Noxosi were detained.

Nearby, the former capital of the Ciskei, **Bisho** is the newly-elected capital of the Eastern Cape province, into which it has now been incorporated. The Department of Aviation can make reservations for local hiking trails, including the Amatola and the 64km (40 mile) Shipwreck trail, along the desolate coastline which became the grave for many wrecked ships — including seven in one day on 26 May 1812.

Take the R346 to Stutterheim, a lovely little town surrounded by mountains, woodlands and rivers making the area perfect for walks and trails. The river provides excellent fishing and boating.

Take the N6 north in the direction of **Queenstown**, the principal town of the Border region, which is known as the 'Rose Capital of South Africa' because of its numerous rose gardens. It was named after Queen Victoria in 1853, and the town centre was laid out in the form of a hexagon so the streets could be defended by directing cannons and guns along any of the six principal thoroughfares. The town contains the **Queenstown and Frontier Museum** and the **Municipal Art Gallery**, as well as the **Queenstown Collectors Museum** featuring displays of over thirty different types of hobby.

Further along the N6 on the banks of the Orange River is **Aliwal North**. The town has grown around hot springs which have developed into a spa. The spa, which is signposted from the town centre, contains an indoor pool with a constant temperature of 34°C. It also has an Olympic-size pool, a 93m (305ft) water slide, and accommodation on-site with a self-service restaurant.

The **Garden of Remembrance and Blockhouse** in Barkly Street was erected in honour of the British and colonial soldiers who died during the Anglo-Boer War. The **Buffelspruit Game Reserve** offers a good view of the town and the reserve is home to several species of antelope.

The majority of the restaurants are steakhouses and the Steak Baron at the Balmoral Hotel is the most popular.

The route leaves the Cape province and enters the Free State — formerly the Orange Free State — an area that was traditionally an Afrikaner stronghold. The Voortrekkers were the first to settle here when they left the Cape Colony on the Great Trek in 1836 in search of their own land away from the British rule. After crossing the Orange River they established their homes and cultivated the unsettled land between the Vaal and the Orange rivers. In the process they decimated most of the wildlife in the area, leaving the legacy that today the Free State has only one national park — the Golden Gate National Park.

The Voortrekkers were, however, still technically subjects of the Cape colony and a series of bitter feuds ensued after their arrival. Many headed north of the Vaal River and founded the Transvaal (meaning 'across the Vaal'). After years of conflict the British finally agreed in 1854 to recognise the Orange Free State as an independent Boer state. However, the Anglo-Boer War brought renewed fighting and much of this occurred in the Orange Free State, as the Boers fought to retain their newly-found independence. At the end of the war, it returned to British rule until in 1910, when Orange Free State regained its former status after the formation of the Union of South Africa. As a measure of its importance, it was made the judicial capital of South Africa.

The Free State is surrounded by the Cape Province, Lesotho, Gauteng and KwaZulu-Natal. Its natural boundaries are the Vaal River in the north, the Orange River in the south and the Maluti mountains in the east. The days are sunny and warm, but in winter the nights become very cold and snow falls in the mountains.

The land is primarily farming country with endless fields of crops in the vast flatlands that make up the Free State.

Overleaf: Bloemfontein is home to the distinctive Tweetoringker Church (meaning 'church with two spires').

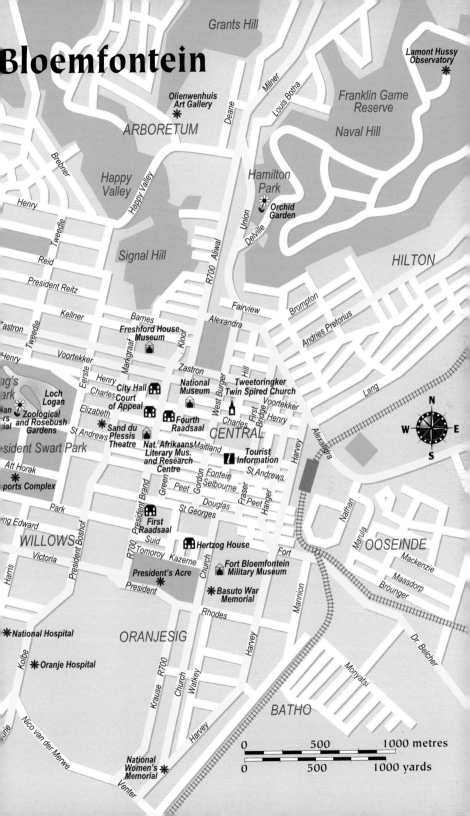

Bloemfontein

Grants Hill

Lamont Hussy
Observatory

Milner

Louis Botha

Olienwenhuis
Art Gallery

Franklin Game
Reserve

ARBORETUM

Naval Hill

Deane

Brebner

Happy
Valley

Hamilton
Park

Henry

Happy Valley

Union

Orchid
Garden

HILTON

Tweedle

Signal Hill

Reid

Delville

Aliwal

R700

President Reitz

Brompton

Fairview

astron

Kellner

Alexandra

Andries Pretorius

Barnes

Tweedle

Henry

Voortekker

Freshford House
Museum

Markgraaf

Kloof

Zastron

Lang

Eerste

Hill

Tweetoringker
Twin Spired Church

N

City Hall
Court
of Appeal

National
Museum

West Burger

Voortekker

Charles

First Bridge

Henry

W   E

ng's
ark

Loch
Logan

Henry

Elizabeth

Zoological
and Rosebush
Gardens

St Andrews

Fourth
Raadsaal

CENTRAL

Charles

Maitland

Harvey

Alexandra

S

sident Swart Park

Sand du
Plessis
Theatre

Nat. Afrikaans
Literary Mus.
and Research
Centre

Tourist
Information

St Andrews

Att Horak
ports Complex

Green

Peet

Fontein

Selbourne

Nathan

Fraser

Peet

Hanger

Gordon

Park

Douglas

Marula

OOSEINDE

ing Edward

St Georges

First
Raadsaal

President Boshof

President Brand

Mackenzie

WILLOWS

Suid

Maasdorp

Victoria

R700

Tomoroy

Kazerne

Hertzog House

Fort

Brounger

Harris

Church

Fort Bloemfontein
Military Museum

Kolbe

President's Acre

Mannion

Dr. Belcher

President

Basuto War
Memorial

National Hospital

Rhodes

ORANJESIG

Monyatsi

Oranje Hospital

Harvey

Krause

R700

Church

Walkley

BATHO

Nico van der Merwe

National
Women's
Memorial

Harvey

Venter

0   500   1000 metres

0   500   1000 yards

BLOEMFONTEIN

Continue on the N6 to **Bloemfontein**, the judicial capital of South Africa, more commonly referred to simply as 'Bloem'. Its turbulent history for control of the region has left a wealth of historical buildings, museums and other places of interest. Bloemfontein is built around the Franklin Game Reserve which is perched on Naval Hill and offers panoramic views of the city. Satour has an office at the Sanlam Parkade and the city has a good bus service with timetables available from the main bus terminal beside the Tourist Office.

The city was founded in 1840 by the Voortrekker Johann Brits who discovered a natural spring in the dry plains. He made his home on land beside the spring and named the area Bloemfontein meaning 'blooming fountain'. Soon this little town became home to the early European pioneers who had headed into the interior from the Cape to escape British rule. After the Anglo-Boer war, Bloemfontein fell under British rule and the mix of Boer and British influence around the city is noticeable. The discovery of the gold-fields in the northern Free State was the catalyst that changed this small agricultural town into the city it is today.

The Information Office on **Hoffman Square** provides a useful brochure entitled *On Foot Through Old Bloemfontein*. The city is based on a grid system, which makes it easy to find the majority of historical buildings and museums, all of which are within walking distance of the city centre.

Bloemfontein is home to over thirty-six monuments, historic buildings and museums. The **Military Museum** of the Boer Republics has an extensive collection of artifacts and exhibitions including actual weapons used during the war. It also houses a collection of items made by Boer prisoners-of-war depicting the lifestyle of the thousands of victims who were incarcerated by the British in the concentration camps. The **National Women's Memorial**, at the end of Church Street, is dedicated to the 26,370 women and children who died during the Anglo-Boer war. The obelisk features a mother holding a dying child and another woman gazing out across the Free State. The obelisk is surrounded by a 'whispering wall' and the smallest sound made anywhere around the wall can be heard clearly on the other side. The ashes of Emily Hobhouse, an English-woman who worked for the welfare of the prisoners, are interred here.

The **National Museum** on the corner of Charles and Aliwal Streets houses one of the largest collections of fossils and archaeological displays in South Africa. The displays include the famous Florisbad skull of primitive man, the fossil remains of a dinosaur and a bushman exhibition.

The **Old Raadsaal** in St George Street is the oldest building in Bloemfontein. The small building with its thatched roof and dung floor originally served as a school before becoming the meeting place of political assembly. It was built in 1849 and is preserved today as a national monument housing a small museum.

The **Fourth Raadsaal** in President Brand Street is where the provincial council of the Free State now sits. It was opened in 1893 and was seat of the Republic until 1899. Opposite the Fourth Raadsaal is the **Appeal Court** which is noted for its impressive wood panelling. The nearby **City Hall** is also worth a visit for its marble and woodwork interior.

The old government buildings are in Maitland Street and a statue of President Brand who served a twenty-five year term of office stands outside the gate. The **National Afrikaans Literature Museum and Research Centre** is housed here and stores the works of many well-known Afrikaans authors. The Old Presidency, on the junction of President Brand and Eunice Street, is a national monument. It was the official residence for three past presidents and now houses a museum and cultural centre.

Bloemfontein is home to the distinctive **Tweetoringker Church** (meaning 'church with two spires'). It is situated on the corner of Radloff and Hill streets and serves as a notable landmark around the city.

The **Anglican Cathedral** in George Street dates back to 1850 and features many fine stained glass windows.

The **Sand du Plessis Theatre** is worth a visit, and information on the entertainment programme can be found in the local press. It is an impressive, modern building with an excellent display of various art forms in the foyer.

Bloemfontein lives up to its name and there are numerous parks and gardens within the city. **Kings Park** is well laid out and has a lively artists' flea market on the first Saturday of each month. The **Orchid House** in **Hamilton Park** at the bottom of Naval Hill houses over 3,000 types of orchid. It is beautifully designed with water-falls, bridges and pools used to display the orchids in their full glory. The **Zoo** in the park is worth a visit to see the largest collection of monkeys in South Africa, as well as the liger — a cross between a lion and tiger. There are night tours.

Naval Hill offers panoramic views across the city and forms part of the **Franklin Game Reserve** which provides a sanctuary for various species of antelope. The **Lamont Hussey Observatory** on the hill is now used as a small theatre by the Performing Arts Council of the Free State.

President Swart Park houses the **Free State Stadium** with swimming and tennis facilities.

There a large number of hotels which cater for all budgets. The four-star Bloemfontein Hotel is reputed to be the best in the city, while the Holiday Inn Garden Court is rated three-star and is excellent value. There are some delightful guesthouses with-in the city limits, most notably in the suburb of Westdean which offer evening meals as well as bed and breakfast.

The Carousel restaurant in the city offers a wide selection of gastronomic delights, while Schillachi's lively restaurant in Zastron Street offers a delicious array of fresh Italian cuisine.

Bloemfontein to Maseru, Lesotho 143 km (89 miles)

Leave Bloemfontein on the R64 head-ing to Maseru. After 60km (37 miles) one reaches the area of **Thaba 'Nchu** which until recently, was the southern-most section of the fragmented former homeland of Bophuthatswana. The first Voortrekker government was elected here in December 1836 at the convergence of the trek parties. A pro-clamation was decreed by President Brand in 1884 to annex Thaba 'Nchu to the Orange Free State and it was later declared a sub-district of Bloemfontein — a decision that was later reversed.

The main attraction is the **Maria Moroka National Park** which covers an area of over 3,400 hectares (8,400 acres) within a natural amphitheatre formed by the majestic Thaba 'Nchu mountain and a number of smaller hills. The environment is ideally suited to the springbok, eland, zebra and other game indigenous to the area.

The **Moutloloaste Setlogelo Dam** attracts large numbers of heron, duck, geese, kingfisher and over 200 identified bird species. Birds of prey

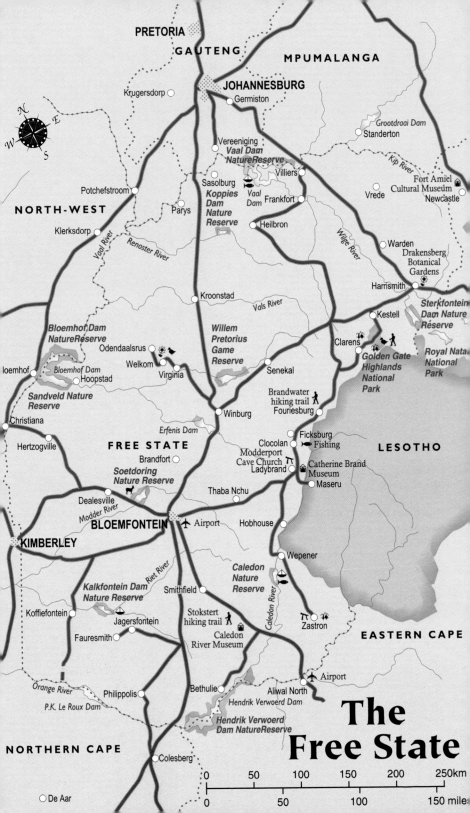

are common sights including the fish eagle, and buzzard. Visitors must enter the park on foot and there are two excellent hiking trails plus pony rides.

Dr S J Moroka's residence and surgery is open to visitors at **Ragkoko Farm**. The doctor studied medicine in Edinburgh and Vienna before becoming politically active in the ANC when the organisation adopted the 1949 Programme of Action. He was very active in community development and died in 1985.

LESOTHO

Continue on the road to Maseru and cross the border into Lesotho at the **Ladybrand/Maseru Bridge** which is open daily between 6am and 10pm. **Lesotho**, sitting high above South Africa which surrounds it on all sides, has earned itself the name 'kingdom in the sky'. It covers an area of approximately 30,000 square kilometres which makes it nearly the same size as Belgium. Seventy-five per cent of the area is mountain, at no point less than 1,000m (3,280ft) high, and includes the highest mountain in southern Africa, Thabana-Ntllenyan at 3,841m (11,417ft).

The history of the area dates back to prehistoric times and there are fine examples of dinosaur footprints and bushman paintings. The kingdom was formed between the years of 1815 and 1820 by Chief Moshoeshoe when he led a large number of Sotho-speaking cattle owners away from the oppression of the Zulu and Matebele tribes. He gradually formed a powerful autonomous kingdom with its own language and army, and established a fortress capital at Thaba Bosiu. By the 1840s, his kingdom extended well into the Orange Free State.

In 1852, a 2,500-strong British force launched an attack on the kingdom in response to the continual rustling of livestock belonging to the settlers in the Orange Free State. Several other attacks followed, and in 1865 the settlers assumed control of most of the land, except for the impenetrable fortress at Thaba Bosiu. In 1868, Moshoeshoe sought assistance from the British, and the following year Lesotho became a British protectorate. Its name was changed to Basotholand and the capital was moved to Maseru.

In 1871 the kingdom was declared part of the Cape Colony, and in a series of wars known as the 'Gun Wars', rebellion ensued as the Basotho refused to surrender their weapons. British rule was ultimately restored in 1884. When the Union of South Africa was formed in 1909, the Basotho sent a delegation to London to plead their case to retain colonial status. They remained a colony until 1966, when Lesotho regained its independent sovereignty under Moshoeshoe's great-great-great grandson, King Moshoeshoe II.

In the 1970s, the Prime Minister, Chief Jonathan, annulled the elections and ruled illegally for several years. King Moshoeshoe was sent into exile until he was allowed to return on condition that he would not participate in any political dealings. Chief Jonathan's dictatorship ran into trouble when South Africa imposed sanctions on Lesotho after discovering their sympathies lay with the communist regimes in Mozambique, Cuba and with ANC guerrillas. In 1986, the South African government, backed by General Lekhanya, finally overthrew the dictatorship and restored King Moshoeshoe to the throne. In 1990, along with his fellow supporters, Moshoeshoe was ousted for his refusal to support the government's policies, and today King Letsie III is the reigning monarch.

Christian missionaries have worked in Lesotho since the 1930s and their influence is still evident today in the educational institutes and Christian teaching. Like many African cultures, Lesotho embraces traditional beliefs of ancestral worship along with their Christianity. Boys and girls still undergo initiation ceremonies although this practice is decreasing in importance as they become more westernised.

Circumcision signifies the end of childhood and is followed by intensive coaching on the laws and customs a boy must follow in his new manhood. After the ceremony, they are confined to a specially-built hut for one month, before being marked with white clay on their faces and sent out to fend for themselves for a period. Girls undergo an initiation period at the time of the new moon when they run to the river and symbolically wash away their girlhood. They cover themselves with dark ash, paint clay on their faces and wear a traditional costume of grass, beads and sheepskin.

To tour Lesotho extensively can prove to be a considerable challenge, as away from the main routes, the roads are mostly gravel which become dangerous in the rain or snow. A unique way to travel is by Basotho pony as many waterfalls, rock paintings, dinosaur footprints and mountain villages can be accessed by bridle-path only. Despite being one of the world's poorest nations, the Basotho are a friendly and generous nation with a third of the population still living unsophisticated lives in mountain villages. Lesotho is economically dependent on neighbouring South Africa and over half its workforce are employed in South Africa in order to support their families back at home. Part of the cultural heritage of Lesotho is expressed through the weaving, pottery and handicrafts industries which are very much in evidence throughout the countryside.

Visitors will also see the Basotho horsemen wrapped in traditional multicoloured blankets and wearing cone-shaped Basotho hats. The Basotho pony is a sturdy mount, and for the locals the main mode of transport. The ponies are believed to be descended from the Shetland pony which a British settler brought with him from Scotland in 1840.

Lesotho has a very healthy climate with clearly defined seasons because of the altitude. In the lowlands, temperatures range from 13°C in winter to 32°C in summer. Snow may fall any time throughout the year in the high mountains, but especially between June and August when roads can suddenly be cut off. Rain is unpredictable but is particularly heavy between October and April.

The city of **Maseru** in the valley of the Caledon River was chosen as the new capital in 1869, in preference to King Moshoeshoe's Thaba Bosiu mountain fortress. The Moshoeshoe I International airport is 20km (12 miles) south of Maseru at Thoteng-ea-Moli and there are regular flights to international connections and within southern Africa. As the road crosses the bridge from the border it enters Kingsway, the main road through Maseru. Kingsway is always a hive of activity with local people selling handicrafts and local produce. The tourist Information Office is on the left.

The new buildings blend gracefully with the colonial-style architecture, but there is little to do or see in town except to use it as a base from which to visit the other attractions in the area. The Royal Palace is worth viewing from the outside although photography is not permitted.

A statue of King Moshoeshoe is on the hill near the government offices.

Lancer's Gap is 4km (2 miles) from ✳ Maseru and is where the British cavalry were defeated in 1852. There is an excellent view of the town from here. There are a number of craft shops to which the Tourist Office can provide directions and an open-air handicraft market on Saturday mornings beside St John's Church.

The Moteng and Thorkild Weaving Centre make tapestries, carpets and place mats and visitors are welcome to visit the workshop and watch the craftsmen at work. Royal Crown Jewellery uses silver, gold, copper, brass and semi-precious stones to make beautiful ethnic jewellery.

Pony Trekking

The **Basotho Pony Trekking Centre** is at **Molimo Nthuse**. As the route twists through the **Bushman's Pass** around the mountainside, one begins to truly appreciate the term 'kingdom in the Sky'. The 'God Help Me' pass is very difficult to negotiate and cars are often overtaken by horsemen.

All levels of horsemanship are provided for and trips must be booked in advance. Treks last between one hour and seven days and only run in summer because of the bitter winter temperatures. Reservations can be made through the Basotho Pony Trekking School. The origin of the school lies in a breeding programme between Ireland and Lesotho where Connemara stallions were crossed with Basotho ponies.

To Thaba Bosiu

Heading south from Maseru, turn left at Masianokeng and again at HaMakhalanyane where the road reaches Moshoeshoe's fortress at **Thaba Bosiu**. The fortress is a short walk from the village of Ha Rafutho, and is situated on a flat topped hill 1,600m (5,248ft) above sea level, looking out across the **Phuthiatsana River Valley**. It is a national shrine for

the Basotho people and provided a formidable defence line during enemy attacks. It was never taken by an enemy force, although the Basotho were forced to seek assistance from the British after a long drawn out siege by the Boers. The footprint of Maleka, the King's son, is visible where he drew around his own foot before tragically jumping to his death, after being forbidden to marry his true love.

Return to the main road heading south and follow the signs to Mafeteng. The road passes through **Thota-Ea-Moli**, the former seat of the traditional Basotho parliament at **Fika-le-Mohala** near the airport. Further along this road is **Matsieng**, the King's country home and the old village of Chief Letsie. There is a trail from here to dinosaur tracks.

Roma was established in 1862 as the site of the first Roman Catholic mission. It now houses the **National University of Lesotho** and attracts students from all over Africa.

On of the world's rarest birds, the Lammergeyer (bearded vulture), inhabits the **Maphotong Gorge** in the Roma valley.

Semonkong is 68km (42 miles) from Roma and the main attraction is the highest waterfall in southern Africa — the **Libihan Falls** which tumble 192m (630ft) over a cliff. A good way to see them is on horseback which can be arranged through the lodge here.

Maseru to Fouriesburg
152 km (94 miles)

Leave Maseru on the Hlotse road in the direction of **Teyateyaneng** (more commonly known as 'TY') 32km (20 miles) further along. At the St Agnes Mission visitors can watch the weavers at work using traditional methods. The mission was originally established in 1886 as the British administration camp, but today the area is best known

Above: Lesotho women wearing their traditionally-colourful dress.
Opposite top: Golden sunrise over the deserted hills in the Free State.
Opposite: Vast cherry crops in the area around Ficksburg.

for its variety of craft centres producing carpets, tapestries, bags, shawls and pottery. The Kolonyama potter, on the Hlotse road produces some unusual stoneware and the pottery gardens are very attractive. There are bushman rock paintings near the mountain road which runs from Teyateyaneng to Mohatlanes. Although they have faded considerably, they are the most accessible in the kingdom.

Hlotse is 52km (32 miles) from Teyateyaneng. It is the main administrative centre of the Leribe district and was founded in 1876 when Reverend John Widdicombe established a mission here. In 1879, it was the scene of heavy attack when the Basotho refused to surrender their arms to the Cape government and the original fort

still stands today. The British General, Gordon of Khartoum, stayed here in a rondavel for a short period which is still preserved today.

Approximately 8km (5 miles) from Hlotse on the road to Buthe Buthe is the **Subeng River** where clearly preserved dinosaur footprints are a short walk from the road. Stop the car just beyond the river and follow the river bed to the footprints in the sandstone of these prehistoric creatures which roamed the earth over 200 million years ago.

Buthe-Buthe meaning 'the place of safety' was given its name because it was the first mountain stronghold of Moshoeshoe. It lies 1,993m (6,340ft) above sea level and the temperature becomes noticeably cooler as one approaches the area. From here the road starts a steep climb up to **Oxbow**

which is becoming an increasingly popular ski-resort because it is one of the few places where South Africans can ski. The season is unpredictable and snow can fall at any time between July and August, although sometimes only just enough for a few days skiing. Beyond Oxbow on the road to **Mokhotlong**, the **Lesotho Highlands Water Project** is under construction on the Senqu (Orange) River. This joint project between South Africa, the World Bank and the EEC will take advantage of the abundance of water in Lesotho and the size of the project has already helped economic growth and employment in the kingdom. It will not only supply Lesotho with its own hydro-electricity scheme, but will also export water to South Africa.

Discussions are underway to establish a tourist development close to the dam which will provide a large source of revenue for the kingdom. From Mokhotlong one can make the journey to the **Sani Pass** but a 4WD vehicle is necessary to cross from here into South Africa. The road climbs past Thabana Ntlenyana which is southern Africa's highest peak to the Mountaineers Chalet — the highest licensed premises in southern Africa.

Leave Lesotho at the **Buthe-Buthe/ Fouriesburg border** (open daily between 8am and 10pm) and follow the signs to Fouriesburg. Either stay overnight here or make a detour of 20km (12 miles) towards **Ficksburg** and stay in one of the three mountain lodges signposted down a sandy road to Rustlers Valley. **Fouriesburg** is the start of the famous Brandwater hiking trail which covers 60km (37 miles) in five days. The route leads through picturesque river valleys and dramatic ravines to high mountain ridges which afford spectacular views across the Maluti, Rooi and Witteberg mountains, and Salpeterkrans, the largest sandstone cave in the southern hemi-

sphere. The **Meiringskloof Nature Park** is 2km (1.5 miles) from town and is the start and end of the Brandwater trail. It also offers a number of shorter hikes to visit bushman caves or to the main dam which supplies the town — although this involves a steep climb up a chain ladder.

Take the R26 to Ficksburg heading towards **Rustlers Valley** (named after the valley where local tribes used to hide the cattle they had stolen from neighbouring farmers) and three mountain lodges with facilities for every taste and budget.

The Rustlers Valley Resort is completely unique and a number of visiting artists and crafts people have been encouraged to leave their mark here. The approach has proved to be effective and the resort is considered home from home for the young or the young at heart. The valley also offers the Nebo Resort where the emphasis is on comfort, and the Franschoek Resort for hiking enthusiasts.

Each November, Ficksburg holds a cherry festival which is worth the detour if one is in the area. Virtually the entire country's cherry crops are grown in the area and the town is very beautiful during the spring when the cherry blossom is in flower.

Fouriesburg to Royal Natal 163 kilometres (101 miles)

Leave Fouriesburg on the R711 in the direction of **Clarens**. The town (known as the 'Gem of the Free State') nestles at the foot of sandstone hills offering breathtaking views of the Maluti mountains. The town square features the work of many artists, craftsmen and women living here. It is also the unlikely home of the eccentric Cinderella's Castle, a miniature castle built from 55,000 beer bottles.

At neighbouring **Shaapplaats** there are some well-preserved bushman paintings, and it is also close to the site where in 1976, palaeontologists discovered five fossilised dinosaur eggs.

Take the Clarens road to the **Golden Gate Highlands National Park** which is situated in the foothills of the Maluti Mountains. It is named after the blazing shades of gold which the sun casts on the sandstone cliffs at sunset. The park covers an area of 11,630 hectares (28,726 acres) and rises to an altitude of 2,770m (9,085ft). The climate is invigorating and snow falls in the winter.

Although the reserve provides a sanctuary for various species of animal and birdlife, including the rare Lammergeyer, (bearded vulture), Cape vulture, Burchell's zebra and eland, it is the geology which is the main attraction in the park. The massive cliff at the southern entrance to the park which is shaped like a human face with a large prominent nose is known as Gladstone's Nose. There are numerous hiking trails which provide the ideal way to experience the unrivalled beauty of the park. The camp offices provide maps and information on the many trails. There are two rest camps as well as camping facilities..

Take the road to **Witsieshoek** which was the former capital of the self-governing homeland of **Qwa Qwa**, now part of the Free State. Qwa Qwa means 'whiter than white' and was the name the San people gave to the huge sandstone mountain north of the Amphitheatre. The **Amphitheatre** is a wall of rock over 5km (3 miles) long and over 1,500m (4,870 feet) high with has deep ravines carved into its surface through years of erosion. There are a number of hiking trails in the area and an educational cultural village opened here in 1994 to educate other tribes and visitors about the Basotho people.

From here take the R712 road towards **Harrismith** and follow the road to the Drakensberg resorts in KwaZulu-Natal. The **Mount Everest Game Reserve** is located on the outskirts of Harrismith and the 1,000 hectare (2,470 acre) reserve of glorious scenery is home to over twenty species of game. This is a perfect area for both hiking and mountain climbing.

The **Drakensberg** is part of the escarpment which separates the coastal range from the interior and is the largest mountain range in South Africa. It stretches from the Eastern Cape across to the north-eastern corner of the republic over 1,600km (994 miles). The Zulus call the mountains Quathlamba meaning 'barrier of spears' — an appropriate name for an area of high peaks and pinnacles divided by deep ravines and chasms.

The area offers a host of opportunities for walking, hiking, horse-riding or simply enjoying some of the most spectacular scenery and invigorating climatic conditions in the country. In summer, expect warm sunny days with afternoon thunderstorms and cool nights. In winter, the days are crisp and cool and the nights very cold. Snow can fall at any time on the Berg during the year. Climbers and hikers should exercise considerable caution as weather conditions can change quickly and heavy cloud can suddenly obscure safe trails or routes. Visitors wishing to climb must either

Overleaf: The Drakensberg is part of the escarpment which separates the coastal range from the interior and is the largest mountain range in South Africa.
Page 119 (*top*): The Amphitheatre is a wall of rock with deep ravines carved into its surface through years of erosion.
Page 119 (*below*): The Tugela Falls is the second highest waterfall in the world after the Angel Falls in Venezuela.

be a member of a mountain club or be able to satisfy the Natal Parks Board of their experience and that they have all the necessary equipment.

A mountain register is kept at the Visitors Centre which must be completed by any person wishing to climb over a certain altitude or stay overnight in the open. It is also necessary to obtain a permit to enter the wilderness area and these are available at the access point on arrival.

 There are numerous trails throughout the Drakensberg, ranging from the challenging two-day Mont-aux-Sources trail to gentle one-hour walks, as well as swimming and trout fishing in the rivers. One of the most popular hikes is to the summit of the Mont-aux-Sources which was named in 1830 by two French missionaries because of the numerous streams which sprang from its plateau.

The Mont-aux-Sources is the source of the Tugela River and the **Tugela Falls** — the second highest waterfall in the world after the Angel Falls in Venezuela. They cascade 850m (2,788ft) down the escarpment wall of the Amphitheatre and the view from here is quite breathtaking.

There are two chain ladders which lead to the summit and from the top of the ladder it is approximately 1,600 metres (5,248 feet) to the top of the mountain. Ideally the trip requires two days which includes one night spent at the cave on the summit and should only be attempted by the physically fit. The number of visitors are restricted so it is essential to book for overnight camping through the warden's office or the Qwa-Qwa Tourist Officer.

Another popular walk is the Tugela Gorge hike which begins at the Tendele Hutted Camp. This hike lasts for approximately six hours and is regarded as one of the best walks in the Drakensberg. It follows a path along, above and parallel to the Tugela River.

The walk through the Gorge involves crossing the river three times and climbing a chain ladder through a tunnel to the Amphitheatre. It is important to watch the changing weather conditions on this route as heavy rain can suddenly turn the Gorge into a raging torrent.

For the less energetic, the Natal Parks Board operates a stable at the Rugged Glen camp. Horseback riding is a popular way to see the region and information can be obtained from the camps, most of which have riding facilities.

The reserve is one of the richest areas in San rock art, and combined with the Ndedema area, it contains over forty per cent of all the known rock art in South Africa. One of the more popular walks, lasting just thirty minutes, is to the **Main Caves and Site Museum** where there are over 500 paintings depicting the traditional San way of life.

The Bushman or San people of the late Stone Age occupied the area now known as the Drakensberg for thousands of years. Towards the end of the fourteenth century, tribes from the north began to move into the area and forced the San into the mountains. After the Great Trek, the whites settled and started hunting in the Bushman territory. The Bushmen retaliated by raiding their farms until, in 1859, the Natal authorities attempted to curb these attacks by establishing specific Bantu locations. This was unsuccessful and the whites mounted an organised campaign to drive the Bushmen from the Berg. A small number ultimately sought refuge in Lesotho.

The last group of Bushmen were seen near Mont-aux-Sources in 1878, and the only legacy left from these original inhabitants are the prolific cave paintings which are the work of the Bushman *shamans* (medicine men). It is believed the *shamans* would enter an induced trance during which they would communicate with the spiritual world. When they returned from the trance state they would paint the visions they had experienced and these paintings have been acclaimed as some the finest artistic achievements of the human race. The rock art was the means by which a clan communicated with the outside and spiritual world and are known as 'images of power'. According to legend, anyone who either sleeps in a cave decorated with rock art, lights a fire, or tries to damage the paintings will be cursed by the powers that reside in the cave.

The best paintings can be seen at the main caves in the **Giants Castle Reserve** where there are over 500 in a single shelter. The paintings are extremely fragile and should not be touched by visitors.

The road leads to the **Royal Natal National Park**, the main camp of the Drakensberg which is a sanctuary for many species of wildlife and birds. The park offers a variety of accommodation including two five-star hotels, the Karos Mont-aux-Sources Hotel and the Royal Natal National Park Hotel. There are also a number of hutted camps and camp sites. The scenery en route is breathtaking and offers spectacular views of the Amphitheatre which is flanked by the two peaks of the Eastern Buttress and the Sentinel.

Royal Natal to Giant's Castle 155 km (96 miles)

Take the Harrismith Road, turning right onto the R74 towards Bergville and Winterton. Turn right towards Cathedral Peak and left onto the R600 towards Dragon's Peak. After 13km (8 miles) turn left towards **Loskop** at the large information board and follow the signs to Giant's Castle. Within the reserve are two hutted camps —

Giants Hutted Camp and Injasuti — as well as two camping grounds, three mountain huts and two caves which also offer accommodation.

The attractive Injatsu Camp is situated in the northern section of the Giant's Castle Reserve. The name derives from 'eNjesuthi' — the name given by the Nguni tribe to the valley where the food was so prolific that even their dogs were well fed. It is surrounded by some majestic scenery and is dominated by Cathkin Peak, Monk's Cowl and Champagne Castle. The two caves — Lower Injasuti Cave and Fergy's Cave — are good overnight stops for hikers en route to Giant's Castle but must be booked through the Parks Board. It is always necessary to make advance reservations for cabins, campsites and caves at Injasuti.

Cathkin Peak is very popular with mountaineers, although its summit is difficult to reach as it is surrounded by treacherous cliffs. At 3,370m (10,970ft) the highest point of the area is Champagne Castle. There are many good hotels in the area including the Champagne Castle and the Cathkin Peak Hotel.

The Rainbow Gorge walk from the Cathkin Peak Hotel is a photographer's dream and covers a total distance of 11km (7 miles) which takes approximately four hours to complete. It leads through dense forest, enchanting caves and eventually into **Rainbow Gorge**.

The Hillside Camp is primarily the base for all horse trails within the reserve and is situated 32km (20 miles) from the main camp. Two- and three-day trails under the supervision of the officer-in-charge are undertaken at certain times of the year.

From this point it is 231km (144 miles) back to Durban via Mooi River and Pietermaritzburg. This route is covered in more detail in Chapter One.

PLACES TO VISIT

Durban

Art Gallery
City Hall, Smith Street
Open Monday-Friday: 9.30am-5pm
Wednesday: 9am-2pm
Sunday: 2.30pm-5pm
☎(031) 300 6234

Crocworld
No 110 off-ramp N2
Open daily: 9am-5pm
Zulu dancing daily 12.15pm except Sat
☎(0323) 21103

Durban Museum
1st Floor
City Hall, Smith Street
Open daily
☎(031) 300 6234

Killie Campbell Africana Museum
220 Marriott Road
Open Monday-Friday: 8.30am-4.30pm
by appointment only
☎(031) 2073432

Local History Museum
Aliwal Street
☎(031) 300 6214

Minitown
Snell Parade, North Beach
Open daily: except Monday

Seaworld Oceanarium
Marine Parade
Open daily: 9am-9pm
☎(031) 374079

Natal Playhouse Complex
☎(031) 304 3631

Natural History Museum
City Hall, Smith Street
Open Monday-Saturday: 8.30am-5pm
Sunday: 11am-5pm
☎(031) 399 6214

Natal Maritime Museum
Small Craft Basin
Lower Aliwal Street
☎(031) 306 1092

Natal Sharks Board
Umhlanga Rocks Drive
Tours: Tuesday: 9am; Wednesday: 9am,
11am and 2.30pm, Thursday: 9am
First Sunday of each month: 2.30pm
☎(031) 561 1001

Old House Museum
31 St Andrew's Street
☎(031) 300 6250

PheZulu Assagay Safari Park
Botha's Hill
Open daily: 9am-4pm
☎(031) 7771405

Snake Park
Snell Parade
Open daily: 9am-4.30pm
☎(031) 376456

Sugar Terminal
Maydon's Wharf
Corner Mayden and Leuchers Roads
Open daily
☎(031) 3010331

Umgeni River Bird Park
Riverside Road

Whysall's Camera Museum
33 Brickhill Road
Open daily: 8.30am-12noon
☎(031) 371431

OTHER PLACES TO VISIT

Bathurst

Summerhill Farm
Open Tuesday-Sunday: 9am-5pm
☎(0464) 250833

Fort Beaufort

Military Museum
Bell Street

King Williamstown

Kaffararian Museum
Albert Road
☎(0433) 23450

Bloemfontein

Queen's Fort
Monument Road
Open Monday-Friday: 9am-4pm
☎(051) 475478

War Museum & National Women's Memorial
Open Monday-Friday: 8am-5pm
Saturday: 9am-5pm, Sunday: 2pm-5pm

National Museum
Corner Charles and Aliwal Streets
Open Monday-Saturday: 8am-5pm
Sunday: 1pm-6pm
☎(051) 479609

First Raadsaal
St George Street
Open Monday-Friday:10.15am-3pm
Saturday & Sunday: 2pm-5pm

Fourth Raadsaal
President Brand Street
Appointment only
☎(051) 478898

City Hall
Appointment only
☎(051) 4058911

Old Presidency
Corner President Brand and Eunice Streets
Open Tuesday-Friday: 10am-12noon & 1pm-4pm
Weekends: 2pm-5pm

Sand du Plessis Theatre
Corner Markgraaf and St Andrews Streets
☎(051) 47771

Orchid House
Union Avenue
Open Monday-Friday: 10am-4pm
Weekends: 10am-5pm

East London

Ann Bryant Art Gallery
Corner Oxford and St Luke's Roads
Open Monday-Friday: 9.30am-5pm
Saturday: 9.30-12noon
☎(0431) 24044

Calgary Wagon Museum
Macleantown Road
Open Wednesday-Sunday: 9am-4pm
☎(0431) 387244

Gately House
Park Gate Road
Open Tuesday-Thursday: 10am-5pm
Friday: 10am-1pm, Saturday: 3pm-5pm
☎(0431) 22141

Mpongo Park
Mpongo River Valley
Open daily
☎(04326) 669

Museum
Upper Oxford St
Open Monday-Friday: 9.30am-5pm
Saturday: 9.30am-12noon
Sunday: 11am-4pm
☎(0431) 430686

Queens Park and Zoo
Open daily: 9am-5pm
☎(0431) 21171

Grahamstown

Albany Natural History and Science Museum
Somerset St
Open Monday-Friday: 9.30am-1pm & 2pm-5pm, Saturday: 9am-1pm
☎(0461) 22312

History Museum (formerly 1820 Settlers)
Somerset Street
Open Monday-Friday: 9.30am-1pm & 2pm-5pm, Saturday: 9am-1pm
☎(0461) 22312

Observatory Museum
Bathurst St
Open Monday-Friday: 9am-1pm & 2pm-5pm
Saturday: 9am-1pm
☎(0461) 22312

Provost
Lucas Avenue
Open Monday-Friday: 10am-5pm
Saturday: 2pm-5pm
Closed lunchtime
☎(0461) 22312

Port Shepstone

Banana Express
Wednesday, Thursday, Saturday, Sunday
☎(03931) 76443

Umtata

Transkei National Museum
York Street

Uvongo

Uvongo Bird Park
Open daily: 9am-5pm
☎(03931) 74086

Queenstown

Collectors Museum
Reservoir Road

Maseru

Basotho Pony Trekking Centre
Tel : (266) 31 4165

Basotho Pony Project
PO Box 1027

Bloemfontein

Franklin Game Reserve
Naval Hill
Open daily

Grahamstown

Shamwari Game Reserve
PO Box 91
Paterson 6130
☎(042) 8511196

Port Shepstone

Oribi Gorge and Nature Reserve
Natal Parks Board
☎(0397) 91753

Thaba 'Nchu

Maria Moroka National Park

Sehlabathebe National Park
Conservation Division
PO Box 24
Maseru
☎(266) 323600

Golden Gate Highlands National Park
Private Bag X03
Clarens 9707
☎(058) 256 1471

Durban

Train Enquiries
☎(031) 361 7692

Greyhound
☎(031) 37 6478

Trancity/Translux
☎(031) 361 7461

Taxis
☎(031) 9121099

Mynah buses
☎(031) 3094126

Ride-a-While (bicycle hire)
15 Tyzack Street
☎(031) 3245295

Airport Bus
☎(031) 3056491

Bisho

☎ 0401 952115

Bloemfontein

Information Office
Hoffman Square
☎(051) 405 8489

Satour
Shop 9, Sanlam Parkade
Charles Street
PO Box 3515
Bloemfontein 9300
☎(051) 471362

Durban

Greater Durban Marketing Authority &
Satour
Tourist Junction
160 Pine Street
☎(031) 304 4934

Durban Unlimited
106 Marine Parade
☎(031) 322595 or 608

Greater Durban Marketing Authority
Durban International Airport
☎(031) 420 400

Drakensberg

Publicity Office
Tahsens Road
Bergville
☎(036) 4481557

East London

**East London Metropolitan Tourism
Association & Satour**
Old Library Building
35 Argyle Street
☎(0431) 26015

Grahamstown

Information Office
Church Square
☎(0461) 23241

Harrismith

Tourist Information Office
Municipal Hall
☎(01436) 21061

Margate

South Coast Publicity Office
Panorama Parade
Margate Beachfront
☎(03931) 22322

Umtata

National Tourism Board
Old Radio Transkei   Building
Corner York Road & Victoria Street
☎(0471) 312885

TDC & Wild Coast   Reservations
Development House
Corner York Road and Elliott streets
☎(0471) 25344

Qwa Qwa

**Tourism and Nature Conservation
Board**
☎(01432) 5886
Lesotho

Tourist Board
(beside Hotel Victoria)
Kingsway
☎(266) 326273

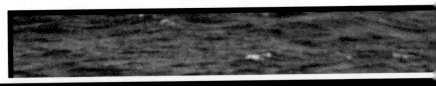

East and Western Cape Garden Route

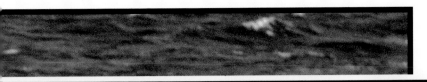

nd the

3

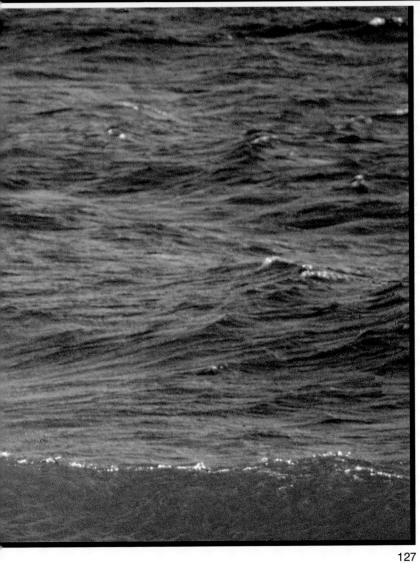

This itinerary will appeal to visitors wishing to enjoy the coastline, the mountains, hiking and watersports. The route explores the Eastern Cape province and meanders through lush valleys, mountain passes, and charming seaside towns and villages. Starting in Port Elizabeth, South Africa's fifth largest city, it winds through the renowned Garden Route into Cape Town, the southernmost city in Africa. It continues through the Karoo region, via the wine routes of the Western Cape, the magnificent game reserves and onward through spectacular scenery and historical towns before returning to Port Elizabeth.

PORT ELIZABETH

Port Elizabeth was named by Sir Rufane Donkin in memory of his deceased wife, Elizabeth. In 1799, the British who already controlled the Cape, wanted to protect Algoa Bay from the French and built a small, stone hilltop fort named Fort Frederick. A garrison was stationed here and subsequently barracks and a military hospital were built. The 1820 settlers landed here in search of a new life away from the slump in Britain which followed the Napoleonic Wars. They were afforded this opportunity by the British government who were keen to increase the number of inhabitants in the area to create a human buffer zone against the vast colony of Xhosa who lived beyond the Great Fish River — the eastern frontier of the Cape colony. Many settlers ventured inland in search of good farming land and subsequently opened up the Albany district around Grahamstown. The original settlement gradually grew into a substantial town, as increasing numbers of settlers built their homes on the slopes near the fort.

Port Elizabeth is an extremely popular holiday destination on the Indian Ocean coast and is often dubbed 'the friendly city'. It has the third largest port in South Africa and lies on a stretch of coastline known as the Sunshine Coast. Known as 'PE' by South Africans, it has some long, sandy beaches with perfect conditions for windsurfing and surfing. Port Elizabeth has a reputation for being the 'windy city', although summers are hot with an average temperature of 22°C. The winters are usually cold and wet with an average temperature of 12°C.

The main bus services around the city leave from Market Square Station which is beneath the Norwich Union Centre building. Taxi ranks can be found at the Victoria Quay, Fleming Street, the Railway Station and Beach Road.

Start at **Market Square** in the historic heart of the city where a replica of the **Diaz Cross** (erected at Kwaaihoik in 1488 by Bartholomew Diaz) stands in front of **City Hall**.

Close by in **Castle Hill** lies the entrance to the **Feather Market Hall** which was originally used for auctioning ostrich feathers from nearby ostrich farms in Oudtshoorn. Today it is used for exhibitions and concerts.

The area around the **Donkin Reserve** is interesting and the Publicity Association and Satour office are located inside the lighthouse. The monument beside the lighthouse was built by Sir Rufane Donkin in memory of his wife and bears the inscription '. . . to one of the most perfect human beings'. Donkin Street is a row of restored terraced houses dating from the early Victorian era. All are national monuments, but only No 7 is open to the public and is today a cultural history museum.

Although many shops are found in and around **Main Street**, the heart of

Port Elizabeth's commercial centre, Greenacres Shopping Centre, 2km (1.5 miles) from the city centre off Cape Road, has become the liveliest and most modern complex in the city. There is an eight-screen cinema complex, as well as a host of shops, good restaurants and snack bars.

The attractive **St George's Park** is situated on the hill overlooking the city centre and an arts and craft market is held here on the first Sunday of each month. There is an athletics stadium which holds a variety sporting events throughout the year, as well as a large open-air public swimming pool. The **King George VI Art Gallery** is at the entrance to the park.

South of the park is the 54 hectare (130 acre) **Settlers Park Nature Reserve** which has many indigenous plants and streams, along with an interesting variety of birdlife, trees and shrubs. The Guinea Fowl trail takes between two and three hours to walk around the reserve and is quite easy.

On Cape Road at the junction of Russell Road is the impressive **Horse Memorial**, erected in memory of the horses which perished in South Africa during the Anglo-Boer War. It bears the inscription: 'The greatness of a nation consists not as much in the number of its people or the extent of its territory as in the extent and justice of its compassion'.

The 52m (170ft) **Campanile** stands at the harbour entrance and was built to commemorate the landing of the 1820 settlers. The red-brick design is based on the Campanile of Venice, and the viewing platform at the top of the 204-step spiral staircase offers excellent views across the city.

Fort Frederick on Belmont Terrace is the oldest stone building in the Eastern Cape and overlooks the mouth of the Baakens River.

One of Port Elizabeth's main attractions is the 3km (2 mile) stretch of white sands known individually as Kings Beach, Humewood Beach and Summerstrand. All these beaches are popular and become extremely busy during the high season. There are a number of restaurants where visitors can eat and drink *al fresco* while watching the activities along the water's edge. Throughout the year, the water temperature seldom drops below 16°C, and 22°C during the summer months. There is safe bathing along this stretch of coast, as well as excellent opportunities for windsurfing and boardsurfing. The Windsurfer Class National Championships are held here every July. Scuba diving is popular around Port Elizabeth and experienced divers may dive to the *SAS Harlem*, one of the many shipwrecks in the area.

Summerstrand is home to the **Port Elizabeth Beach Yacht Club** and the area is very popular at weekends.

Happy Valley is situated on Beach Road. This sheltered garden valley of lawns, lily ponds and winding paths is very pleasant to stroll around at night when the area is illuminated. The neighbouring **Port Elizabeth Museum** complex consists of an oceanarium, a museum, a tropical garden and snake park. The oceanarium has twice-daily dolphin and seal performances. The snake park has an extensive collection of indigenous snakes, and inside its **Tropical House**, birds, reptiles and fish live in an exotic environment of tropical vegetation. The museum features several cultural and natural history displays and its maritime hall tells the history of seafaring through the centuries. There are also video shows of wildlife programmes at specified times.

Port Elizabeth has one of the few remaining narrow-gauge railway lines in the world. The **Apple Express**, which runs from Port Elizabeth to Thornhill through some spectacular

Port Elizabeth

Algoa Bay

Charles Malan Quay

Pleasure Cruises

Deep Sea Fishing Excursions Available

Kings Beach

Summerstrand Beach

Humewood Beach

Oceanarium and Snake Park

Tropical House and Museum

Happy Valley

Boet Erasmus Stadium

HUMEWOOD

SOUTH END

Elizabeth Donkin Hospital

Victoria Park

Settlers Park Nature Reserve

Great War Memorial

King George VI Art Gallery

St George's Park

Arts Hall

Mike's Diving Shop

CENTRAL

Upper Hill St Houses

Fort Frederick

Main Library

Tourist Information

Donkin Heritage Trail (Walk)

Feather Market Hall

Opera House

Cultural History Museum

Campanile

Air Terminal

Walmer Boulevard

Forest Hill

North Union

Perrott

La Roche

Driftsands

Chalmers

Marshall

Windermere

Ferndale

Humewood Beach

Poole

Pier

Mitchell

Heugh

Fordyce

Alister Miller

H E Yonward Airport

M9

M11

M9

M11

Parliament

Russel

Clyde

Havelock

Rose

Pearson

Western

Deare

Cuyler

Bird

Gordon

Cuyler

Annerley

Valley

Military

Produce

Bakers

Whites

Castle

Hope

Daljosafat

Chapel

Prospect

Belmont

Tawhites

Britannia

Donkin Reserve

Upper Hill

Donkin

Alfred

Whitlock

Tander

Palmerston

Rodney

Kemp

Belmont

Municipality

Larsen

Brickmakers Kloof

Macintosh

R102

Peel

Albany

Devon

Callington

Glen

Somerset

Lansdowne

Bain

St Phillips

Zareba

Stanley

Litman

Raleigh

Campbell

M4

N

S

E

W

0   500   1000 metres

0   500   1000 yards

Top: The Donkin lighthouse beside the monument built by Sir Rufane Donkin in memory of his wife.
Above: Summerstrand is one of the popular beaches in Port Elizabeth and home to the Port Elizabeth Beach Yacht Club.

mountain and forest scenery via the Van Staden's River bridge. The trips run on either a Saturday or Sunday once a month and every few days during the high season. The **Diaz Express** runs a shorter trip between the Port Elizabeth harbour and King's Beach on an extended narrow-gauge line during the peak season.

Port Elizabeth is full of activity in September during the Great Train Race. Relay teams of runners attempt to beat the Apple Express over its 73km (45 miles) journey to Loerie. The event attracts many of the country's top athletes, as well as amateur teams from all over the city.

Anybody wishing to visit an African township should contact the Institute for a Democratic Alternative for South Africa (IDASA), a non-profit making organisation that runs awareness tours aimed at educating the local people and tourists about daily life in a township. The tours also includes a visit to the 'coloured' locations, the more affluent areas and the squatter areas.

The days and times for the tours vary, so it is advisable to telephone in advance for information.

The coastline stretching from Port Elizabeth has numerous deserted beaches. From Skoenmakerskop and Sardinia Bay 24km (15 miles) west of the city, there are two reserves — the **Sardinia Bay Sea Reserve** and the **Sylvis Nature Reserve**. The area is maintained to measure the impact of human encroachment on dune life and coastal flora. The **Sacramento Trail** starts at Schoenmakerskop and is approximately 3km (2 miles) in each direction.

There is a host of accommodation along the Summerstrand beachfront and at Humewood. Hotel and self-catering apartments are available which range from luxury to moderate prices.

Port Elizabeth offers a host of excellent restaurants to suit every budget, and there is a very active social life in the city. Many of the restaurants and bars have live music in the evenings and some offer regular specially-priced meals or drinks, details of which can be found in the local newspapers. There are three Spur franchises located at Cape Road, Newton Park and the Kine Centre in Rink Street. The beachfront has become a very popular place for eating and drinking.

TRIPS FROM PORT ELIZABETH

The **Island Forest Reserve** is situated en-route to Van Stadens River Mouth. It is primarily indigenous, sub-tropical coastal forest which offers sanctuary to bushbuck, the rare blue and grey duiker and verdent monkeys. A circular 16km (10 mile) path known as the Bushbuck trail has been established here.

Seaview Game Park, is approximately 25km (15 miles) from Port Elizabeth and offers an opportunity to see cheetah, lion, zebra, rhino and giraffe in a lovely hillside setting with a stunning views across the coast. The nearby **Cape Recife Nature Reserve** is a good spot for picnics and angling and there are some charming tea-shops in the area.

Addo Elephant National Park is about 72km (45 miles) north of the city and visitors are virtually guaranteed sightings of elephant in their natural habitat. These pachyderms once roamed freely in great herds throughout the area, but their reputation for raiding farms led to them being hunted to near extinction.

The park was proclaimed in 1931 to save the surviving elephant herds, and at the same time to provide refuge to the few remaining Cape buffalo. There is also a sanctuary for black rhino in the park. Today there are approximately 180 elephants in the park and several good hides at watering holes making it possible to see them at close range. The park ultimately aims to increase their numbers to 500 in order to ensure survival. The Addo elephants are smaller than equatorial elephants, and one peculiarity is that the female elephant has no tusks. There is some accommodation available here which must be booked through the National Parks Board.

The **Mountain Zebra National Park** is located 280km from Port Elizabeth. It was proclaimed a national park in 1937 to save the mountain zebra from extinction. The park has proved to be a tremendous success and zebra are now sent from here to other parks and reserves throughout the republic. There are also klipspringer, black wildebeest, caracal and over twenty species of birds in the park. There are cottages available for overnight stays and camping is permitted.

The Swartkops River is only 10km (6 miles) from the city centre and is a popular place for all watersports — particularly windsurfing and sailing. There are often yacht races along the river estuary. The villages of **Swartkops** and **Amsterdamhoek** are on the banks of the river near the estuary.

Uitenhage is the oldest town in the Eastern Cape and lies in the foothills of the rugged Winterhoek mountains. Established in 1804, the town with its wide tree-lined streets of jacaranda and oak, has retained a latter-day charm with many carefully preserved fine old buildings. Uitenhage is primarily an industrial area and home to the giant car manufacturer — Volkswagen. It is also a large wool processing centre.

The **Drostdy Museum** in Caledon Street was built in 1809 and now houses an Africana museum. The **Cuyler Manor Museum** is a cultural museum housed in an old homestead which has been authentically restored and furnished. The old railway station has been converted into a railway museum where souvenirs of the steam era are on display.

The Gamtoos River Valley is one of the most beautiful valley areas in the country and is totally untouched by tourism. The valley originally belonged to the Khoikhoi, and Gamtoos is believed to mean 'wily as a lion'.

Today, it is a rich agricultural area which the farming community has opened up, and on the first weekend of each month they welcome visitors to enjoy its natural beauty and their hospitality. The hiking trails around the area offer spectacular views.

From Port Elizabeth, follow the road west and take the R331 to Gamtoosmond/Hankey. The road continues into **Baviaanskloof** which is equally impressive and, although the road is gravel, a good car and safe driving will lead through some fabulous scenery.

Port Elizabeth to Storms River Mouth 215 km (133 miles)

Leave Port Elizabeth on the N2 towards Cape Town. The 300km (186 mile) coastal strip between Riversdale and Storms River is known as the Garden Route because of its lush beauty in comparison to the dryness of the neighbouring Karoo. The rugged coastline is interspersed with a succession of bays, beaches, cliffs, and coves linking one beautiful resort with another, and is bordered in the north by majestic mountain ranges.

The waves of the Indian Ocean lapping at the long stretches of golden coastline; the dense forests and verdant valleys watered by year-round rainfall; the serene lagoons and

Opposite top: The Apple
Express is one of the few
remaining narrow-gauge
railways in the world.

Opposite: The impressive
Storm's River bridge on
the Van Staden's Pass.

Above: The Tsitsikamma
National Park is popular
with hiking enthusiasts.

Right: The popular surfing
beach of Supertubes at
Jeffrey's Bay.

meandering rivers make the Garden Route the perfect outdoor holiday destination. Spring is a particularly beautiful time when the area is prolific with brightly-coloured fields of wildflowers in full bloom.

From the sophisticated holiday playground of Plettenberg Bay to the several hiking trails along the coast, the Garden Route has activities and accommodation to suit all tastes and budget. It is advisable to book well in advance for the peak holiday season each December and January. Surfing, water-skiing, diving and fishing are particularly popular and there are plenty of facilities and localities for these sports.

On the R102 **Van Staden's Pass**, drivers can travel down to the old bridge to obtain a good view of the new bridge above. Return to the N2 and continue to **Jeffrey's Bay** where a wonderful view of the town can be seen from the brow of the hill before descending into the valley below. Take the turning for Jeffrey's Bay and drive into town along the beachfront road. The beach is considered by surfing enthusiasts to have the 'perfect wave' and the area provides excellent surfing, swimming and sailing. The resort is extremely busy during the peak season and at weekends, when it is packed with holidaymakers, visitors and surfers from all over the world.

The most popular surfing beach is **Supertubes** which is named after the surf break'. **Magnatubes**, near the Beach Hotel, also has fast and powerful surf breaks. **Kitchen Windows**, near the water-skiing club is more suited for beginners.

For the less energetic, there are wonderful seashells to be found on the beaches due to the mix of the cold Benguela and warm Agulhas currents. The **Shell Museum** in the library near Main Beach has one of the finest shell collections in the world.

There are some excellent factory shops here, particularly for beach wear and the Tourist Information Office can provide more details.

From Jeffrey's Bay take the road to **Humansdorp** and follow the signs to **Cape St Francis**. Its long golden beach offers excellent surfing, sailing and other watersports. The Point is excellent for fishing and there are always *choka* or squid boats here as this is a good breeding spot. St Francis Bay is a sophisticated resort that has developed around an inland waterway system. Unusually, the houses, although vastly different in shape and size, all have white exteriors and grey thatch or slate roofs. It is a much sought after place to own a holiday home.

Return to the N2 via Humansdorp and turn left. The Tsitsikamma Lodge is approximately 77km (48 miles) further along and makes an ideal base from which to explore the forest. En route the road crosses the Storms River on the impressive 200m (650ft) single-span **Paul Sauer** suspension bridge, which until recently was the highest bridge in southern Africa. A few kilometres from the bridge follow the signpost on the right to the **Big Tree** — a giant yellowwood believed to be over 800 years old.

There is some reasonably-priced accommodation in the small town of **Storms River**, or alternatively continue along the N2 turning left towards **Storms River Mouth**, where the **Tsitsikamma National Park** offices are located. They can provide a range of facilities, but it is wise to make reservations in advance as the area is popular with hiking enthusiasts keen to explore the coastal section of the park. The wettest months are May and October and the driest are June and July.

There are a variety of different hikes, and one of the more interesting is a short, outdoor museum walk through indigenous forest along which trees and plants are labelled. It leads to a suspension footbridge bridge which crosses the river mouth.

The 46km (28 mile) five-day Otter trail is one of the most popular walks in South Africa and runs along the rugged coastline from Storms River Mouth to **Nature's Valley**, across ravines, through thick forest and along golden beaches. It is essential to book in advance with the National Parks Board as numbers are limited and there is usually a long waiting list.

In 1964, the area was proclaimed South Africa's first Marine National Park in response to the first world conference on national parks held in Seattle, USA. The protected coastal strip run for 80km (50 miles) from Grootrivermond, near Humansdorp, to Nature's Valley.

Tsitsikamma is the Khoi word for 'clear water', and dolphins and whales are often sighted along the wild and rocky coastline. The area is also home to a wide variety of animal life including the Cape clawless otter, baboon, rock-rabbit, bushbuck, Cape greysbok and blue duiker.

Storms River Mouth to Plettenberg Bay 67 km (42 miles)

Return to the N2 and take the R102 turning in the direction of George and Coldsteam. This stretch of road was completed in 1885 by Thomas Bain and winds through two spectacular river gorge passes — the **Groot Rivier Pass** and the **Bloukrans Pass**. The Bloukrans Pass snakes its way over a distance of 7km (4miles) down into the gorge, before winding back up towards Bloukrans Forest Station, and the beginning of the scenic **Marine Drive** which offers spectacular views of the surrounding area down towards Plettenberg Bay. Further along at the bottom of the Groot Rivier Pass is

Nature's Valley, a charming seaside town on a small lagoon at the mouth of the Groot Rivier. It is a secluded spot with many walking trails and a beautiful beach.

Leave on the R102 towards Plettenberg Bay and rejoin the N2 toll road heading towards George. Approximately 8km (5 miles) before Plettenberg Bay is the Keurbooms River mouth and long stretches of pristine beach. It is a popular place to stay and there are a number of natural trails, forest walks as well as boat hire, fishing and water-skiing.

Plettenberg Bay was named in 1718 after the Dutch Governor Joachim van Plettenberg who tried to establish a port here. It was originally a whaling station, but today 'Plett' as it is more commonly known, has become one of most sophisticated resorts along the Garden Route. In the summer the population swells from 10,000 to around 40-50,000 as the rich and fashionable party-goers arrive in droves for the sun and summer fun. Plettenberg Bay was once voted by *National Geographic* as having the most temperate climate in the world.

There are numerous nature trails for either cycling, walking or horseriding through the forest, beside the lagoon or along the river. Anglers may hire fishing rods at the Plett Mountain Trout Farm for use in either of its two dams.

The three beaches along the 12km (7 mile) stretch of coastline provide safe bathing and tourists can dive for oysters. It is possible between the months of May and September to see the whales which come into the bay to calve.

The centrepiece of Plettenberg Bay is the rocky islet of **Beacon Island**, separated from the mainland by the estuary of the Piesang (Banana) River. Beacon Island was originally a whaling station but has been

Above: Plettenberg Bay isone of most elegant resorts along the Garden Route.
Opposite top: The Knysna lagoon is framed at the southern end by two huge sandstone cliffs known as 'The Heads'.
Opposite: Bird's-eye view of the Knysna lagoon.

transformed into a popular luxury hotel.

There is a large arts and crafts fraternity in the town, and an art, craft and culture route has been developed. The Old Nick Pottery beside the N2 has some beautiful pottery, jewellery and hand-spun woollen items. Visitors can watch the potter at work and it is also a good place to stop for a cream tea.

The Whale Shop is unusually decorated and offers a wide variety of gifts with an underwater theme including starfish candles, seahorse ornaments and a good selection of literature on marine life.

The **Jerling Collection** in the **Municipal Building** displays fine examples of Ming pottery and artefacts from the *San Gonzales* shipwreck which was discovered during exca-

vations at Robberg. In 1630, the survivors lived in Robberg for six months while they built two boats from the wreckage. One reached Portugal , but the second was wrecked within sight of Lisbon and most of the survivors of the *San Gonzales* drowned.

Robberg Nature Reserve ('Seal Mountain') was named after the many seals which once basked on the shores of this spectacular 6km (4 mile) red, sandstone peninsula. Paths traverse the reserve and offer stunning views of the area. On the southern side there is a large cave where an excellent selection of seashells can be found. The reserve is rich in birdlife and is popular with locals for fishing, cycling and picnics. There is an 11km (7 mile) circular coastal walk and permits can be obtained at the Nature

Conservation offices in Zenon Street between 8am and 10am from Monday to Saturday.

The **Nelson's Bay Cave** is where archaeologists discovered the skeleton of a twelve-year-old child estimated to date back to around 700BC.

There is plenty of accommodation in the area to suit all budgets, although it is essential to book during the peak periods.

Plettenberg Bay to Knysna
32 km (20 miles)

It is not necessary to stay overnight in **Knysna** as the sights can be easily enjoyed on a day trip from Plettenberg Bay. However, Knysna does have a unique charm and it is worth taking some time exploring the area. Take the N2 the short distance between these two resorts, and just before Knysna follow the left turn to Noetzie down a gravel road, which winds through pine forest down to a car park on the coast. Along the steep private road one encounters Spanish-style castles overlooking the small, secluded beach. It is an interesting find but the currents are dangerous for swimming and there is a steep climb back to the car from the beach.

Knysna was established in 1804 by George Rex, a mystery character who arrived with a party of friends in a coach bearing his coat of arms. It was believed that he was the illegitimate son of King George III of England, and although this has never been authenticated, his flamboyant lifestyle added substance to the rumours.

Knysna is the Hottentot word for 'place of wood' because of the beautiful indigenous yellowwood and stinkwood trees from which local craftsmen make furniture and household items. The **Knysna Forest** is also home to the few remaining rare Knysna elephant which are different in appearance to both the Indian and African elephant.

Knysna is an extremely attractive resort situated at the heart of the Garden Route with an exceptional combination of forest, sea and a vast estuarine lagoon. The lagoon is framed at the southern end by two huge sandstone cliffs known as **The Heads**. It provides safe waters for sailing, swimming, fishing and many other watersports.

The Publicity Office on the main road can provide maps and information on the area. There is plenty of accommodation in town, as well as a number of forest lodges and farm resorts on which the Publicity Office can provide further details.

There are several paths leading to different vantage points at the Heads where there are striking views of the surrounding area. One very steep drive to the top of the East Cliff on Coney Glen Road offers a breathtaking panoramic view of the town, lagoon and sea.

The **Featherbed Nature Reserve** and tavern on the western bank of the Heads make a nice excursion. A regular ferry service runs from the Municipal jetty to the reserve where there is a Bushbuck trail and lunch is served at the restaurant on the side of the lagoon. John Benn and Lightleys operate pleasure cruises on the lagoon to the Heads four times a day during the peak season, and at 1pm and 5pm other times of year. At the end of the jetty in the middle of the lagoon is a *Tapas* bar which makes a perfect place to watch the activities taking place on the lagoon. It is a popular spot and many locals arrive by boat to either drink or dine here or in the seafood restaurant upstairs. Cranzgots Pizzeria has an enviable location at the end of the western Head road, with a excellent view of the Heads, the channel, and across the lagoon.

Mitchell's Brewery offers free tours to watch the brewing process of the four different beers produced here — Foresters, Bosuns Bitter, Raven Stout and Millwood Mild.

Knysna is the home of the oyster farming industry, and the Oyster Tasting Tavern situated on the jetty at the end of Long Street, serves the freshest oysters in the town.

Knysna has some excellent craft shops where one can find unusual gifts made from pottery, wood, beads or leather. The **Knysna Museum** is situated at the **old Gaol Complex** and houses South Africa's only angling museum.

There is plenty of hotel and self-catering accommodation in Knysna. The Caboose offers budget accommodation in mock train compartments which are good value, but somewhat cramped. Papino's Italian restaurant has an excellent atmosphere and is very popular with the locals.

There are also tours of local furniture factories which can be arranged through the Publicity Office.

The Knysna Forest is the largest indigenous forest in South Africa and stretches from George eastwards along the foothills of the Outeniqua and Tsitsikamma mountain ranges, over a distance of approximately 170km (106 miles). The forest was originally home to large herds of the unique Knysna elephant, but excessive hunting during the eighteenth and nineteenth centuries decimated their numbers to near extinction.

As a result, the few surviving herds now live deep in the forest and are rarely seen. In a controversial attempt to increase the numbers, elephants have been introduced from Addo Elephant Park to cross-breed with the remaining Knysna elephants.

Take the R339 off the N2 after leaving the Knysna Lagoon and follow signs for **Prince Albert's Pass**.

Twenty-two kilometres (14 miles) further along is the **Diepwalle Forest Station** where the 18km (11 mile) Elephant trail begins.

The **Outeniqua Choo-Tjoe** train is an old steam locomotive used primarily as a goods train. It has one passenger coach which carries fifty people on a delightful journey through tunnels and forest; along valleys and coastal shores; over bridges and the Knysna lagoon.

It was built in 1924 and was considered at the time to be the most expensive piece of railway line in the world — particularly the section from Victoria Bay to Wilderness, where three tunnels had to be blasted through mountainside, and the long curved bridge over the Kaaimans River had to be constructed.

The train runs in both directions during the peak season. At other times of the year, it runs from Knysna only and the return journey is on a shuttle bus.

Brenton-on-Sea is on the other side of the western Head and offers a sandy beach with a popular hotel and restaurant. On the road from Knysna, the road leads past **Belvedere Church**, a tiny Norman-style church built by Captain Thomas Duthie, who was married to George Rex's daughter, Caroline. A retirement village, luxury hotel and restaurant have been built around it.

The **Old Millwood** gold mining area is about 32 km (20 miles) away from Knysna. Follow the signs to Millwood and Jubilee Creek through the beautiful Gouveld forest to the remains of a gold rush town which grew up when gold was discovered in a nearby stream. Nowadays very little remains of the town, (which once had twenty-five shops, six banks and three newspapers) except for a dusty museum, some mining trails and a few of the old mines.

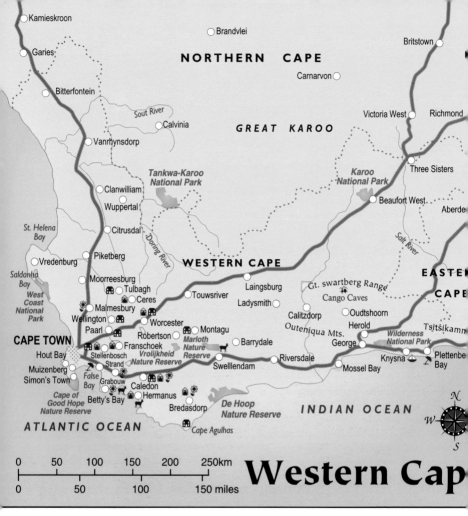

Map labels (Northern Cape region):

Kamieskroon
Brandvlei
Britstown
NORTHERN CAPE
Garies
Carnarvon
Bitterfontein
Sout River
Victoria West
Richmond
Calvinia
GREAT KAROO
Vanrhynsdorp
Three Sisters
Tankwa-Karoo
National Park
Karoo
National Park
Clanwilliam
Beaufort West
Wuppertal
Aberde
St. Helena
Bay
Citrusdal
Doring River
Salt River
Vredenburg
Piketberg
WESTERN CAPE
EASTE
Saldanha
Bay
Moorreesburg
Laingsburg
Gt. swartberg Range
CAPE
West
Coast
National
Park
Tulbagh
Touwsriver
Cango Caves
Ceres
Ladysmith
Malmesbury
Calitzdorp
Oudtshoorn
Wellington
Worcester
Herold
Outeniqua Mts.
Tsitsikamm
Paarl
Robertson
Montagu
Wilderness
National Park
Marloth
George
CAPE TOWN
Franschoek
Nature
Barrydale
Knysna
Plettenbe
Hout Bay
Stellenbosch
Vrolijkheid
Reserve
Riversdale
Bay
Muizenberg
Strand
Nature Reserve
Swellendam
Mossel Bay
False
Simon's Town
Bay
Grabouw
Caledon
Cape of
Good Hope
Nature Reserve
Betty's Bay
Hermanus
Bredasdorp
De Hoop
Nature Reserve
INDIAN OCEAN
ATLANTIC OCEAN
Cape Agulhas

| 0 | 50 | 100 | 150 | 200 | 250km |
| 0 | | 50 | 100 | | 150 miles |

Western Cap

Knysna to Mossel Bay
111 km (69 miles)

After leaving Knysna, there is a left turning to **Buffels Bay**, a holiday resort 10km (6 miles) away. The Buffalo Valley Game Farm, which offers short game drives, is along this stretch of road. From Buffels Bay, it is possible to walk all the way along the beach to Brenton-on-Sea and relax in the hotel gardens on the headland which overlook the beach.

The next town along the N2 is **Sedgefield** which is situated on the edge of a lagoon that links the Swartvlei lake with the sea. This quiet village is becoming increasing popular because of the fishing, boating, water-skiing and windsurfing opportunities on the lakes. This area is part of the **Wilderness National Park** and is known as the Lake District because it incorporates five rivers, four lakes, two estuaries and 28km (17 miles) of Southern Cape coastline. The lakes are

Opposite top: Seal Island near Mossel Bay is home to thousands of seals and penguins.
Opposite: The Goukamma Nature Reserve is a popular area for birdwatching.

bordered by the verdant green slopes of the coastal plateau, and sand dunes which separate them from the sea.

The Serpentine River connects the Upper and Lower Langvleis lakes with the Touw River making it possible to reach the Wilderness lagoon by boat. There are plenty of good places to stay including two National Parks Board camps. Take the turning marked 'George via the Lakes' and follow a scenic route on an untarred road through the lakes area. The route passes a small art gallery housed in a farmhouse, and for a time runs parallel to the railway line used by the Choo Tjoe.

The nearby **Goukamma Nature Reserve** is nearby and is extremely popular with birdwatchers. The scarlet-winged Knysna Lourie is one of the many protected species in this region. Horse riding trails can be arranged through the forest.

Take the N2 towards George which leads into the town of **Wilderness**, home of ex-State President P W Botha. There is a specially-constructed look-out point on the N2 leading out of town, which offers excellent views across the 8km (5 mile) long Wilderness beach with its unusual tiered flow of waves.

The road winds beside the Kaaimans River and into **George**, the principal town on the Garden Route, named in 1811 after the English monarch, King George III. It is a spacious town built in the foothills of the Outeniqua mountains with beautifully landscaped gardens and tree-lined streets.

The Information Office is in the old library building in York Street, and the **Old Slave Tree** outside is where slave auctions were held. There is a manacle from these days embedded in a nearby tree which has now been declared a national monument.

The quaint **St Mark's Cathedral** is the smallest cathedral in South Africa and is beautifully maintained.

The **Dutch Reformed Church** is noted for its stinkwood pulpit and yellowwood ceiling carved out of wood from the forests at Plettenberg Bay and Knysna. In the **Old Drostdy Building**, the **George Museum** houses an impressive collection of antique musical instruments, as well as an exhibition of medals and gifts presented to ex-President P W Botha from foreign dignitaries.

The **George Crocodile Park** off the Oudsthoorn/Knysna Road runs tours every hour and feeding time is at 3pm.

The challenging 137km (85 mile) eight-day Outeniqua hiking trail begins at the **Witfontein State** forest near George.

Leaving George, take the R102 old Mossel Bay road which passes through the two resorts of the Little and Great Brak River. **Great Brak River** was founded in 1852 by the Searle family who operated the toll at the causeway across the river. Charles Searle made boots and shoes for sale to passersby, and by reinvesting his profits in various enterprises, the town was gradually established. Today, many of the residents are connected to the Searle organisation and the town is noted for manufacturing high-quality mens footwear. The homes are built on islands in the Brak River and it is a 'dry town' where the sale of alcohol is prohibited.

The Portuguese explorer, Bartholomew Diaz first landed in South Africa at **Mossel Bay** ('mussel bay') after rounding the Cape in 1487. Diaz named the town the 'Watering Place of St. Blaize', until in 1602, the Dutch navigator, Paulus van Caerden renamed it after finding a huge collection of mussel shells in a cave at the headland of **Cape St Blaize**.

Each summer sees a huge influx of holidaymakers, but Mossel Bay has also increased in population since the inception of the Mossgas Off-Shore Natural Gas and Oil Operation. It is still a popular resort, although the oil operation is an eyesore and detracts from the town's natural beauty. For those interested in the project there is an information centre open to the public.

The **Bartholomew Diaz museum complex** houses the **Maritime Museum** and displays a replica of the caravel which belonged to Diaz, along with many other aspects of early Portuguese maritime history. The **Shell Museum** has an exquisite collection of shells, while the local **History Museum** displays the cultural heritage of the town and district. The milkwood tree outside the complex once had a seaboot nailed to it and was used by sailors to collect and post mail. It is over 500 years old and is today known as the **Post Office tree**. There is a boot-shaped postbox beside the tree and all mail posted from here receives a special postmark.

The stone cross nearby is known as the padrao and was donated by the Portuguese government to commemorate the first chapel in South Africa to practise Christianity.

There are regular boat trips from the harbour across to **Seal Island**, the home of thousands of seals and penguins. There is an oyster hatchery in the old aquarium building and these marine delicacies are a local speciality. A perfect evening is to enjoy a sunset cruise while sipping sparkling wine and sampling a feast of fresh oysters. The fish festival in September is the main event of the year.

There is a Khoi-san cave at **The Point** which is known locally as 'Bat's Cave' where artefacts dating back 80,000 years have been discovered. Inside the cave is 'Gladstone's Nose' a formation which is considered to resemble the profile of Gladstone, a former prime minister of Britain. From here, visitors can see a cross which is a symbolic representation of the early cross planted by a Portuguese explorer over 400 years ago.

The St Blaize hiking trail begins at the cave and ends at Dana Bay. It is an excellent way to enjoy the coastline and golden sandy beaches.

The Publicity Association provides comprehensive details of all accommodation available, including bed and breakfast, farms, hotels, chalets, and campsites.

The Santos restaurant in the Santos Hotel is highly recommended for its fresh seafood and its location directly on the beach. There is a Spur restaurant which has pretty views overlooking the bay.

Mossel Bay to Swellendam 173 km (107 miles)

Leave Mossel Bay on the R102 heading towards the tiny mineral mining town of **Albertinia**. It has grown in popularity during the last few years since the introduction of bungy and bridge jumping.

People launch themselves from the nearby Gourits River bridge and participants can either book in advance with one of organisers, or just wait in line on a Sunday.

The small farming town of **Riversdale**, at the official end of the Garden Route, sits at the bottom of the Sleeping Beauty peak in the Langeberg mountain range. Riversdale is noted for honey produced here from heather and other veld flowers, and the air around the town is saturated with the antiseptic aroma of various species of the aromatic *Agathosma* shrub.

Take a short detour on the R322 shortly after leaving **Heidelberg** which leads down to the two adjoining resorts of **Witsand** and **Port Beaufort** at the mouth of the Breede River. The

Above: Erica — one of the many tropical flowers to be found along the Garden Route.

is situated on the river bank and organises fishing trips and champagne sunset cruises.

Either return to Heidelberg on the tarred road, or take the gravel road directly to Swellendam which saves approximately 30km (19 miles). **Swellendam** is an attractive town built in the foothills of the Langeberg mountains with four peaks named ten, eleven, twelve and one o'clock. It is South Africa's third oldest town after Cape Town and Stellenbosch and became the last outpost of civilisation for travellers venturing into the unknown of the interior. The town developed on the old Cape wagon road — the only road between Cape Town and the far-off eastern parts of the Dutch East India Company. Even today, it remains a popular refuelling and refreshment stop.

The 76km (47 mile) Swellendam hiking trail begins here and lasts for six days; there are also shorter walks for the less energetic.

A detailed leaflet available from the Information Office lists all the old buildings around the town. The **Dutch Reformed Church** is definitely worth a visit, as well as the **Old Drostdy** which is a fine example of rural Cape architecture and reflects the lifestyle of the latter-day inhabitants. The thatched-roof buildings of Crafts Green are home to crafts dating back to the frontier days — including a blacksmith, a cobbler and carpenter.

The National Parks Board's **Bontebok National Park** is 6km (4 miles) from Swellendam and was established to protect the Bontebok from extinction. There are also grey rhebuck, Cape grysbock, steenbok, red hartebeest and Cape mountain zebra, as well as numerous species of birdlife. There are two short nature trails and a variety of guest houses including the Klipperivier Homestead which offers charming bed and breakfast facilities.

little fishing village of Witsand takes its name from its long stretch of white sandy beach. The area is very popular with fishermen as the Breede River is navigable for 60km (37 miles) through the wheatlands of the southern Cape. The best months for fishing are from June to November.

At **Malgas**, 30km (19 miles) upstream, it is possible to cross the river on the old hand-operated bridge which joins the Swellendam and Bredasdorp roads.

The Breede River Lodge caters mainly for anglers, but nevertheless has a charming atmosphere. The lodge

Above: Cape Agulhas is the point at which the Indian and Atlantic oceans meet, depending on the tidal currents.

Swellendam to Hermanus
297 km (145 miles)

Take the R319 from Swellendam to **Bredasdorp** which leads through sheep and grain country. There is a Wool Route for those interested, and a brochure is available which provides full details.

From here one can visit the **De Hoop/Potberg Nature Reserve** which is unique for having seven eco-systems. Many endangered species are protected in the reserve and between May and November it is possible to glimpse sightings of the Southern Right whales. Entry permits to the reserve are available at the gate which is open from 8am-4pm. The main attraction in Bredasdorp is the **Shipwreck Museum** which houses remnants of many wrecks that

foundered along this treacherous coastline.

The Bredasdorp Foot of Africa Marathon takes place each October and there is a Wild Flower Show, as well as a Beer and Bread Festival, each September.

Nine oil fields have recently been discovered near Bredasdorp which will undoubtedly bring about future commercial growth in the area.

From Bredasdorp take the R316 to **Waenhuiskrans (Arniston)**. The name *waenhuiskrans* means wagonhouse cliff and refers to an enormous cave eroded into the cliff-face which is capable of sheltering several wagons. Its second name of Arniston is after a ship that capsized here in 1815 and in 1983 its wreck was declared the first under-water national monument.

The mouth of the cave faces the sea

and can be reached at low tide by walking across the sand past rock pools, or by following the footpath from the parking area.

Nearby **Kassiesbaai**, a restored fishing village, attracts many artists, and prehistoric fish traps can still be seen on the coast along with part of the wreck of the *Clan McGregor* which date back to 1902.

Struisbaai ('ostrich bay') runs from here to **Cape Agulhas** and is bordered by a long sandy beach. The fishermen's cottages with their typical straw roofs have all been restored and declared national monuments, and occasionally one can see ostrich roaming on the farmland close to the road. One has to return to Bredasdorp in order to reach the southernmost tip of Africa at Cape Agulhas. It is at this point that the Indian and Atlantic oceans meet, depending on the tidal currents. It is unclear how Cape Agulhas (meaning 'needles' in Portuguese) was named, although it is possibly after the needle-like reef and sunken rocks here that have proven to be so perilous. The lighthouse dates back to 1848 and has been restored as a national monument.

From Cape Agulhas return to Bredasdorp and take the R316 towards **Caledon**, turn left onto the R326 and right onto the R43 towards **Hermanus**. This is the best place in South Africa to spot the whales and it is a popular resort which attracts many tourists. There is a cliff walk from the new harbour along the coastline to the lagoon at **De Mond** where it is possible to see whales giving birth only 200-300 metres out to sea. The best time for sightings is between May and November.

Hermanus has the only whale crier in the world and he can be heard at the old harbour each morning. A collection of old fishing boats, some dating back over 100 years, have been restored and are on display at the Old

Harbour Museum. There is no shortage of seafood here and abalone, mussels and crayfish can be purchased from the fish shop at the new harbour nearby. The best times to visit are either in March, when the town has a Festival of the Sea, or the end September/early October when there is a week-long Whale Festival.

Hermanus has a total of thirty-three restaurants offering a variety of international cuisines to suit all tastes, including the unusual Bientang's Cave which is located in a cave in the cliff.

The Windsor Hotel on Marine Drive is a popular place for tourists and very central for the town centre. The Ken Jockity offers bed and breakfast accommodation and also caters for backpackers. The Accommodation Centre offers a wide range of flats, houses, chalets and guesthouses.

There are dozens of coves to explore and the beaches are safe for both swimming and surfing, especially Voelklip and Grotto beaches. East of the town, the lagoon has a wide stretch of sandy beach and safe bathing. The **Fernkloof Nature Reserve** offers over 45km (28 miles) of good hiking and walking trails up the mountain slopes as well as are pleasure cruises on the Klein River.

Hermanus to Cape Town
156 km (97 miles)

Take the R43 from Hermanus which leads into the R44 heading for Cape Town. Between Hermanus and Cape Town the road winds around the side of **False Bay** and a few small resort towns. **Kleinmond** is primarily a holiday resort for farmers from the nearby areas, and the **Bot River Marsh** and **Kleinmond Coastal Nature Reserve** are popular for sailing and hiking. Nearby **Betty's Bay**, originally a whaling station, is now an enchanting, small village popular with fishermen and nature lovers. The **Harold Porter Botanical Garden** stretches up the mountainside to the waterfall at **Dia Kloof** and is noted for its wildflowers — particularly the rare disa which blooms in summer.

The coastline from Hermanus to **Gordon's Bay** incorporates a stretch of treacherous waters, which despite the unpredictable tides, is popular with fishermen. There are a number of plaques along the road to commemorate those who died here. The fishing village of Gordon's Bay has one of the prettiest harbours along the coast and is a popular meeting place in summer for owners of small boats. The white GB anchor sign on the mountain slopes stands for General Botha, not Gordon's Bay. Nearby, **Steenbras Dam** is a charming place to visit with its colourful gardens and waterfalls. The protea, the national flower of South Africa is grown here. Visitors must obtain a permit from the municipality office in Gordon's Bay before visiting the dam.

The neighbouring resort town of **Strand** is popular with local fishermen and the 3km (2 mile) **Milk Bay Beach** offers safe bathing, water-skiing, surfing, and windsurfing. The beachfront is dominated by the imposing Strand Pavilion timeshare complex,. From Strand take the N2 into Cape Town which is detailed further in Chapter Four.

Cape Town to Oudtshoorn
425 km (264 miles)

Leave Cape Town on the N1 heading towards Worcester or alternatively, combine part of this itinerary with the tour of the wine route detailed in the Cape Town section of Chapter Four. From Franschoek follow the R45 over the **Franschoek Pass** and turn left on the R321 towards Worcester.

Worcester is situated at the entrance to the **Hex River Valley** and is named after a family title of Lord Charles Somerset, Governor of the Cape in 1818. The area is the country's biggest wine and brandy producer and is the capital of the Breede River valley district. The town has a rich cultural heritage which uniquely combines the old town with a vibrant business centre. The **Drostdy** is the oldest building in town and served as the magistrate's office until 1891. It is now a national monument that is used as a hostel and can therefore only be viewed from the outside.

The **Kleinplasie Open-Air museum** is 1.5km (1 mile) from the town centre in the direction of Robertson. It is a living museum which authentically recreates the lifestyle of the early Cape farmers. There are two restaurants in the grounds, along with an extensive wine cellar which stocks wines from the many cooperatives in the area. The **KWV Brandy Cellar** here is the largest brandy distillery of its kind in the world, and on weekdays there are four guided tours a day.

Robertson is one of the largest wine-producing areas of the Cape and is also where most of South Africa's top racehorses are bred. Take the road towards **Montagu** and continue along the R62 to Oudtshoorn. The route passes through delightful countryside and a number of small, pretty towns. This area is known as **Little Karoo** and is exceptionally charming. There are a variety of interesting small wine routes and tours of cheese factories, as well as hot springs, hikes and walks.

On the road from Ladysmith to Caltizdorp are the Zoar and Amalienstein missionary stations established on adjacent farms by the South African Missionary Society and the Berlin Missionary Society respectively.

In spring and summer the air in **Calitzdorp** is filled with the heady

Opposite top: The Hex River Valley is the country's largest wine and brandy producer.

Opposite: The verdant hills and lush agricultural land around the Franschoek Valley.

Above: Steenbras Dam has colourful gardens and the Protea, the national flower of South Africa is grown here.

Right: The ostrich farms in Oudtshoorn have the best breeding records in the world.

fragrance of jacaranda and the gardens are a mass of colour. The police station has an unusual garden with neatly manicured lawns and a variety of brightly-coloured farming implements.

The area has a number of excellent estates producing top-quality wines at prices that are considerably lower than the more well-established routes near Cape Town. A trip to the Spa here makes a refreshing stop.

✳ The ostrich farms in **Oudtshoorn** have the best breeding records in the world and this is the only place worldwide where these birds are farmed on such a large scale. The industry began in 1869 when a farmer perfected the design for an ostrich egg incubator which permitted hatching control. The feathers became the height of fashion in Europe and large sums were paid for quality ostrich feathers. By 1880, this industry was more profitable than any other farming product in the country and successful farmers built themselves 'feather palaces' from their profits, an example of which is *Welgeluk* at the Safari Ostrich farm. This opulent property incorporates five different styles of architecture and has a bath which takes 100 litres of water.

World War I, and changes in fashions, caused the bottom to drop out of the market and the demand for feathers never recovered. Today farmers have adapted by selling the ostrich meat for steaks and biltong, the skin for expensive leather goods and the exceptionally clear corneas are used for human eye transplants. The ostrich is often portrayed as a comical figure, but this powerful bird can reach speeds of nearly 70 kph and can kill a human with their powerful forward kick. Most of the birds are raised communally in paddocks.

Ostriches will mate for life and although a 'widow' will find a new partner, 'widowers' will not. The male is ready to mate when their necks and legs turn red and the female will make a clucking sound when she is ready. The female will lay between fourteen and sixteen eggs in a hollow which she has scraped in the ground and she and her mate then take turns over the next forty-two days to incubate the eggs.

There are three farms which run organised tours for the public. The tours usually last approximately one-and-a-half hours and provide a wealth of information on this flightless bird. It is also possible to ride an ostrich which is far harder than it looks.

On the road to Mossel Bay, the **Safari Ostrich Farm** and the **Highgate Ostrich Farm** are the two oldest farms in the area. Their guides are very knowledgeable and tours are conducted throughout the day between 8am and 4pm. The Safari Farm has the added benefit of a 'feather palace' — one of the few remaining palatial mansions constructed from the latter day profits of the ostrich feather industry.

Oudtshoorn is the best place to sample ostrich steak, ostrich liver paté, an ostrich omelette or ostrich soup and Headlines restaurant is one of the better establishments to visit. There are several hotels including the Holiday Inn Garden Court.

The **C P Nel Museum** was named after Charles Paul Nel, a local businessman whose hobby was collecting medals and regimental insignia. As his collection increased in size, he eventually opened a museum, which on his death was passed to a board of trustees and moved to its present site. Whilst all the medals are still on display, along with a large collection of dolls, the main theme of the museum is now the ostrich and the industry that surrounds them. It also houses a synagogue where services are occasionally held.

The newest farm, **Cango Ostrich**

Farm is located on the road to the **Cango Caves** along with the **Cango Crocodile Ranch** and **Cheetahland**. The tours leave every half hour and last approximately one hour. They provide a fascinating insight into the habits of these ancient reptiles, and many of the myths and legends surrounding the crocodile are clearly explained. There is also a enclosure where visitors can play with tame cheetahs in return for a donation to the Cheetah fund.

The 74m (21ft) **Rust-en Vrede** waterfall is reached by taking the Raubenheimer Dam turning on the road to the Cango Caves. It is quite a distance off the main road but is an excellent spot for swimming.

Continue on to Cango Caves — some of the most spectacular calcite caves in the world and certainly the best in South Africa. There are more than eighty chambers extending along over a kilometre of passages. A guide conducts an interesting sound-and-light show where fantastic limestone formations are described and high-lighted with colourful spotlights. Some of the stalactites and stalagmites are believed to be over 200,000 years old. The second part of the tour is entertaining but is not for either the claustrophobic or the larger person, as there are some very tight squeezes along the way.

Oudtshoorn to Beaufort West 206 km (128 miles)

Leave Oudtshoorn on the R328, Cango Caves road heading towards Prince Albert. The road into the Great Karoo leads over the **Swartberg Pass**, which climbs to a height of 1,585m (5,200ft) above sea level, and the views down across the arid savannah are quite exceptional. Several kilometres from the summit, a road leads off to **Gamkaskloof**, previously known as

'the Hell' — a name coined by Piet Botha, a cattle inspector who used to regularly travel the 57km (35 mile) bumpy road around hairpin bends and almost vertical drops. This is a deep, narrow valley which was inhabited for several generations by descendants of the early trek-Boers (nomadic farmers) who spoke their own language and shut themselves off from civilisation. Apart from the occasional trip to Calitzdorp, 43km (27 miles) away, they were totally self-sufficient. Today, the valley is virtually deserted as most of the residents became too old to live alone and moved to Prince Albert. There are plans to turn the area into a living museum.

Nestling at the foot of the Swartberg mountains is the small town of **Prince Albert**, which is often likened to a diminutive version of Graaff-Reinet. It was founded in 1802 and named in honour of the Prince Consort, Queen Victoria's husband. There are many beautiful examples of Cape and Karoo-style architecture, many of which bear a 'Prince Albert' gable and a visit to this pretty village is like travelling into a bygone era. The town clerk can provide information on the many walks and trails in the area. The hotel is one of the oldest licensed premises in the country and a national monument.

Take the R353 towards the N1 and turn right into **Beaufort West**. This is a popular resting point for travellers between Cape Town and Johannesburg, although there is very little to see here. The museum in Donkin Street houses a permanent exhibition to the town's most famous sons — the heart transplant surgeons Christian and Marius Barnard. Among the exhibits is a collection of gifts from around the world presented to these brothers after their first successful transplant in 1967.

The Royal Hotel, the Oasis, the Karoo Lodge and the Wagonwheel Motel all have their own restaurants

and offer comfortable accommodation.

The **Karoo National Park** is 4km (2 miles) south on the N1 and is one of the largest natural ecosystems in South Africa. There are fifty different species of mammal here, including the Mountain Zebra, as well as several species of bird. The park is renowned for its fossil treasures of the Central Karoo and the skeletons of prehistoric and extinct reptile groups. There is a fossil walk which includes a study of fossilised bones from mammal life that lived 240 million years ago.

The three-day Springbok hiking trail which is open from late February to the middle of October follows a circular route of the park. Accommodation is provided in the two rest camps.

Beaufort West to Graaff-Reinet 209 km (130 miles)

Take the R61 towards Aberdeen and the R57 to Graaff-Reinet. The town is situated on a horseshoe bend in the Sundays River which provides irrigation for the local farming of Merino sheep, Angora goats, cattle and horse stud farms.

Graaff-Reinet is the fourth-largest town in South Africa and was established as the local seat of administration for the new eastern frontier district in the Republic in 1786. It was named after the Governor of the Cape at the time, Cornelius Jacobus van der Graaff and his wife Reinet.

Today this prosperous farming area is known as the 'Gem of the Karoo'

Opposite: The Cango Caves are the best calcite caves in South Africa.
Top: Springbok in the Karoo National Park.
Above: The Owl House Museum at Nieu Bethseda.

because of its authentically-resorted buildings and wide jacaranda-lined streets. A tour of the town should begin at the **Hester Rupert Art Museum** which is housed in the **Old Dutch Reformed Mission Church** in Church Street. It is one of three remaining churches built in the traditional cruciform plan, and is now a national monument. There are excellent displays of contemporary South African art and exhibitions held here throughout the year.

Next door, the **Old Library Museum** houses displays of fashions dating back to the 1800s, San paintings, an excellent collection of nineteenth century photographs, as well as the fossilised remains of reptile skulls found in the Karoo.

The houses in Parsonage Street are all constructed in a typical Karoo-style and have been faithfully restored. **Reinet House Museum**, on the corner of Parsonage and Murray Streets, is a beautiful Cape Dutch house with an interesting collection of eighteenth and nineteenth century yellowwood and stinkwood furniture. The building was damaged by fire in 1980, but has since been carefully restored. It was the home of Reverend Andrew Murray who, together with his family, had a great influence on the town after his arrival from Scotland in 1824. Behind the house is a unique double-curved stairway and a massive grapevine of the Black Acorn variety which was planted in 1870 by Reverend Charles Murray, and is reputed to be the largest in the world. The museum has a special postmark depicting the vine.

The Residency is an annexe of the museum which served as the magistrate's residence from 1916. The H-plan homestead has now been declared a national monument.

The **John Rupert Little Theatre** at the southern end of the street served as a place of worship for the coloured community for 120 years and has now been converted into a theatre. The original pulpit can still be seen in the foyer.

The **Drostdy and Stretch's Court** was built in 1805 by French architect Louis Thibault. In 1855, Captain Charles Lennox Stretch, an Irish soldier of high repute, acquired a large piece of land at the rear of the Drostdy and constructed the cottages to house emancipated slaves. It is now a hotel complex which is made up of small cottages located behind the main building.

At the top of Church Street on **Church Square** stands the **Groote Kerk**, a strikingly beautiful early Gothic-style church, built from local stone along the lines of Salisbury Cathedral in England.

The **Graaff-Reinet Pharmacy** at 24 Caledon Street was established in 1870. It retains a distinctive Victorian atmosphere and is now an unusual national monument.

The Drostdy is a charming hotel with a delightful *a la carte* restaurant. The Panorama Swiss Guesthouse is very popular and offers a carvery every Sunday, and set meals or *a la carte* during the week. The Andre Stockenstrom restaurant offers fine Karoo-style cuisine, and as the restaurant is unlicensed, diners can bring their own wine.

Trips from Graaff-Reinet

The 15,000 hectare (37,070 acre) **Karoo Nature Reserve** surrounds Graaff-Reinet and has four easy walking trails. However, it is primarily known for the **Valley of Desolation** which was proclaimed a scenic monument in 1935. Take the Murraysburg Road and follow signs to the Valley, 14km (9 miles) from Graaff-Reinet. It is accessible via a tarred, winding road leading to the hills of the west. At

1,400m (4,593ft) above sea level there are lookout points over the endless plains of the Great Karoo. There are fascinating examples of 200 million years of erosion where cliffs and rock pinnacles have been carved in the shale and sandstone.

An interesting trip from Graaff-Reinet is to the village of **Nieu-Bethesda**. It is reached by following the road to Middleburg and is off the R57. The 25km (15 mile) journey on a gravel road passes through the Sneeuberge mountains into a fertile valley surrounding this picturesque village with its elegant white church and pretty Karoo houses. On the main road into the village there is a signpost to the **Owl House Museum**. The house is a shrine to the memory of Helen Martin, a teacher who returned to the village to nurse her ailing parents. After their death, she became a virtual recluse and turned her cottage into a shrine for her father. She was fascinated by light and throughout the cottage, among her incredible array of personal possessions, the walls and ceilings are covered with tiny pieces of coloured, crushed glass. The workshop has been left as it was when she died and there are hundreds of bottles containing different types of glass.

Outside in Camel Yard, her devotion to eastern philosophy is displayed in an extraordinary collection of statues of peacocks, camels and prophetic figures all facing east. In 1978, on discovering her sight was deteriorating, she committed suicide by swallowing caustic soda. Her life was celebrated in a play by South African writer, Athol Fugard, and today the house is maintained by the Friends of the Owl House who believe it to be an important monument to an artist's life.

From Graaff-Reinet take the R63 which becomes the R75 to Uitenhage/Despatch and follow the signs to Port Elizabeth. It is an easy 255 kilometre (158 mile) drive.

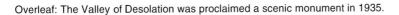

Overleaf: The Valley of Desolation was proclaimed a scenic monument in 1935.

PLACES TO VISIT

Beaufort West

Museum
Donkin Street
Open Monday-Friday: 9am-12.45pm
& 2pm-4.45pm

Bredasdorp

Shipwreck Museum
Independent Street
Open Monday-Friday: 9am-4.45pm
Saturday: 9am-12.45pm
Sunday: 10.30am-12.30pm
☎ (0284) 41240

Cape Agulhas

Agulhas Lighthouse
Open Monday-Saturday: 9am-5pm
Sunday: 9am-12noon

George

Choo-Tjoe Steam Train
☎ (0441) 738288

George Crocodile Park
York Road
Open daily: 9am-5pm
☎ (0441) 734302

The George Museum
Old Drostdy Building
York Street
Open Monday-Friday: 9am-4.30pm
Saturday: 9am-12.30pm
☎ (0441) 735343

Outeniqua Hiking Trail
☎ (0445) 23027

Graaff-Reinet

Hester Rupert Art Museum
Church Street
Open daily: 10am-12noon & 3pm-5pm
Saturday & Sunday: 10am-12noon
☎ (0491) 24248

Old Library Museum
Corner Church & Somerset Street
Open weekdays: 9am-12noon & 3pm-5pm
Saturday: 9am-12noon
Sunday: 10am-12noon

Reinet House Museum
Parsonage Street
Open weekdays: 9am-12noon & 3pm-5pm
Saturday: 9am-12noon
Sunday: 10am-12noon

Owl House
Nieu Bethesda
Open daily: 9am-5pm
☎ (04923) 667

Hermanus

Old Harbour Museum
Marine Drive
Open Monday-Saturday: 9.30am-5pm
Sunday: 9am-12noon
☎ (0283) 21475

Knysna

Angling Museum
Queen Street
☎ (0445) 826138

Choo-Tjoe Steam Train
☎ (0445) 21361

John Benn Cruises
☎ (0445) 21693

Knysna Oyster Hatchery
Teason Island
☎ (0445) 22168

Knysna Museum
Old Gaol Complex
Queen Street
☎ (0445) 826138

Mossel Bay

Bartholomew Diaz Museum
Market Street
☎ (0444) 911067

Mossgas Information Centre
Santos Road
☎ (0444) 911115

Seal Island
☎ (0444) 3101

Shell Museum
Market Street
☎ (0444) 911067

Oudtshoorn

Safari Ostrich Show Farm
R328 to Mossel Bay
Open daily: 7.30am-5pm
☎ (0443) 227311/2

Hoopers Highgate Ostrich Farm
10 km (6 miles) from Outdshoorn off R328
Open daily: 7.30am-5pm
☎ (0443) 227115/6

Cango Ostrich Farm
Cango Cave Road
Tours between 9.30am & 6pm
☎ (0443) 224623

**Cango Crocodile Ranch &
Cheetahland**
Cango Cave Road
Tours daily from 8.00am
☎ (0443) 225593

Port Elizabeth

The Campanile
Main entrance to harbour
Open Monday, Tuesday, Thursday,
Friday: 9am-1pm & 2pm-4pm
Wednesday & Saturday: 8.30am-12.30pm

Cultural History Museum
7 Castle Hill
Open Tuesday-Saturday: 10am-1pm
Daily: 2pm-5pm
☎ (041) 522515

Feather Market Hall
Main Street, Central
☎ (041) 555514

King George VI Art Gallery
Park Drive, Central
☎ (041) 561030

Opera House
Whites Road
☎ (041) 562256

Port Elizabeth Museum
(including Oceanarium)
Beach Road, Humewood
Open daily: 9am-1pm & 2pm-5pm

Riversdale

Julius Gordon Africana Centre
Open Monday-Friday: 10am-12noon

Worcester

Kleinplasie Open-Air Museum
Open daily: 8.30am-4.30pm
☎ (0231) 22225

KWV Brandy Cellar
Church Street
Open weekdays & Saturdays in season
☎ (0231) 20255

NATIONAL AND PROVINCIAL PARKS

Beaufort West

Karoo National Park
PO Box 316
Beaufort West 6970
☎ (0201) 52828/9

Graaff-Reinet
Karoo Nature Reserve
Murraysburg Road and follow signs
Dept of Nature Conservation
Box 349
☎ (0491) 23453

Knysna
Buffalo Valley Game Farm
Buffelsbaai Road
Open daily: 11am-3pm except Saturday
In season daily 9am-5pm
☎ (0445) 22481

Wilderness National Park
PO Box 35
Wilderness 6560
☎ (0441) 91197

Plettenberg Bay

Robberg Nature Reserve
☎ (0445) 32151

Port Elizabeth

Addo Elephant National Park
PO Box 52, Addo 6105
Open daily
☎ (0426) 400556

Seaview Game Park
25km (15 miles) west to Buffelsfontein
Open daily
☎ (041) 741702

Settlers Park Nature Reserve
Halock Street
☎ (041) 336794

St Georges Park
Park Drive
☎ (041) 559711

Tsitsikamma National Park
PO Box Storms River 6308
☎ (042) 541 1607

Zuurberg National Park
12km (7 miles) north of Addo Elephant Park
☎ (0426) 400583

Swellendam

Bontebok National Park
PO Box 149 Swellendam
☎ (0291) 42735

LOCAL TOURIST AUTHORITIES

Beaufort West

Tourist Information
Museum
☎ (0401) 4082

Bredasdorp

Publicity Association
Dirkie Uys Street
☎ (02841) 42584

George

Tourist Office
Old Library Building
124 York Street
☎ (0441) 744000

Graaff-Reinet

Publicity Association
Museum Building
☎ (0491) 24248

Hermanus

Publicity Association
105 Main Road
☎ (0283) 22629

Jeffrey's Bay

Publicity Association
Oosterland Street
☎ (0423) 932588

Knysna

Publicity Association
40 Main Street
☎ (0445) 21610

Mossel Bay

Marketing Association
Corner Church & Market Street
☎ (0444) 912202

Oudtshoorn

Tourist Bureau
Seppie Greefs Building, Voortrekker Street
☎ (0443) 222221

Plettenberg Bay

Publicity Office
Victoria Cottage, 12 Kloof Street
☎ (04457) 34065

Port Elizabeth

Publicity Association & Satour
Lighthouse Building
Donkin Hill, Central
☎ (041) 521315

St Francis Bay

Publicity Office
The Village Centre
☎ (0423) 940076

Swellendam

Information Office
26 Voortrekker Street
☎ (0291) 42770

The Cape, North-West Provinces

n and Gauteng

This itinerary begins in the beautiful city of Cape Town in the Western Cape province and continues up the Atlantic coast, through picturesque fishing villages, past sparkling lakes, mighty dams, dramatic mountains and quaint farms and vineyards. Between the months of September and October the Cape flora bursts into a magnificent medley of colour as the spring flowers make their annual appearance.

From Cape Town, the route travels across to the majestic Augrabies Falls and onto the remote desert of the Kalahari Gemsbok National Park on the borders of Namibia and Botswana. It continues to Kuruman, the former home and mission of Dr David Livingstone and onto the scene of the siege of Mafikeng.

The route draws to a close at the magnificent Sun City, one of the country's main tourist attractions with four luxury hotels within its complex. The Palace is reputed to be one of the finest hotels in the world and was the surreal setting for the last three Miss World contests. Visitors can then end their journey in Johannesburg or possibly return to Cape Town either by air or on the luxurious Blue Train.

CAPE TOWN

When Sir Francis Drake first sighted the South African Cape coast he described the landscape as '... the most stately, the fairest Cape we saw in the whole circumference of the earth.' **Cape Town** certainly enjoys one of the most beautiful settings in the world and ranks in elegance and grace with other breathtaking cities like Sydney, San Francisco and Rio de Janeiro.

From its small beginnings, when the first market garden was established for passing ships in 1652, the city has become the jewel of South Africa and now stretches over an area of 300 sq km (118 sq miles). Cape Town is often spoken of as 'Mother City' by South Africans and it is dominated by **Table Mountain** and **Table Bay**. The flat-topped mountain is so vast that it is sometimes visible as far as 200km (124 miles) out to sea and has acted a perfect landmark to seafarers.

Cape Town combines a perfect blend of natural beauty with a lively cosmopolitan atmosphere where a variety of cultures co-exist in harmony in an almost village-like atmosphere. The city centre is busy without being overcrowded, and close at hand are vast stretches of beautiful sandy beaches, lush winelands or spectacular walks along the peninsula. The mixed international community have all leant their influence to the wide assortment of food served here, and the area is a culinary delight with its abundance of fresh seafood, bountiful fresh produce and its close proximity to the winelands.

Cape Town has one of the healthiest climates in the world. The south-easterly wind which blows from October to February takes with it the summer smog and pollution and, for this reason, it is referred to locally as the 'Cape Doctor'. The busiest time is from mid-December to mid-January when the area is very popular with people from all over South Africa. Summer lasts from November to March and is clear, bright and dry with temperatures averaging from 13°C (55°F) at night to 26°C (77°F) during the day. The south-easterly wind blows along the western shores of the peninsula and provides good surfing conditions, while the beaches of Clifton and The Boulders are more sheltered and offer some protection from the winds. Autumn lasts from March to May and is considered by many to be the best time of the year to visit as the wind has dropped and the sea is warm and calm. In winter, between June and September, the weather becomes distinctly European with temperatures ranging from 8°C (48°F) to 18°C (65°F). The north-easterly wind blows and the weather alternates between damp and rainy to crisp, bright warm days. There is some excellent surfing available for those brave enough to stand the chilly water. Spring last from August to October during which the wildflowers bloom and Cape Town is at its most beautiful.

Cape Town is easily accessible by road, rail or air. The international D F Malan Airport is 22km (14 miles) east of the city on the N2 freeway and a number of international airlines run regular scheduled services directly here. It is approximately two hours flying time from Johannesburg and there are daily flights between the cities. There are regular coach services from all across South Africa and a train service from Pretoria via Johannesburg and Kimberley — which includes the luxury **Blue Train**. The railway station and coach station are in the heart of Cape Town.

There is well-established public transport system within Cape Town, as well as a number of tour companies. Taxis do not cruise the streets, but can be picked up at any of the three main ranks situated outside the Post Office in Parliament Street; the railway station; and St George's Cathedral at the top of Adderley Street. The *tuk-tuk* is a three-wheeled taxi which looks like a cross between a milk float and a motor cycle and can be flagged down on the streets. It is a fun way to see the city sights in fine weather. There are always black kombi buses lined up at central station some of which are marked with their destination and others will shout out where they are going. They can also be waved down in the street, but take heed, they pack passengers in like sardines and it is not the most comfortable form of trans-

port. The main bus terminal is at **Grand Parade** and there are numerous bus routes around Cape Town operated by City Tramways. It is worth buying a ten-trip clipcard for visitors planning a few trips.

Once outside the city centre, it is advisable to hire a car to enjoy the true essence of the area. Alternatively, there is an efficient train service around the peninsula to Wynberg, Fish Hoek, Simon's Town and Muizenberg. However, Seapoint, Clifton and Hout Bay on the Atlantic side are only served by bus.

The Cape is an important part of the tourism industry and a department called Captour has been established which is wholly-devoted to promoting the area. They have a number of different offices around the city which can provide a wealth of information on the area along with copies of their monthly *What's On* publication.

There is a roundabout in the **Heerengacht** with a fountain and ornamental pools where the bronze statue of Jan van Riebeeck, and a nearby statue of his wife tower over the city they founded. A small bronze ship in front of the **Medical Centre**, where Adderley Street leads into the Heerengracht features a moving testimony to Robert Falcon Scott. Cape Town was Scott's last stop before he sailed to the Antarctic in the early 1900s.

The pastel-coloured **City Hall** in Grand Parade was built in 1905 and today houses the city library. It was on the steps of this magnificent building that Nelson Mandela made his historic speech to the world when he was first

Overleaf top: The skyline of Cape Town is dominated by the spectacular Table Mountain.
Overleaf: The Houses of Parliament, are the seat of legislative government.

Cape Town

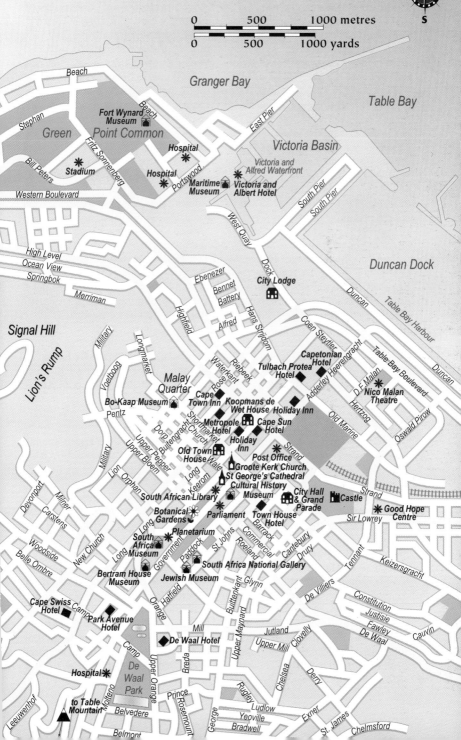

N
W E
S

0   500   1000 metres
0   500   1000 yards

Granger Bay

Table Bay

Beach

Stephan

Green

Fort Wynard
Museum

Point Common

Beach

Fritz Sonnenberg

East Pier

Victoria Basin

Bill Peters

Stadium

Hospital

Hospital

Portswood

Victoria and
Alfred Waterfront

South Pier

South Pier

Western Boulevard

Maritime
Museum

Victoria and
Albert Hotel

West Quay

Dock

Duncan Dock

High Level
Ocean View
Springbok

Ebenezer

Bennet

Battery

City Lodge

Duncan

Table Bay Harbour

Merriman

Highfield

Hans Strijdom

Alfred

Coen Steytler

Duncan

Signal Hill

Lion's Rump

Military

Longmarket

Voetboog

Waterkant

Riebeek

Rose

Capetonian
Hotel

Tulbach Protea
Hotel

Adderley Heerengracht

Table Bay Boulevard

D.F Malan

Nico Malan
Theatre

Duncan

Malay
Quarter

Bo-Kaap Museum

Cape
Town Inn

Koopmans de
Wet House

Holiday Inn

Hertzog

Oswald Pirow

Pentz

Dorp

Buitengracht

Shortmarket

Church

Metropole
Hotel

Cape Sun
Hotel

Old Marine

Upper Pepper

Long

Keerom

Old Town
House

Holiday
Inn

Strand

Lion

Orphan

Upper Bloem

South African Library

St George's Cathedral

Groote Kerk Church

Post Office

Cultural History
Museum

City Hall
& Grand
Parade

Castle

Strand

Military

New Church

Botanical
Gardens

Parliament

Town House
Hotel

Barrack

Sir Lowrey

Good Hope
Centre

Devonport

Milner

Carstens

South
Africa
Museum

Planetarium

Government

Paddock

St Johns

Commercial

Roeland

Canterbury

Druy

Tennant

Keizersgracht

Woodside

Belle Ombre

Long

New Church

Bertram House
Museum

Jewish Museum

South Africa National Gallery

Glynn

De Villiers

Constitution

Cape Swiss
Hotel Camp

Park Avenue
Hotel

Orange

Hafield

Buitenkant

Upper Maynard

Justisie

Fawley

De Waal

Cauvin

Camp

Mill

De Waal Hotel

Breda

Jutland

Upper Mill

Clovelly

Chelsea

Derry

Hospital

De
Waal
Park

Upper Orange

Prince
Rosemount

Rugley

Ludlow

Yeoville

Bradwell

George

St. James

Chelmsford

Leeuwenhof

Toleno

Belvedere

Exner

to Table
Mountain

Belmont

released from his life prison sentence. The offices of Captour and the Tourist Rendezvous Centre are located here and can provide detailed information on the surrounding area, as well as make travel and accommodation reservations.

The **Castle of Good Hope** is South Africa's oldest building and dates back to 1665. Its distinctive five-pointed star shape was designed to make it impregnable against invading forces. Today, the **Kat Gallery** in the castle houses the **William Fehr Collection** of paintings, porcelain, carpets and furniture from the colonial days of the Cape and there are daily guided tours. The Castle is also the headquarters of the Western Province command.

The **Koopmans de Wet House** is a townhouse dating back to the Cape neo-classical period and contains one of the finest collections of colonial Dutch antiques in the country.

Bertram House is the city's only surviving redbrick Georgian town house, and is furnished in the style of the early nineteenth century. The **Jewish Museum** dates back to 1862 and displays the history of Jewish communities in the Cape. It is situated in the first synagogue to be constructed in South Africa. The **Old Town House** houses the Michaelis Collection, a permanent exhibition of seventeenth century Dutch and Flemish paintings.

The **Company Garden** is close to the library, and is where Jan van Riebeeck set up the market garden for passing ships, which heralded the beginning of the Cape settlement. It is now a botanical garden with exotic trees and shrubs from many parts of the world. It is the main park of the city and also features an aviary, tropical flowers, fountains and a statue of Cecil Rhodes pointing north, bearing the inscription 'Your hinterland is there'.

The **South African National** Gallery is close to the gardens and houses permanent exhibitions of contemporary work by local and international artists. There are film shows, lectures and special exhibitions throughout the year.

The **South African Museum** opposite is the Republic's oldest museum and has Bushman paintings among its many anthropological and natural history exhibits. It also houses the imaginatively designed planetarium — the **Theatre in the Sky**.

The **Cultural History Museum** in nearby Adderley Street was originally built as a slave lodge for the Dutch East India Shipping Company and later became the Supreme Court. Today it houses a display of early Greek, Egyptian and eastern empires and the history of the Cape. The tombstones of Jan van Riebeeck and his wife are in the courtyard, although their remains are in the Far East where they died.

The **Groote Kerk** in Upper Adderley Street is the mother church of the Dutch Reformed Church of southern Africa. Dating back to 1704, it is the oldest church in South Africa and has a beautiful hand-carved wooden pulpit. **St George's Anglican Cathedral** in Wale St is famous for its stained-glass windows and is similar in design to St Pancras Church in London. The **South African Library** behind the cathedral is the oldest public library in the country.

The **Houses of Parliament**, the seat of legislative government, are situated on Government Avenue and visitors may obtain tickets to watch the parliamentary session between January and June. During the recess from July to December, guided tours are available. Smart dress and passports are required when parliament is sitting. The elegant building of the **Tunhuys** (Garden House) is the office of the State President and is located next door.

The **Malay Quarter** is a short walk from Wale Street and is the original home of the workers indentured from the east in the seventeenth century by the Dutch East India Company. It is worth visiting this unique Islamic area of old mosques with their sparkling minarets, enigmatic shrines and narrow cobbled streets. The **Bo-Kaap Museum** was built in 1763 and is part of the **Cultural History Museum**. It is one of the oldest houses in Cape Town which survives in its original form, and is furnished as a typical late nineteenth-century Muslim home.

Continuing back along Buitengracht, one reaches **Table Bay Harbour**, the second-largest harbour in South Africa after Durban. It has undergone major redevelopment in recent years and is now one of the major tourist attractions of the city.

The **Victoria and Alfred Waterfront** is packed with restaurants, bars, specialist craft and jewellery shops and is a lively place throughout the day and evening. It offers some of the finest live music in the city and has become extremely popular with young people out to enjoy the excellent food and entertainment here. The harbour houses the **Royal Yacht Club** and the **Maritime Museum** which has two floating exhibits, the *SAS Somerset* and the *Alwyn Vincent*.

The old **Penny Ferry**, a small rowing boat which has been in use since the early 1900s, will take visitors from one pier to another. Sealink has offices in the harbour from where boat excursions can be arranged and Court Helicopters run trips over the city.

Table Mountain was proclaimed a national monument in 1964 and was subsequently declared a nature reserve which is home to over 1,470 species of plants. On a clear day the views from the top are breathtaking, although the 'tablecloth' of cloud, which sometimes shrouds the summit but makes an impressive sight from the bottom, often hampers views from the top. The aerial cableway takes only a few minutes to the summit in good weather, from where it is a one-hour walk to the highest point, **Maclears Beacon** (1,087m), along a signposted footpath. There is an abundance of tame hyraxes (rock rabbits) running around the viewpoints.

A dazzling variety of wildflowers bloom on the mountain including a species of orchid known as the Pride of Table Mountain. There is a restaurant which serves snacks and reasonably-priced meals and the post office at the top will frank outgoing mail 'Table Mountain'.

It is advisable to be at the cable station by 9am in the summer season as it is usually extremely busy. Alternatively, during the December-January holidays, use Captour's advance reservation service.

For the more adventurous, there are numerous ascents to the summit including over 300 footpaths which range from easy scrambles to dangerous climbs. A map indicating these different ascents is available from Captour, and the Mountain Club of South Africa can offer helpful advice. The mountain is floodlit at weekends throughout the year and nightly between December and April.

Table Mountain is bordered by Devil's Peak, Signal Hill and Lion's Head. **Signal Hill** provides one of the best vantage points of the harbour and city — particularly of the lights at night. The 335m (1,098ft) summit is **Lion's Battery** which is used to fire salutes to passing ships and for ceremonial occasions. Every day at noon,

Overleaf top: The aerial cableway which runs to the summit of Cable Mountain.
Overleaf: The Cape of Good Hope.

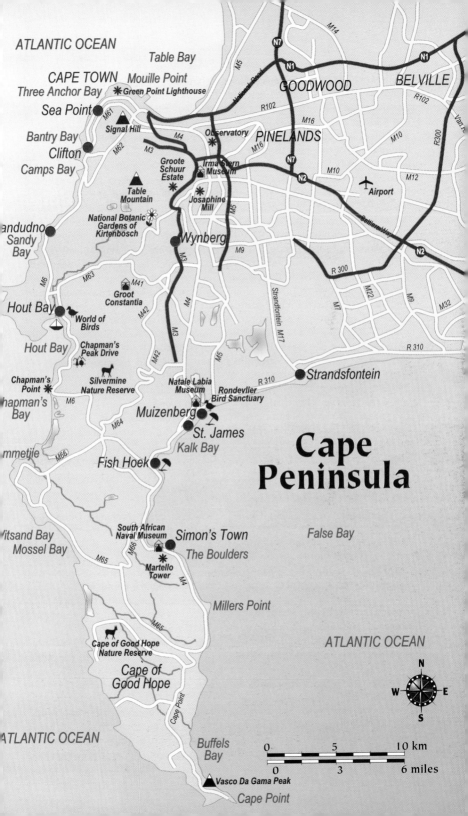

except Sunday, a gun is fired from the summit which sets the time for the republic. The 669m (2,194ft) sugar-loaf peak, connected to Table Mountain by the saddle of land known as the **Kloofnek**, is called **Lion's Head**. It is believed that the last lion of the peninsula was shot here, hence its name. The summit can be reached by footpath from where there is a breathtaking 360° view of Table Mountain, the mountain range of the Twelve Apostles, the city and ocean. **Devil's Peak** flanks the eastern side of Table Mountain and was named after a Malay legend which connects the 'tablecloth' of cloud to a smoke cloud created by a pipe-smoking contest between Van Hunks, a retired pirate and the devil. The contest continues throughout the summer and only ceases in the winter when Van Hunks is stricken with rheumatism and is unable climb the mountain, at which point the 'tablecloth' mysteriously disappears. The peak was originally named Wind Mountain as it whipped the south-easterly wind to gale-force speed.

A TRIP AROUND THE CAPE PENINSULA

Until sixty million years ago, the peninsula of the **Cape of Good Hope** was once an island. The water then receded to expose a low lying sandy arm of land known as the Cape Flats which connected the island to the mainland. This 75km (47 mile) peninsula is dotted with small, charming towns and resorts all the way to its tip at the Cape of Good Hope. The main drive around the peninsula, between Hout Bay and Camps Bay, runs along the foot of the mountain range known as the Twelve Apostles. The range was named by the British Governor, Sir Rufane Donkin who believed he could identify the various apostles in their shapes.

On sunny days the area is reminiscent of the French Riviera with picturesque resorts and hosts of semitropical flowers. The drive around the entire peninsula covers 143km (89 miles) although there are many short routes to also follow.

Take the M61 out of the city centre towards the residential area of Green Point and Three Anchor Bay which is noted for the massive waves here when the north-easterly storms rage in the winter. The next town is **Seapoint**, a lively, but congested cosmopolitan area, which a few years ago claimed to have the highest concentration of restaurants in the world. It is a fashionable place to live because of its close proximity to the centre, and large sums are paid for properties overlooking the sea. There is a hedge maze on Beach Road which is floodlit until 11pm every night.

The road passes along the rocky coastline of **Bantry Bay** to **Clifton** which has four sandy beaches and is ideal for sunbathing and surfing as the beaches are protected from the summer south-easterly wind. It is possible to sunbathe here until 8pm on warm summer evenings, but swimming is inadvisable as the waters are bitterly cold due to the Benguela current which brings in waters from the Antartic. A feature of Clifton is that it is perched on the side of Lion's Head, and the apartments are supported by concrete stilts. The beaches can be reached from the road by a steep flight of steps.

The road winds around the coast past the lawned promenade of **Camps Bay** with its magnificent backdrop of the Twelve Apostles on the left and the white sandy beach on the right. Camps Bay is an excellent beach for sunbathing, but the undertow can make swimming dangerous and the sea is cold. The cove of **Glen Beach**, which adjoins Camps Bay is famous for surfing.

The road passes through **Bakoven** with views over to the small residential area of **Llandudno** on the right. There is a lovely beach here but swimming is dangerous. From here it is a short walk through lush coastal woodland to beautiful Sandy Bay — now unofficially a nudist beach.

Hout Bay is a charming historic fishing port where an abundance of fresh fish, including crayfish, is sold. The harbour is dominated by the **Mariner's Wharf** on the quay; a unique seafood emporium housing a fresh fish and lobster market, a restaurant and a nautical souvenir and gift shop. The fish and chips here are excellent quality.

There are regular boat trips from Hout Bay to **Seal Island** where visitors can view fur seals. The trips last thirty minutes except for the evening champagne cruises which last two hours. The **World of Birds** in the bay is a sanctuary for 5,000 exotic and indigenous birds all of which are kept in large walk-through aviaries.

From here take the **Chapman's Peak Drive** which is rated as one of the world's most stunning scenic drives. For 10km (6 miles) the drive cuts through cliffs around the mountain peak and along sheer ravines which drop into the sea. There are several vantage points which offer exceptional views and there are a number of mountain climbs and walks worth taking. When travelling away from Hout Bay the best view is to the rear, so it is best to make use of the lookout points.

The wreck of the 1,500 ton *Kakapo* lies half-buried on the beach at Chapman's Peak. The ship ran aground in 1900, and all attempts to refloat it since have failed. It was used as a set for the film *Ryan's Daughter*.

Take the turning to the M65 towards **Kommetjie**, a quiet, attractive village and seaside resort which is a popular surfing spot in summer when the south-easterly wind brings a strong shoreward swell.

The coastline stretches for almost 40km (25 miles) through some of southern Africa's most dramatic scenery. The peninsula divides at the tip into three points: the Cape of Good Hope being the most southerly; Cape Maclear (named after Sir Thomas Maclear, the nineteenth-century astronomer) and Cape Point, the furthest east, on which a lighthouse and radio beacon have been built. There are breathtaking, panoramic views from the lookout which involves a steep ten-minute climb from the car park.

The **Cape Point Nature Reserve** encompasses an area of 7,500 hectares (19,100 acres) and was proclaimed in 1939 to protect the flora and fauna of the peninsula There are over 8,000 plants here and a small number of antelope including eland, bontebok, springbok and hartebeest. The reserve produces a fact sheet in a variety of languages which gives detailed information on the area. Cape Point is often believed to be the place where the Atlantic and Indian Oceans meet, but this is actually at Cape Agulhas, 200km (124 miles) to the east.

There are tidal swimming pools at nearby Buffel's Bay which provide an ideal place to escape the wind that blows virtually all year round.

Join the N4 in the direction of Simon's Town on leaving the reserve. **The Boulders** is very popular with locals for its clear, protected waters

Overleaf top: Hout Bay.
Overleaf: Freshly-caught rock lobsters.
Page 175 (*top*): The elegant Rhodes Memorial in Rondebosch.
Page 175 (*below*): Cape Point Nature Reserve.

that are dotted with massive rocks which resemble huge beached whales. It is excellent for swimming, diving, canoeing and fishing but is accessible only by foot from Seaforth.

Simon's Town is the headquarters of the South African Navy. This attractive town, which is steeped in history, is named after the former Governor of the Cape, Simon van der Stel who founded the port. The British developed the town as a base for their South Atlantic squadron and many naval personalities visited or were based in the town. The **Martello Tower** at the Naval Dockyard was built by the British in 1796 as a defence against the French. It is now a maritime museum which includes in its exhibits a copy of the *Times* newspaper from November 1805 that records the death of Lord Horatio Nelson and the victory at the Battle of Trafalgar.

The Scratch Patch at **Mineral World** is located nearby, and visitors may purchase a bag to fill by scratching around ankle-deep in millions of semi-precious gemstones. It is possible to tour the factory and watch the polishing process, or visit the gemstone mine to see the stones in their natural environment. There is also a Scratch Patch at the Waterfront in the harbour.

Fish Hoek was originally a farm situated on the road which connected the naval base at Simon's Town with Cape Town. Fearful that the area would become a den of iniquity, the British governor, Lord Charles Somerset prohibited the sale of liquor on the property. This old municipal by-law is still in existence and it is impossible to find any bars or liquor shops in the town. There is excellent surfing and yachting and the beach offers the safest swimming in the Cape. From Fish Hoek the beach stretches several kilometres towards Clovelly.

Kalk Bay means 'lime bay' and this small fishing port takes its name from the kilns that were built here in the seventeenth century to produce the lime required to manufacture paint. This quaint town with its cobbled streets is worth a visit—particularly to the quay at midday where the catch of the day is sold to the highest bidder. Part of the old railway station has been converted into a popular restaurant and pub called the Brass Bell and features regular live jazz bands.

St James is a pretty village which was named after the first church built here in 1874. It is popular with visitors because of its tidal swimming pool which offers protection from the infamous 'Cape Doctor' wind.

Muizenberg is one of the most popular holiday resorts in the area because the sea is shallow with little undertow and few strong currents. In summer, if there is no south-easterly wind, it is an ideal place to relax and soak up the sun, and in winter the north-easterly wind builds up perfect waves for beginners in surfing. The colourful Victorian changing booths lend the air of an English seaside resort to the beach.

The **Natale Labia Museum** was named after Count Natale Labia who presented the building to the South African National Gallery in 1983. It contains fine furniture and works of art. The thatched cottage where Cecil Rhodes died is on the outskirts of Muizenberg, in the direction of St James, and contains many of his possessions. **Rondevelei Bird Sanctuary** is a leading ornithology research station where visitors can watch the birds from observation platforms. It is open all year round.

The **Silvermine Nature Reserve** covers an area of 2,000 hectares (5,000 acres) and enjoys some of the most spectacular mountain scenery the country has to offer.

False Bay was named because ships

heading east often confused Cape Hangklip with the Cape of Good Hope. This huge inlet of sparkling, blue water is bordered by a 35km (22 mile) stretch of sandy beach and lies between the mountains of the Cape Peninsula and the Hottentot's-Holland range. In winter the area is popular for surfing, but it is also one of the world's major angling areas and of great importance to marine biologists.

The Suburbs

The **Groote Schuur Estate** covers the whole slope of Devil's Peak and includes the Cape Town residence of the President of South Africa, the **University of Cape Town** (UCT) along with its medical school, and the **Groote Schuur hospital** where the first heart transplant was performed by Professor Christian Barnard in 1967.

Rondebosch is one of the more fashionable suburbs and is dominated by the impressive **Rhodes Memorial** which marks the spot where Cecil Rhodes used to sit and enjoy the view of the Cape Flats across to the mountains beyond.

Newlands is considered to be one of the finest suburbs in Cape Town despite having the highest rainfall in the peninsula. It is home to the Western Province Rugby Club which has its own museum with rugby memorabilia dating from 1891. The excellent open-air Newlands swimming pool close to the grounds.

Follow Rhodes Drive along the bottom of the slopes at the back of Table Mountain. This scenic drive passes through an extremely gracious residential area and is home to a number of famous people including Archbishop Desmond Tutu. Rhodes Avenue leads past the entrance to the **Kirstenbosch Botanical Gardens** which were founded in 1913 on the property Cecil Rhodes presented to the nation. The gardens which incorporate a forest reserve house 5,000 of the 20,000 plants in southern Africa and are a garden for all seasons. It is a wonderful place to explore, and the open-air cafe here is a popular place to meet. There is a splendid gift shop which is similar to the National Trust shops in the United Kingdom, and there are free guided garden walks every Tuesday and Saturday at 11am. Thirty minute 'happy tractor' rides take visitors around the entire gardens.

Wynberg is Cape Town's largest suburb and features quaint cottages that many artists and would-be artists have made their homes and studios. **Maynardville Park** here has a popular open-air theatre.

The **Constantia Wine Route** is clearly marked from the road and runs between Groot Constantia, Klein Constantia and Buitenverwachting. **Klein Constantia** was part of the original estate of Constantia until the farm was divided in 1712 after Commander Van der Stel's death. The vineyard was created by Ernst le Roux of the prestigious Nederberg estate, and together with the expertise of Ross Gower, also from Nederberg, a select range of wines have been cultivated. **Buitenverwachting** (meaning 'beyond expectations') was built in 1796 and the beautiful homestead, gardens, cellars and outbuildings still stand today. There is also an exclusive restaurant of the same name.

There are a variety of tour companies within Cape Town, but 'One City Tours' run by a Xhosa named Paul offers a comprehensive tour of the entire city including a trip through some of the townships in a kombi bus. There is even a night tour to a *shabeen* for the adventurous.

It is worth visiting Cape Town during some of the shows and festivals, and the best of these include

Top and above: Namaqualand blooms carpet the ground in glorious colours.
Opposite: The Kirstenbosch Botanical Gardens were founded in 1913 on the
property which Cecil Rhodes presented to the nation.

the Cape Coon Carnival in January when 12-14,000 brightly-dressed minstrels dance through the streets of the city and the J & B Metropolitan Stakes at the Kenilworth racecourse. February and March hosts the Cape Show; the Kirstenbosch Annual Sale of Indigenous plants; and the Argus Pick Cycle tour around the peninsula.

The scenic Ohlsson's Two Oceans 56km (35 mile) road marathon takes place each April and July sees the annual KWV Berg River Canoe marathon. The Cape Town Proms are held each October and the Rothmans Regatta in December.

There are numerous hotels and guesthouses within the Cape Town Area. The Victoria and Alfred Hotel is popular on the Waterfront as well as the Breakwater Lodge. The Mount Nelson Hotel in the city centre is a first class hotel offering luxurious rooms and facilities. Captour provides a detailed booklet of all accommodation in the peninsula.

There is a large concentration of restaurants in the near vicity of the Victoria and Alfred Waterfront and at nearby Seapoint. The Observatory also offers several lively restaurants and bars. The Kaapse Tafel is a well-established restaurant serving authentic Cape cuisine, which is definitely worth sampling whilst visiting the area.

DAY TRIPS FROM CAPE TOWN

There are so many specialised routes within the Cape that it is advisable to discuss particular requirements with Captour. They will help in planning out routes with the assistance of maps and leaflets on places of interest. There are a number of art routes in Cape Town and around the Cape Peninsula where once a month artists and craftspeople open their doors to visitors. The fruit routes takes in the local farming co-operatives and factories, and the wool route gives a taste of farm hospitality. There is also a mission route which tours old mission stations along the west coast as well as a flower route and wine route.

A trip up to **Kagga Kamma** makes a long day out as it involves a 260km (161 mile) trip in each direction. Kagga Kamma ('the place of the bushmen') is situated 120km (74 miles) from Ceres in the midst of the Cedarberg mountains. Accommodation is expensive, but it is possible for day visitors to participate in a game drive. Kagga Kamma is a private game reserve where bushmen from the surrounding areas have been relocated in an attempt to preserve their cultural heritage by supporting themselves through eco-tourism. There is a tourist complex with organised safari drives, and leopard and lynx live naturally in the area.

There are some excellent examples of bushman paintings, some of which date back 6,000 years. The bushmen also demonstrate the age-old skills of hunting, fire-making, dancing and story-telling.

Take the N1 from Cape Town towards Worcester and the R43 left to Ceres. The town was named after the Roman goddess of agriculture and is a popular holiday resort with visitors who enjoy the outdoor life. The summers are warm, but the winters can get so cold that it will sometimes snow.

The entrance to **Ceres** is via the beautiful **Mitchell's Pass** which opened in 1848. The tollhouse here is now a national monument and home to a restaurant and country shop. There are both long and short hiking trails from the nearby nature reserve which are marked along the route.

About eighty percent of the fruit juice in South Africa is produced at the

CFG cold storage complex, including *Liquifruit* and *Fruitree* brands. Visits to the complex can be arranged, and the kiosk here sells fruit trees, dried and fresh fruit. It is possible during November and December to visit the Klondyke Cherry farm. The farm also grows apples and pears and visitors may pick their own fruit after 1 November by prior arrangement. There is a cherry festival in the last week of October.

From here, follow the signs towards Calvinia and then Kagga Kamma. It is worth including a trip to Tulbagh on the way to or from the reserve. Surrounded by mountains and vineyards, **Tulbagh** is one of the most attractive villages in the country. In 1969, an earthquake destroyed large parts of the town including thirty-two of the buildings in Church Street. These have been restored to form the largest concentration of national monuments in the republic and it is worth taking a stroll around to enjoy the atmosphere and architecture.

At the **Oude Drotsdy**, there is a collection of early Cape furniture and local art. Visitors can enjoy a glass of locally-produced sherry while viewing examples of Louis Thibault's work. The **Drostdy Wine Cellar** which is famous for its sherries and a range of wines, offers conducted tours at 10am and 3pm everyday except Sunday. The Paddagang Restaurant and Winehouse in Church Street is open from 9am to 5pm. It was the first winehouse in the country and is a popular venue for its excellent restaurant where they serve their own label 'Padda' wine.

Cape Town has its own ostrich show farm which is twenty minutes from Cape Town off the N7. Guided tours leave every thirty minutes and visitors can observe all aspects of ostrich breeding and ranching, as well as have their photograph taken with an ostrich.

Fruit

The pretty villages of **Grabouw** and **Elgin** enjoy an ideal climate for growing apples, and supply a large percentage of the fruit that is exported from South Africa. Take the N2 from Cape Town towards George over **Sir Lowry's Pass** (named after Sir Lowry Cole, the Governor of the Cape) to the fruit producing region of the Elgin Valley. There is a spectacular view across the peninsula down to the coast from the 402m (1,318ft) summit. Before the pass was constructed in 1838, traders and travellers used to cross the Hottentot-Holland's mountain range by wagon and it is possible to still see wagon-wheel tracks just beyond the summit.

The **Four Passes Fruit Route** begins at Grabouw and Elgin and includes the fruit producing areas of Vyeboom, Villiersdorp and Franschoek set amidst incredible mountain scenery. Captour has a leaflet on this route.

The **Elgin Apple Museum** complex is situated on the banks of the Palmiet River and details the history of the industry along with modern-day techniques. They can also arrange visits to the farms and apple-packers in the area.

On the last Sunday of each month the local craftspeople on the Akeddis art route open their home to visitors. There is no pressure to buy and visitors are encouraged to relax and enjoy the hospitality of these artists while viewing their work. Naturally, there are many fruit stalls in the area as well as an assortment of charming inns serving traditional afternoon tea. The Houw Hoek Inn is at the foot of the **Houw Hoek Pass**, just before Botrivier. It has been a stopping point for travellers since 1779, and is the oldest existing licensed hotel in South Africa. The farm stall here sells fresh bread, cakes, fruit and vegetables.

Above: The Hottentot-Holland's mountain range is surrounded by the fruit-producing region of the Elgin Valley.

Whales

The Whale route encompasses the coastal strip which runs between Arniston in the east and Saldanha in the north west. It is a breathtaking experience to watch the habits of these majestic creatures at such close quarters when they come into these waters between the months of August and November to breed.

Captour produce a brochure on those most likely to be seen, which include Southern Rights, Humpbacks, Bryde's and very occasionally Killer whales. Captour also provide reports of the previous day's sightings.

The coastline between Cape Town and Hermanus is one of the best places for viewing (see Chapter Three).

Flowers

When the rains bring the spring flowers into bloom, a good day trip from Cape Town is to take the R27 coastal road north to **Mamre** to the quaint Rhenish Mission station and home to the few surviving Khoikhoi tribes. From here continue to **Darling** and its magnificent flower reserves and farms where each spring local farmers open their homes to visitors. The Sandveld flora is famous for its colourful daisies, ixias and gladioli. The **Tinie Versveld Flora Reserve** on the Yserfontein road hosts a wild-flower show each year in the third week of September and is renowned for its wild flowers typical of the Sandveld area.

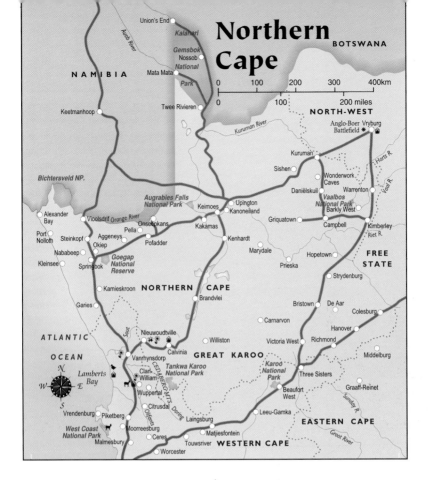

Guide To Viewing The Flowers

The best flowers bloom from early August to mid-September with weather patterns determining the length of the flower season.

Telephone the Flower Hotline to check where the rains have been good and the best blooms have appeared, and be sure to make hotel reservations before travelling. The flowers bloom for such a short period that the sudden influx of visitors usually makes accommodation scarce.

The flowers are at their best during the warmest part of the day — usually between 11am and 4pm and remember it is illegal to either pick them or remove any plants.

Winelands

The Cape Winelands lie only a thirty-minute drive east of Cape Town. The area is renowned for the excellent wine produced here, as well as its elegant Cape Dutch architecture, wide streets lined with shady oak trees, enchanting valleys and scenic routes.

There is a combination of private estates, wine cooperatives and wine tasting centres throughout the region which offer guided tours and wine tasting. Many estates offer a range of meals, from a vintners platter of local cheeses and *vetkoek* — a delicious, deep fried bread — through to *a la carte* Cape cuisine. Naturally, each dish is accompanied by an excellent selection of locally-produced wines.

Wine production in the area dates back to the early Dutch settlers before the process was subsequently refined by the expertise of the French Huguenots who arrived in 1685, fleeing religious persecution in France. Today, the Cape wine routes have a strong European flavour as they were inspired by the *Routes du Vin* in France and the *Weinstrassen* in Germany.

The quality of South African wines is noted throughout the world and they often win prestigious wine awards. The demand for the wine has increased in recent years — most notably when the country regained its status as an acceptable trading partner with the rest of the world.

The wine estates can be visited throughout the year but visitors during February and March have the added advantage of seeing the harvesting and bottling.

Stellenbosch lies 42km (26 miles) east of Cape Town on the N1 in a fertile valley beside the Eerste River. It is one of the foremost wine producing areas in the country, and was founded in 1679 by Cape Governor, Simon Van der Stel who moved wine farmers into the area. He also initiated the planting of the oak trees that now line the avenues and parks around town which inspired its secondary name 'Town of Oaks'.

Stellenbosch is South Africa's second oldest town and has splendid examples of Cape Dutch architecture with a total of seventy-one buildings preserved as national monuments. A university was established in 1918 and the town became an educational and cultural centre for Afrikaans speaking people.

It is situated on level plains and cycling has proved to be a popular way to see the area. Bicycles can be hired from either Stellenbosch Railway Station or from the Information Centre. Alternatively, it is possible to take horse trails, including moonlight trails, through some of the striking scenery in the area.

There is also a 12km (7 mile) vineyard hiking trail which begins at the Stellenbosch Farmers Winery and meanders through the verdant vineyards of the nearby well-known estates.

The Information Centre in Plein Street can help visitors plan their day. There are too many wineries to visit in one day and they are also a fair distance apart. The *Stellenbosch and its Wine Route* guide provides detailed maps of the town centre and the wine routes. The *Discover Stellenbosch on Foot* leaflet guides visitors on a walking tour around the town which takes approximately five hours and incorporates old colonial houses of varied architectural styles.

Oom Samie Se Winkel at 84 Dorp Street is a shop which trades in the foods and memorabilia of yesteryear and there are some unusual bargains to be found. The **Village Museum** is made up of four period houses dating from 1709-1850 which have been faithfully restored and furnished in the style of a different period. **Stellenryck Wine Museum** and **Oude Meester Brandy Museum** are both excellent places to discover more information on the historical development of wine and brandy. They both display examples of antique equipment and glasses, and the historical development of bottling techniques.

The **Stellenbosch Wine Route** opened in 1971 and now incorporates nearly thirty wineries within 12km (7 miles) of the town. The route leads off the four major roads from Stellenbosch and each winery is clearly signposted. Visitors can pay informal visits to each winery, but it is advisable to check the wine route guide for opening times, tour times and when lunch is served. The **Farmers Winery Centre** on the

R310 is also a useful information source. Their lunches are good value and on a clear day there are impressive views of the peninsula and Table Mountain.

The **Bergkelder** close to the town centre offers twice daily tours, including a slide show. Visitors can lay wine down in oaks in the mountainside and receive regular updates from the cellar master until it reaches maturity. The **Van Ryn Brandy Cellar** off the R310 towards Cape Town offer one hour tours along with free tasting of the various types of brandy produced here. Visitors can watch the production process including the cooper making vats by hand.

The Simon Van der Stel Festival in the last week of September offers wine and food tasting.

On the outskirts of town, the **Oude Libertas winery** has its own amphitheatre dedicated to promoting the performing arts. Operas, ballets and musicals are performed between December to mid-March and free wine is served during the intervals. Tickets can be purchased through Computicket.

Take the R45 for 30km (19 miles) from Stellenbosch to the charming village of **Franschoek**. The town was originally known as Oliphantshoek because of the elephants that continually migrated to the area up to the early nineteenth century. It was renamed Franschoek by the French Huguenots who established themselves in the valley in 1688, where for the last three centuries local farmers have concentrated on wine production and distilling brandy. A map of Franschoek estates can be found at the information office or the wine route office. Visits to certain estates in the area must be made by prior arrangement, so it is advisable to check the map for tour times before setting out. There are some lovely old homes,

antique shops and cafes serving mouthwatering cream teas.

The **Huguenot Memorial Monument** at the end of the main street was built to commemorate the 250th anniversary of the arrival of the French, and the adjacent museum contains a detailed history of the Huguenot families.

The 300-year-old **Boschendal Estate** is fascinating and the tours include a comprehensive slide show, and wine tasting beneath huge oak trees. There is also an excellent restaurant which serves delicious meals. A shop is also situated in the grounds.

Take the R45 from Franschoek to **Paarl**, the town where Nelson Mandela spent a large portion of his last few years of imprisonment. It was named in 1657 by a small party of explorers who described the granite domes of Paarl Mountain as 'giant diamonds and pears' when they glistened in the sun after the rain. The town developed in 1700 after the Dutch farmers and French Huguenots planted vineyards and today, amongst other well-known estates, the headquarters of the South African wine industry is located here. KVW provides more than fifty percent of all brandy produced in South Africa and exports to more than twenty-five countries. It was established in 1918 to stabilise the cape wine industry and has over 5,000 producing members. Tours are conducted daily at 9.30am 11am, 2.15pm and 3.45pm in a variety of languages.

A booklet from the information office provides details on a number of historical buildings which are found mainly in the vicinity of Main Street. The *Guide and Map of the Paarl Wine Way* booklet is available and provides useful information on the town.

There is a odd-shaped monument to the Afrikaans language near to the town. Each April, the Paarl Young

Above: The luxurious Blue Train amidst majestic mountain scenery.
Opposite top: The Hex River Valley has many fine examples of Cape Dutch architecture.
Opopsite: Spectacular view over the Paarl Valley.

Wine Show and Festival heralds the arrival in Paarl of the first wines. It is a wonderful day of festivities worth visiting for those in the area at the time. Reservations can be made through the information office in Paarl or through Computicket.

Cape Town to Clanwilliam 349km (217 miles)

Leave Cape Town on the N1 at the Waterfront and almost immediately take the turning towards **Milnerton**. The road passes through Table View and Bloubergstrand which is immediately recognisable as a popular spot for photographs of Table Mountain. There is a long sandy beach running along this section of coast, and it is a perfect place to enjoy a picnic or a braai in the sand dunes. From here, there is a

view of Robben Island, the high-security prison where Nelson Mandela spent many of his twenty-seven years in prison. It is possible to make arrangements through the Department of Correctional Services to visit Robben Island, although space is limited and advance booking is necessary.

The legacy of the market garden that Jan van Riebeeck established in 1652 becomes increasingly evident on the road heading northwards through the fertile farming area of the Swartland where strawberries, wheat and vegetables flourish in abundance. The journey continues past Citrusdal and along the Olifants River wine route.

In recent years, small resorts geared towards fishing and bird-watching enthusiasts have developed around the tiny fishing villages and farming towns of the west coast. The lagoons, coves and sheltered bays are perfect for water-skiing, sailing and scuba-diving, while the Atlantic Ocean yields a wide abundant marine life and offers some of the best line fishing in the world.

 During the spring, the countryside is covered with blankets of brightly-coloured flowers. Many of these plants are rare and during the months of August and September flower lovers travel from far and wide to witness one of the world's most spectacular botanical sights. Even for visitors with only a passing interest in flowers, it is impossible not to appreciate the miracle of nature here.

A left turn leads to the **West Coast National Park**. The Langebaan lagoon and the islands of Malgas, Jutten, Marcus and Schaapen which cover a total of 18,000 hectares were pro-claimed a national park in 1985. The fishing village of **Langebaan** sits at the head of the tranquil waters of the 26km (16 miles) long, shallow lagoon and in summer the lagoon is inhabited by approximately 55,000 birds, many of whom are migrants from the Arctic circle. Sailing is good all-year-round and part of the lagoon has been demarcated for watersports.

There is excellent swimming from Langebaan beach and the Information Office can provide details on all the latest regulations and permit require-ments. There is limited accommo-dation available at the lodge. The Postberg entrance gate is open only in August and September from 9am-5pm.

The information office can also provide details on the specially arranged lunches and suppers on the beach. The nearby timeshare resort of Club Mykonos is an authentic recreation of a yacht marina and Greek village. It is consists of white villas with brightly coloured doors and shutters and a Greek restaurant at the harbour. There are even several donkeys wandering around the streets.

Fifteen kilometres (9 miles) west of **Hopefield**, between Langebaan and Saldanha on the **Elandsfontein Farm**, is where the Neanderthal fossil of Saldanha Man was found in 1951. Continue up the coast and take the R79 to **Saldanha**. This town was super-seded by Table Bay as South Africa's second-largest natural harbour be-cause of the lack of fresh water here. However, Europeans made vast for-tunes after discovering the value of guano as fertilizer deposited on the mudflats at the southern end of the lagoon by the large population of gannets, cormorants and penguins. Today, Saldanha is primarily an iron and steel port and there are guided tours of the harbour and iron ore loading terminal. It has also developed as a holiday resort because of the excellent sailing in the bay, and because the beaches are safe and the water warmer than the rest of the coast.

The coastline is dotted with several fish processing factories and the seafood here is excellent. It is possible to purchase crayfish, snoek, oysters, mussels and sea-trout here at extre-mely reasonable prices.

Heading back to **Vredenburg**, the attractive fishing village of Paternoster is situated 29km (18 miles) down a gravel road. The white-washed fisher-men's cottages are over 100 years old and the quay is an excellent place to buy lobster cheaply from the fisher-men who are always keen to negotiate prices.

Return to the N2 via the R399 to the town of **Citrusdal**. Fruit is despatched from here throughout the world and there are regular tours, between March and September, in the harvest season of one of the largest orange-packing sheds in South Africa. The **Olifants**

River Wine Route starts at Citrusdal and features a number of interesting wine cellars along the road to Lutzville. The nearby **Pickenierskloof Pass** is very beautiful and it is worth stopping at the mountain resort to visit the Vanmeerhoff farmstall and restaurant. The farmstall sells a variety of local produce including excellent fresh fruit, vegetables and home-made jams.

The **Cedarberg** region was declared a wilderness area in 1973. It is a unique combination of state forest and dramatic mountain ranges traversed with well-maintained hiking trails. The area offers stunning areas of caves, waterfalls, rock paintings and spectacular mountain views. There are incredible rock formations which have been sculpted by the elements and which offer challenging climbs for mountaineers.

The rare snow protea blooms high in the mountains between December and February. The area is excellent for hiking and it is worth allowing additional time here to explore its natural beauty.

Clanwilliam, one of the oldest towns in South Africa, sits at the foot of the Cedarberg mountain range in the Olifants River valley. The valley was originally settled in 1725 by colonists and the area still retains a latter-day charm. Each spring, the town is filled with the intoxicating aroma of evanescent wildflowers which can be seen in abundance at the wild flower garden at the **Ramskop Nature Reserve** and on the banks of the Clanwilliam Dam. Every August a ten-day wild flower show takes place in the Dutch Reformed Church building.

There is some charming accommodation around the **Clanwilliam Dam** and the area is also popular for watersports, including boating and fishing. Reinholds is an excellent steak and seafood restaurant opposite the Clanwilliam Hotel which is open from Wednesday to Saturday. Reservations are essential. The Pizza House is a less formal, but nevertheless, popular venue with the locals.

This is the centre of the Rooibos tea industry and there are regular guided tours of the tea estates. Tours are conducted at 10am, 12noon, 2pm and 4pm from Monday to Thursday and 10am, 12noon and 2pm every Friday. Visitors are shown a video on the tea-grading process as part of the tour. The best time to visit is in March when the crops are being harvested.

The **Leipoldt-Nortier Memorial Library** houses paintings by Hugo Naude and personal possessions of C Louis Leipoldt, a famous South African doctor, epicure and poet.

It is worth contacting the West Coast Tourism Bureau in nearby **Lamberts Bay** who can provide invaluable assistance with travel arrangements, personalised tours and general queries.

Clanwilliam to Vanrhynsdorp 76km (47 miles)

Vanrhynsdorp is the southern gateway to Namaqualand where the semi-desert of the Knersvlakte begins. From here visitors can either continue up to Springbok and onto Augrabies Falls, or travel via Calvinia which is shorter. It is definitely worth travelling via Springbok during the months of August, September and early October as the spring flowers are at their most glorious during this period. Otherwise there are hours of motoring through fairly barren terrain.

There is very little to see in Vanrhynsdorp, although the succulent nursery in Voortrekker Street is interesting. There is a museum in the old prison in Van Riebeeck Street and an Information Office opposite the

189

Above: The Augrabies Falls National Park.
Opposite: The Nieutwoutdville Waterfall tumbles 90m (295 feet) down a deep ravine.

library in the Town Hall. There is a spectacular waterfall 26km (16 miles) out of town on the dirt road that starts at the end of Voortrekker Street. This pleasant drive through farmlands leads to the waters which cascade 125m (410 feet) down a deep ravine. There is a wine cooperative in nearby **Vredendal** which runs tours and sells some of the cheapest wines in the area.

The Caravan Park offers accommodation in the outhouse buildings of a farm. They serve delicious home-cooked breakfast and dinners using fresh local produce. The Lombard's Guesthouse is comfortable, although they do not provide meals. The Namaqualand Country Lodge has a good restaurant and there are a several other places to eat around the main street in town.

Via Calvinia to Augrabies Falls 672km (417 miles)

The **Vanhryns Pass** is located to the east of Vanrhynsdorp en route to **Nieutwoutdville**, and the 820m (2,624 feet) summit offers panoramic views of the surrounding coastal plains. Nieutwoutdville is a pretty village which is distinctive because of its sandstone buildings, and the interesting architecture of the Dutch Reformed church. There is a flower reserve a short distance out of town where the spring flowers bloom into a glorious blanket of vibrant shades.

On the R357 Loeriesfontein Road, there is a turning to a small parking area which offers a breathtaking view of the **Nieutwoutdville Waterfall** as the Doorn River plunges 90m (295 feet)

down a deep ravine. There is a 46km (28 mile) hiking trail at the **Oorlogskloof Nature Reserve** which leads past surreal rock formations, bushman caves with excellent rock paintings and enchanting views of the surrounding area. There are also day hikes from here.

Continue on the R27 to **Calvinia** which is situated in the centre of an important wool producing district. The **Calvinia Museum** is housed in the same building as the *art deco* synagogue built for the Jewish community who lived here between the 1920s and the 1960s. The museum offers a fascinating insight to country life with displays of antiques, clothing and vehicles used by the local community. **Bothasdal**, a private home, has been authentically furnished in the style of the seventeenth and eighteenth centuries and **Die Hantamhuis** is one of the town's first homes and dates back to the 1850s. Both of these homes can be viewed by arrangement with the Hantam Publicity Association.

The Hantam Meat Festival takes place each August and offers sport, dancing and excellent food — especially meat. From here the road passes through the small towns of Brandvlei and Kenhardt. Take the R359 at Neilersdrif to the Augrabies Falls National Park or the untarred road just after Kenhardt.

Vanrhynsdorp to Springbok 256km (159 miles)

There are only small towns situated off the main road to Springbok and the road leads through endless arid countryside. **Springbok** is the capital of the Namaqualand region and it was on this site that the first mining operation in South Africa began. This region has been associated with copper mining from the seventeenth

century when the Dutch governor sank mining shafts 3km (2 miles) south of Caroulsberg. The Van der Stel mine was the first place where ore was mined by Europeans in South Africa.

The **Goenab Nature Reserve** is located 15km (9 miles) south-east of Springbok and is dry and arid for most of the year. After the rains, however, this wasteland bursts forth into a blaze of colour as the Namaqualand daisies carpet the area. It is possible to see gemsbok, ostrich and mountain zebra. The **Hester Malan wildflower garden** in the reserve has an exhibition of rare indigenous succulents, a rock garden and impressive displays of wild flowers. There are several interesting hiking trails of varying lengths through the reserve.

The **Mining Museum** in **Okiep** is 8km (5 miles) north-east of the town on the R64. Okiep once ranked as the richest copper mine in the world and is still an active mining centre. There are several examples of early Cornish-style architecture left by the miners who arrived in droves in the early 1900s. There is also a **Mine Museum** at **Nababeep** 19km (12 miles) south of Springbok which contains relics and photographs of the copper boom era. Clara, an old narrow-gauge steam locomotive which was the last to be used on the track from Nababeep to Okiep and Port Nolloth is also on display.

There is limited accommodation in Springbok and the best places to stay are either the Kokerboom Motel or any of the guesthouses in the area. The Tourist Office can provide full details on guesthouses or bed and breakfast establishments in the area.

BJ's Steakhouse serves steaks, fresh seafood and excellent burgers. The Godfather is also worth a visit for international and Italian cuisine.

Port Nolloth is 145km (90 miles) from Springbok. Its harbour was established to serve the copper mines until diamonds were discovered in 1926 and today it serves the diamond mining operations. The area was purchased by the Diamond Syndicate, headed by Ernest Oppenheimer, when they realised the wealth of the mineral deposits here. The area around **Alexander Bay** has the world's richest deposits of alluvial diamonds and there is a weekly tour of the diamond mine at Alexander Bay which demonstrates open cast, sea and beach mining techniques, the sorting of stones and the diamond safe.

Springbok to Augrabies Falls 320km (199 miles)

From Springbok take the R64 via Pofadder to Augrabies Falls. Just before the road reaches **Keimoes** there is a turning left to the park and it is a further 11km (7 miles) from here.

This area is the Northern Cape, the largest province in South Africa, where vast distances have to be covered across this semi-desert area between towns. There is very little rainfall and summers are extremely hot with an average temperature of 33°C. In winter, the days are sunny and temperatures drop dramatically at night. The best time to visit is between March and May.

There are many rock carvings and bushman paintings in the area, along with examples of the lifestyle of the missionaries from the early nineteenth century. Some of the Anglo-Boer War's most significant battles were fought in the Northern Cape, including the famous sieges of Kimberley and Mafikeng.

The Orange — the largest river in South Africa traverses the harsh landscape and irrigates the agricultural lands, citrus estates and vineyards in the area.

The **Augrabies Falls National Park** is where the Orange River unites from a number of channels, and the flow of the river is forced through a narrow channel over a series of rapids, before torrenting over a sheer drop of 120 metres (390 feet). There are several observation points where visitors are afforded excellent views of the falls and the immense crater-like pool at the bottom of the gorge.

The national park covers 15,415 hectares (38,075 acres) of river landscape but the spectacular falls are the major attraction of the park and rate as one of the five greatest falls in the world. They were given their name by the local Khoi who called it 'the place of great noise'.

It is an arid area with a low rainfall which means that the falls can virtually dry up in the late winter months.

The Aloe and Kokerboom tree are indigenous, as are many other species of aloe. Black rhino, eland, baboon and a number of small antelope, particularly klipspringer, inhabit the park. The dassie or rock hyrax is the most common mammal and predators such as the leopard, and black-backed jackal roam free.

There are several good vantage points of the waterfall around the park for visitors travelling by car, otherwise the **Arrowpoint**, **Moon Rock** and **Potholes** lookouts are all a one-hour walk from the main reception. The 40km (25 miles) three-day Klipspringer hiking trail climbs up steep shale slopes, along doleritic plateaux, over dry stream beds and across arid plains rich in wildlife. It is essential to make advance reservations as numbers are limited.

The average rainfall of 107mm (five inches) occurs mainly between January and April and the best time to visit is considered to be between March and October. In winter the temperature falls to below freezing, but the days can be sunny and bright.

Above: The sun casts interesting shadows on the dunes of the Kalahari.
Opposite: Sociable weavers find the quiver tree an ideal place to build their nests.

Augrabies Falls to Kalahari Gemsbok National Park
567km (352 miles)

On leaving Augrabies Falls head for Upington via the small towns of Kakamas and Keimoes. There is little to stop for but the road leads through fertile vineyards and lush agricultural lands. Grapes were originally planted here in 1914 for the production of sultanas, but gradually the farmers progressed to wine concentrate, and later table wines. The Wine Cellar of the Orange River Cooperative is the second largest wine cooperative in the world and the one of the largest in the country. The wine here is not of the same quality as those found in the Cape but there are some unusual flavours and tours and wine tastings are conducted by prior arrangement. The road leads past attractive islands in the Orange River, the largest of which is Kanoneiland.

Upington is 120km (74 miles) from Augrabies and is a large town which makes a good starting point for trips to the Kalahari and Namibia.

There is a monument to the donkey in front of the **Kalahari Oranje** **Museum** in recognition of the beast of burden's contribution to the development of the lower Orange River valley. There is also a monument to the camel in front of the police station in memory of the mounties and their mounts who patrolled the desert. Le Must restaurant in Schroeder Street is decorated in the style of a French bistro and exhibits paintings by South African artists on its walls.

Sultanas are still a successful business in the area and the 9.45am or 2pm tour of the South African Dried Fruit Cooperative (SAD) offers an opportunity to observe the sorting and packing of raisins and sultanas. There is also a shop where local produce is sold.

It is essential to purchase stocks of anti-malaria tablets before travelling onto the **Kalahari Gemsbok National Park** which is 358km (222 miles) away on the R360.

The park, in the north-western corner of South Africa, is a semi-desert area with sparse vegetation, great extremes of temperature and an annual rainfall of less than 100 millimetres (five inches). It lies adjacent to **Botwana's Gemsbok Park** and was proclaimed a national park in 1931 in an attempt to curtail the poaching activities in the region.

The two parks together form a conservation area of almost three million hectares (seven million acres) and the animals are allowed to roam freely throughout the entire area in search of water. In normal years some species can survive without water by obtaining it from the moisture contained in their food, particularly from the Tsamma, a creeper which bears round fruits similar to the water melon.

Two vital components of the Kalahari ecosystem are the pans and the sand dunes which occur between the two dry river beds of the Aoub and Nossob rivers in the southern part of the park. The Silver Cluster and the Grey Camelthorn trees are the most common trees along the riverbeds and beneath the shade provided by their thorny branches, the animals find shelter from the harsh sun.

Colonies of sociable weavers make huge nests in the camelthorn trees, some of which cause the branches to collapse beneath their weight. Ninety percent of the animals in the park can be found along the dry river beds and these include blue wildebeest, eland, springbok, red hartebeest, camel and ostrich.

There are three rest camps situated at different ends of the park. Twee Rivieren is located at the southern entrance gate to the park at the confluence of the Auob and Nossob rivers. It is the largest of the camps and has a swimming pool, tennis court and telephone. The rest camp at Mata Mata is the smallest and is situated on the bank of the Auob River on the Namibian border. The valley is a perfect place to see cheetah hunting their prey and herds of wildebeest can be seen around the lower section of the valley. Nossob is situated on the banks of the Nossob River on the border of Botswana.

As it takes several hours from the park's entrance to reach either Mata Mata or Nossob, it is advisable to stay at Twee Rivieren for the first day. The rest camps all offer accommodation in the form of family cottages or small huts with communal facilities. Accommodation is cheaper in the summer months, but be warned that the area can become unbearably hot.

The road to Nossob leads through striking scenery to the rest camp 170km (105 miles) from Twee Rivieren. The best game viewing sites are nearby and this is an excellent place to see lion, hartebeest, springbok and gemsbok. The largest pan in the park is Kwang which is about 33km (20 miles) north of Nossob and is particularly favoured by many species of antelope.

There is no access by road to either Botswana or Namibia from the park.

Kalahari to Kuruman 385km (239 miles)

The route back from Kalahari Gemsbok National Park to Kuruman is a long one. Take the R360 south and join the untarred R31 through deserted areas when one can travel for miles without seeing another form of life, except perhaps for the sociable weavers as they fly out of giant nests built on the telegraph poles which they use to escape their predator, the black-necked cobra.

Kuruman is often referred to as 'the fountain of Christianity' after the famous Kuruman 'Eye' which supplies twenty million litres of water every day from its dolomite springs. It was from here that the Moffat family and David Livingstone began their explorations into Africa.

Robert Moffat and his wife Mary arrived from Scotland in 1820 working on behalf of the London Missionary Society. They established the beautiful **Moffat Mission** which is still preserved today and taught the Tswana to read. They translated the Bible into the local language and printed copies on their own press.

Their daughter Mary married the explorer David Livingstone in the church at the mission.

The Cave Shop in Main Street is a fascinating experience as its interior has been built as a series of caves lined with the semi-precious stones.

Most of the hotels in town have restaurants and the Information Office can provide full details on accommodation available in the area. The Royal Steakhouse is popular with locals.

The Second Eye holiday resort is located a few kilometres outside of town on the Vryburg Road where self-contained holiday homes are situated in lawned grounds surrounding a pretty lake.

Kuruman to Mafikeng 298km (185 miles)

Leave Kuruman on the R27 towards **Vryburg**. Situated on the edge of the Kalahari Desert, Vryburg is sometimes known as the Texas of South Africa because ranching is carried out on such a massive scale in the area, including some of the largest Hereford herds in the world, and a progressive Brahman Stud Farm.

The largest cattle auction in the republic is held every Friday morning at 10am at the auction centre. The **Taljaart Nature Reserve** is 25km (16 miles) out of town and is sanctuary to black and blue wildebeest, Cape Buffalo and rhinoceros.

The remainder of the trip will lead through the area which was, until recently, the self-governing homeland of Bophuthatswana. Most people will have either heard of it because of the fabled Sun City, or because of the 1994 riots in Mmabatho that preceded the elections and ensured the homeland's re-incorporation into South Africa.

The formation of **Bophuthatswana** (meaning 'that which binds the Tswana') gave independent status to the Tswana people in 1977. It was the second area to be allowed to govern itself but the homeland was fragmented into seven separate pieces of land scattered throughout the Transvaal, the Cape and the Free State.

The Sotho migrated to this area from Central Africa in search of new lands between the thirteenth and sixteenth centuries, but were scattered during the Zulu *difaqane* under the rule of Zulu King Shaka, when the land was devastated by war and famine and tribes were forced to diversify. Over the subsequent centuries, the Sotho subdivided into three main areas; the Tswana in Bophuthatswana and Botswana, the southern Sotho in Lesotho and Qwa Qwa and the

Opposite top: Elephant herd crowd around a waterhole in the arid surroundings of the Kalahari Gemsbok National Park.

Opposite: Gemsbok and female kudu.

Above: The famous Kuruman 'Eye' which supplies twenty million litres of water every day from its dolomite springs.

Right: David Livingstone's home is now preserved as a museum.

northern Sotho, the Bapedi, in the homeland of Lebowa.

When the new constitution was drawn up under the new government of Bophuthatswana it embraced the western style of democracy of private ownership and free enterprise, whilst maintaining the traditions of the sixteen tribes living within its borders.

The worship of sacred objects known as *totems* plays an important role in the lives of all Sotho groups. Like many other tribes in South Africa, ancestral spirits are revered and sickness, drought and other natural disasters are believed to indicate that the spirits are angry. The amount of cattle owned by one man is still considered an indication of his wealth. The Kgotla is the highest political authority in the tribe and they arbitrate on minor civil and criminal cases and levy fines.

Traditional ceremonies including rain dances still take place, and witchcraft is a widely accepted practice. Bone-throwing is a form of divining in which a handful of bones are thrown, and the way the bones fall determine the interpretation. Coloured beads are used extensively in the jewellery produced here and the patterns which they form tell a story.

The majority of the region's income is produced by tourism, the revenue from Sun City and more recently from hunting. The **Bophuthatswana National Parks Board** introduced a unique system to deter poaching under which rural farmers were encouraged to permit licensed hunting on their land. Two-thirds of the revenue collected in this fashion is paid back to the tribal authority on whose land the hunting takes place. Poaching has thus been virtually eradicated as farmers realised they can earn far more from controlled killing.

Mafikeng is the Molemo word for 'place of stones', and was named because of its location on the rocky northern bank of the Molopo River. Mafikeng was the seat of government of the Bechuanaland Protectorate (including part of present day Botswana) until, in 1980, it was incorporated into Bophuthatswana. It is now the capital of the North-West Province.

During the Anglo-Boer War of 1899, the city of Mafeking (as it was once known) attained worldwide recognition because of the 214-day siege of the town by the Boer forces. When the town was finally relieved in May 1900, the celebrations in London were so exuberant that a new word entered the Oxford English dictionary — *maffick* meaning to 'exult riotously'.

During the siege, Colonel Robert Baden-Powell established the foundations for the Boy Scout movement which was inspired by the young cadets he used for military duties. The museum in the old Town Hall has a superb collection of documents on the history of Mafikeng, the siege and various aspects of past and contemporary Tswana history. The Northern Province Information Office is next to the museum.

Warren's Fort was used during the siege and is situated on the Vryburg Road out of Mafikeng. The fort was originally used as a headquarters for British soldiers who were responsible for establishing the town. The Anglican church was designed by Sir Herbert Baker in memory of the people who died defending the town.

Lotlamoreng Tribal Village was established by well-known *sangoma* and author Credo Mutwa in an attempt to increase the white understanding of blacks and their tribal traditions. He has written a series of books including *Indaba My Children* which recreates fireside legends passed on through the generations. The complex has been constructed as traditional Batswana villages and there are regular demonstrations of ancient rituals. Traditional healers practice their craft here including bone-throwing and herbalism. It is possible to make an appointment to meet with Credo who will entertain with interesting conversation.

Mbabatho was the former capital of Bophuthatswana and is situated close to the town of Mafikeng. It offers impressive examples of contemporary architecture with Tswana designs used extensively on the buildings. A good example is at Ga Rona, the horseshoe-shaped former government complex in the business district of the city.

Mega City is one of the most modern shopping centres in southern Africa and was the scene of violent looting during the 1994 riots. Bophuthatswana TV is a very popular channel that is watched throughout the region wherever it can be picked up.

The 60,000 seater stadium was used for the independence day celebrations. Today is it the pride of the city and is used to host large sporting events.

The University of Bophuthatswana (Unibo) was founded in 1989 and was a proud addition to the city, although architecturally it is fairly uninspiring. The Mmabatho Sun was the first of many Sun International properties to have a casino and it has a very intimate atmosphere.

Mafikeng to Sun City
226km (130 miles)

Take the R27 via Zeerust almost into Rustenberg and then the R565 to **Sun City**. This unique entertainment complex sits at the foot of the Pilanesburg and is southern Africa's equivalent of Las Vegas. There are four luxury hotels in the complex, Cascades, the Sun City Hotel, the Cabanas and the Palace. The Palace cost R830 million (approxi-

mately $170 million) to build and it is rated as one of the world's top resorts. It boasts an exceptional theme area called the Lost City in which a fantasy world has been created around a myth that a tribe migrated from the north and settled in this hidden valley to escape from civilisation. When the tribe eventually died, the jungle took over the city, and as part of the complex a 26-hectare (64-acre) man-made jungle surrounds the resort with exotic plants and trees imported from all over southern Africa. The Palace sits amid hidden waterfalls, streams and pools. There is a golf course designed by Gary Player which includes a lake with live crocodiles.

The **Valley of the Waves** is the most advanced water park in the world and has several waterslides and rides as well as the ability to generate surfing waves up to 1.85m (6ft) high. The **Temple of Courage** is the most daring ride which features a vertical drop of over 18.5m (60ft). There is a beach with palm trees and it is easy to forget that one is about as far away from the sea as possible in South Africa.

The major attraction are the casinos which draw people from all over southern Africa — particularly visitors from Pretoria and Johannesburg in the hope of securing the Grand Slam, the largest jackpot prize which always pays over R5 million.

The 6,000 seater **Superbowl** in the Entertainment Centre has played host to many international artists including Frank Sinatra, Shirley Bassey, Rod Stewart, Elton John and Queen when they bypassed the cultural boycott against apartheid in South Africa.

The **Kwena Gardens Crocodile Farm** is in the Sun City complex amidst waterfalls, dams and lakes.

Waterworld in Sun City is designed for watersport enthusiasts and provides facilities for windsurfing, jet skiing, canoeing and parasailing.

Above: The spectacular Valley of the Waves in the Lost City.

The **Pilansberg National Park** covers 500 sq km (193 sq miles) and opened in 1979. Since this time over twenty different wildlife species have been introduced to the region, which now boats over 8,000 animals. A feature of the park is its Ratlhogo and Kedibone hides situated beside water-holes and its scenic drives through rolling grasslands The park is open from 5.30am and 7pm in the winter and 5am and 8pm in the summer. The best hours to spot game is early morning when it is considerably cooler and the animals venture down to the waterholes to drink.

The site of **Jan Smuts farm** can be visited and there are conducted walks, wilderness trails and geological sites. The geology of the area is unique because of the volcanic activity which rocked the area millions of years ago. The Pilansberg hills are actually the fragmented base of the ancient volcanic crater, at the centre of which is the **Mankwe Lake**.

The Information Centre is housed in a preserved building that was once used as the Pilanesburg Magistrate's Court. Although most visitors stay at nearby Sun City and utilize the game drives provided by the hotels, there are luxurious fully-equipped safari tents at the Manyane camp, which also offers magnificent hot-air balloon flights over the park.

Above: Visitors chance their luck in the casinos at Sun City.

Sun City to Johannesburg 210km (130 miles)

The road to **Rustenberg** leads through an important tobacco producing area, and the largest tobacco handling unit in the country is located here. **Rustenberg Platinum Mine** is the largest platinum producer in the world and one of South Africa's major employers. Rustenberg is also renowned for the production of citrus and other tropical fruits including peaches and watermelons.

Paul Kruger's farm property **Boekenhoutfontein** where he farmed until his exile in 1902 is 25km (15 miles) out of town on the R565 heading to Sun City. There is also a statue of the former President in front of the Town Hall.

Rustenburg Nature Reserve on the northern slopes of the Magaliesburg Mountains has both two-hour or two-day hiking trails which provide good opportunities for game viewing of springbok, hartebeest and waterbuck. It is advisable to make advance reservations for overnight stays.

Continue from Rustenberg to either Johannesburg or Pretoria (see Chapter One for further details) and either drive back to Cape Town following the route via Kimberley or perhaps take the luxury Blue Train. Alternatively there are numerous flights each day between the two cities.

Johannesburg to Kimberley
467km (290 miles)

Take the N12 southbound stopping at **Potchefstroom**, capital of the former Afrikaner-governed South African Republic (SAR), often referred to as 'Potch'. In 1900 the British occupied the town and established a large artillery camp which is today used by the South African defence force. Its importance diminished with the development of the Witwatersrand and President Paul Kruger replaced it as state capital with Pretoria.

The town has many buildings of historical interest including the **Potchefstroom Museum**, on the corner of Wolmarans and Gouws Streets. The museum is packed with Voortrekker artefacts, including one of the original wagons from the Battle of Blood River. There is an old church in front of the Town Hall and the ruins of a fort on the road to Klerksdorp.

Klerksdorp is the oldest white settlement in the Transvaal, although it was little more than a farming town until the discovery of gold on the Witwatersrand turned it virtually overnight into a rapacious rush town. A total of sixty-seven bars and beerhalls sprang up, and the town even had its own stock exchange. Old mining shafts can be seen on the Stilfontein Road, as well as rocks with inscriptions made by members of the British regiments who camped there during the Anglo-Boer War.

There are many old houses in Klerksdorp, most notably around Hendrik Potgieter Road where many Voortrekkers settled in 1837. The museum on the corner of Magaretha Prinsloo and Lombaard Sreets was used as a prison until the early 1970s. Today it houses displays of archaeological and geological exhibits.

When alluvial diamonds were discovered in 1870 the town of Christiana was transformed into a boom town with a raucous population of fortune hunters and diamond dealers. Today it is a busy town, but there is little reason to stop here except to visit the mineral baths resort on the banks of the Vaal River.

Several nature reserves have been established along the banks of the Vaal River including the **Bloemhof Dam Nature Reserve** which covers a total of 14,000 hectares (34,500 acres). There is excellent fishing in the Bloemhof Dam and the reserve is also sanctuary to various species of antelope and white rhino.

The **Wolwespruit Nature Reserve** is also popular for fishing and camping is permitted in the area.

KIMBERLEY

The first recorded discovery of diamonds in the area near **Kimberley** was in 1866 when a young boy found what he believed to be a shiny pebble near Hopetown. A year later, the twenty-one carat 'Eureka' diamond was found and for the next few years diamond diggers concentrated their efforts on the alluvial deposits on the Vaal River about 50km away.

However, in 1869, after diamonds were found on nearby farmlands, over 50,000 people from all over the world descended on the area within weeks. It became known as **Colesberg Kopje** and diggers set up tents and tin shacks everywhere as they strove for fortune amidst the flies, dirt, disease and unrelentless heat.

Cecil John Rhodes described the scene in a letter '. . .imagine a small round hill, at its very highest part 9m (30ft) above the level of the surrounding country, about 541ft broad and 659ft long; all around it a mass of white tents. It is like an immense number of ant-heaps covered with black ants as thick as can be, the latter represented by human beings.'

Over the next forty years the mining continued to create the largest man-made hole in the world, now known as ☀ the **Big Hole of Kimberley**.

This was the 'New Rush' town and from these beginnings grew the city of Kimberley, capital of the Northern Cape, whose name would forever be associated with diamonds.

Men of vision and determination whose wealth from diamonds helped to change the face of South Africa emerged from this era. Cecil John Rhodes arrived from England at the age of nineteen and sold ice and pumped water at the diggings. He gradually acquired claims and finally formed the De Beers Mining Company along with C D Rudd. Barney Barnato was a London East End barrow boy who arrived in Kimberley at the age of twenty. Like Rhodes, he also bought up claims and became a millionaire within a few years. He formed the Kimberley Central Diamond Mining Company which he later sold to Rhodes to form De Beers Consolidated Mines Limited. A later entrant to the city was Ernest Oppenheimer who came to Kimberley in 1902 as the representative of a diamond merchant. His son Harry was born here and was elected as Member of Parliament for the city in 1948 and Chairman of De Beers in 1957.

There are still many fascinating sides to the diamond industry including the street diggers who move in when houses or buildings are demolished in search of diamonds which may have been scattered in the kimberlite.

The only public transport is a tram which runs between **City Hall** and the **Big Hole and Mine Museum**, passing historical and noteworthy buildings along its route. It departs five times a day during the week between 9am and 4pm with seven trips on the weekends and public holidays. It is also possible to hire bicycles from the youth hostel.

The main attraction is the **Big Hole** and **Kimberley Mine Museum**. The Big Hole is 400m (1,312 feet) deep and 500m (1,640 feet) across. During its forty fruitful years, it produced over fifteen million carats of diamonds. Along its rim there is a replica of a section of the old town from the gold rush days along with a display of photographs and diary entries. De Beers Hall in the **Kimberley Mine Museum** is where the original '616' diamond — the largest uncut diamond in the world — and the 'Eureka', the first diamond discovered in South Africa are on display.

The **William Humphreys Art** **Gallery** is considered one of the most important galleries in the republic. It houses British and European works along with a fascinating collection of contemporary South African art. The **Duggan Cronin Gallery** in Egerton Road has been declared a national monument and the photographic exhibitions here by A C Duggan Cronin are one of the most comprehensive studies of tribal life among the black people of southern Africa. Many of his original albums are available to browse through.

The **McGregor Museum** is housed in the original building constructed by Cecil Rhodes which served as a hotel and health resort. During the Kimberley siege, Rhodes occupied two rooms on the ground floor. It subsequently became the Hotel Belgrade, then a convent, and later a school. There are geographical and geological exhibits, as well as information relating to the siege. **The Hall of** ☀ **Religions** is a fascinating insight to the broad spectrum of world religions. The museum can arrange viewing of **Dunluce** at 10 Lodge Road, an elegant period house built in 1897 and **Rudd**

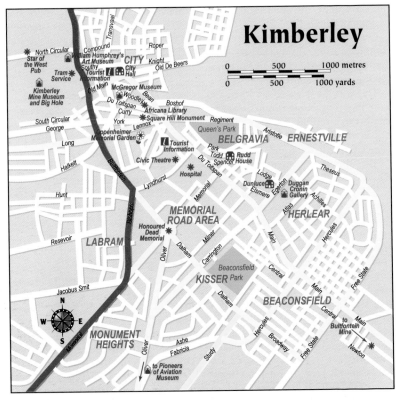

Kimberley

North Circular
Star of the West Pub
Compound
William Humphrey's Art Museum
Roper
Knight
CITY
Old De Beers
South
Tourist Information
City Hall
Tram Service
Old Main
McGregor Museum
Kimberley Mine Museum and Big Hole
Woodley
Bean
Boshof
Du Toitspan
Africana Library
South Circular
Curry
Square Hill Monument
George
York
Lennox
Regiment
Oppenheimer Memorial Garden
Queen's Park
BELGRAVIA
ERNESTVILLE
Long
Tourist Information
Park
Aristotle
Halkett
Civic Theatre
Todd
Spencer
Rudd House
Theseus
Du Toitspan
Lyndhurst
Hospital
Lodge
Dunluce
Egerton
Duggan
Hunt
Elsmere
Cronin Gallery
Achilles
Memorial
Atlas
HERLEAR
MEMORIAL ROAD AREA
Hercules
Honoured Dead Memorial
Milner
Main
LABRAM
Oliver
Dalham
Carrington
Resevoir
Central
Beaconsfield Park
Jacobus Smit
KISSER
Dalham
BEACONSFIELD
Hercules
Central
N W E S
MONUMENT HEIGHTS
Ashe
to Bultfontein Mine
Oliver
Fabricia
Study
Hercules
Broadway
Free State
Main
Newton
Memorial
to Pioneers of Aviation Museum
Bishops
Bultfontein

0   500   1000 metres
0   500   1000 yards

THE **RELIEF** OF KIMBERLEY

Opposite: The diamond mining in Kimberley continued over forty years and created the largest man-made hole in the world.
Above: Along the rim of the Big Hole of Kimberley, there is a replica of a section of the old town from the gold rush days.

House, home of the mining magnate HP Rudd.

The oldest, exclusive residential suburb is Belgravia and there are a several elegant properties which date from 1872 to the present time.

The **Oppenheimer Memorial Gardens** in Jan Smuts Boulevard, opposite the Civic Centre, are noteworthy. The memorial was erected in honour of Sir Ernest Oppenheimer who arrived in Kimberley the year Cecil Rhodes died. He was destined to become the leading figure in South African mining and gain control of all the diamond fields in southern Africa.

The city's five major mines are also symbolised here by a monument of a sieve supported by five diggers at the **Diggers Fountain**. The **Africana Library** is a typical nineteenth century stately home and houses the original printing press that belonged to Robert Moffat who translated and reprinted the Bible from English into Tswana.

It advisable to make advance reservations for an underground tour of **De Beers Bulfontein Diamond Mine**. Dressed in miners clothing visitors descend 860m and walk through diamond-encrusted Kimberlite shafts to the working face of the mine. It is an excellent and fascinating tour but numbers are limited and tours must be booked through De Beers. Alternatively the surface tour of De Beers Recovery and Treatment Plant is interesting and tours leave from the Visitors Centre at the mine at 9am and 11am weekdays.

A unique feature of the town are the two drive-in pubs — one at the Kimberlite Hotel and one at the Halfway House Hotel. These date back to Cecil Rhodes era who never wanted to dismount in order to drink. The Star of the West Pub on the corner of North Circular and Barkly Roads is the oldest pub in town and dates back to the early 1870s. It is now a national monument and is open every day between 10am-11pm except Sunday. Diggers Pub at the Kimberley Sun Hotel offers good value lunches and is open daily from 10am to midnight except Sunday.

Around Kimberley

The site of the **Magersfontein battlefield and Museum** is 31km (19 miles) from town on the airport road. This battlefield is where the British suffered a crushing defeat at the hands of the Boers in December 1899 as they implemented their new military tactics of trench warfare. The battlefield includes three cemeteries and various monuments to commemorate the soldiers who fell there.

The **Memorial to the Pioneers of Aviation** is also located on the airport road on the site of South Africa's first flying school.

At **Nooitgedacht**, 24km (15 miles) along the road from Kimberley to Barkly West, there are **Glacial Pavings** over 250 million years old. The surface rock was scored by stones held in an ice sheet. There are also Stone Age rock engravings on the pavements.

At **Barkly West**, 32km (20 miles) away, prospectors still pan for diamonds in the river between June and September and permits can be obtained from the Mining Commissioners Office in Kimberley. Nearby **Canteen Kopje** is a geological reserve where fossil remains of extinct mammals have been discovered.

Kimberley to Beaufort West 497km (309 miles)

From Kimberley take the N12 south and join the main N1 south at **Three Sisters**. **Hopetown** was where South Africa's first diamond was discovered, but today it is a sheep and cattle farming area. **Victoria West** is a pretty town set against a mountain that was used as a staging post for the thousands of fortune seekers who passed through on the way to the diamond fields. It takes its name from three distinctive mountains in the area. The next major town is **Beaufort West** (see Chapter Three for further information).

Return to Cape Town on the N2. There is not really any reason to stop other than at **Matjiesfontein** 300km (186 miles) before Cape Town. In Victorian times the town was a thriving, popular health resort and today it has been faithfully restored to the style of the era, and is a popular stopping-off point for tourists travelling through the Karoo.

In 1876 a young Scot, James Douglas Logan, left a ship bound for Australia and found employment as a porter at Cape Town Railway Station. He successfully persuaded the authorities to allow him to open a refreshment stop at what is now **Touws River**. The success of this enterprise led to him being granted the railway refreshment concession between Cape Town and Bulawayo. He found that the Karoo air cured his troublesome chest and in 1883 he built a hotel and a Victorian village. Socialites and aristocracy including Lord Winston Churchill, Cecil Rhodes and the Sultan of Zanzibar came from far and wide to enjoy his hospitality and the health-giving air. When Logan died in 1820 ownership of the village changed hands several times until it was sold in 1968 to David Rawdon who completely restored it to its former Victorian glory. There is an English pub — the Laird Arms, a post office, bank and coffee house.

Continue back to Cape Town to finish your trip.

PLACES TO VISIT

Boekenhoutfontein
25km (15 miles) from town on R565
towards Sun City
Open daily except Monday
☎ (0142) 733199

Calvinia

Museum
4 Church Street
Open Monday-Friday: 8am-1pm
& 2pm-5pm, Saturday: 8am-12noon
☎ (02772) 43

Cape Town

Bertram House
Government Avenue
Open: Tuesday-Saturday: 9.30am-4.30pm
☎ (021) 249381

Bo-Kaap Museum
71 Wale Street
Open daily: 9am-4.30pm except Sun & Mon
☎ (021) 24 6485

Castle of Good Hope
Buitenkant Street
Open daily: 10am-4pm
☎ (021) 408 7911

Circe Launches
Hout Bay harbour
Operate daily
☎ (021) 790 1040

Cultural History Museum
Upper Adderley Street
Open daily: 10am-4.30pm
☎ (021) 461 8230

Fort Wynard Museum
Fort Wynard Road
Open daily: 10am-3.45pm

Groot Constantia
off Constantia Road, Wynberg
Open daily: 10am-5pm
☎ (021) 794 5067

Houses of Parliament
Government Avenue, Gardens
Open Monday-Friday except Easter
☎ (021) 403 2911

Koopmans de Wet House
35 Strand Street
Open Tuesday-Saturday: 9.30am-4.30pm
Closed: Good Friday & Christmas Day
☎ (021) 242473

Muizenberg Museum Complex
192 Main Road
☎ (021) 7884106

Natale Labia Museum
192 Main Road, Muizenberg
Open Tuesday-Sunday: 10am-5pm
Closed August
☎ (021) 788 1816

Nico Malan Opera House
☎ (021) 217695

Old Town House
Michaelis Street, Greenmarket Square
☎ (021) 246367

One City Tours
☎ (021) 387 5351

Rhodes Memorial
off Rhodes Drive
Rondebosch
☎ (021) 689 9151

Rhodes Cottage
Main coast road by St James
Open Tuesday-Sunday: 10am-1pm &
2pm-5pm
☎ (021) 788 1816

Robben Island Tours
Public Relations
Department of Correctional Services
Private Bag Robben Island
☎ (021) 4111006 ext. 208

Scratch Patch
Dido Valley Road
Simonstown
☎ (021) 786 2020

Scratch Patch
Waterfront
☎ (021) 419 9429

South Africa Maritime Museum
Dock Road, Waterfront
Open daily: 10am-4pm
☎ (021) 419 2506

South African Museum
Queen Victoria Street
Open daily: 10am-5pm
☎ (021) 24 3330

South African National Gallery
Off Government Avenue, Gardens
Open Monday: 1pm-5pm
Tuesday-Sunday: 10am-5pm
☎ (021) 45 1628

Table Mountain Cableway
Tafelberg Road off Kloofnek
Open: 8.30am-6pm out of season
8am-10pm in season
☎ (021) 24 5148

Western Province Rugby Museum
Boundary Road, Newlands
Open: 9.30am-4pm
☎ (012) 686 4532

West Coast Ostrich Show Ranch
Vanschoordrif Road, off N7
Open daily: 9am-5pm
☎ (021) 972 1905

The World of Birds
Valley Road, Hout Bay
Open daily: 09am-6pm
☎ (021) 790 2730

Clanwilliam

Rooibos Tea Natural Products
Rooibos Avenue
Tours Monday-Thursday: 10am, 12noon,
2pm, 4pm
Friday: 10am, 12noon and 2pm
☎ (027) 4822155

Franschoek

Huguenot Memorial Museum & Monument
Lambrecht Street
Open Monday-Saturday: 9am-5pm
Sunday: 2pm-5pm
☎ (02212) 2532

Boschendal Estate
Tours Monday to Friday
☎ (02212) 41031

Kagga Kamma
Near Ceres
☎ (02211) 638334

Kimberley

Big Hole and Mine Museum
Tucker Street
Open daily: 8am-6pm
☎ (0531) 31557

William Humphreys Art Gallery
Jan Smuts Boulevard
Civic Centre
Open Monday-Saturday:10am-5pm
& Sunday 2pm-5pm
Closed for lunch: 1pm-2pm
☎ (0531) 811724

Duggan Cronin Gallery
Egerton Road
Open Monday-Saturday: 9am-5pm
Sunday: 3pm-5pm
☎ (0531) 32645

McGregor Museum
Atlas Street
Open Monday-Saturday: 9am-5pm
& Sunday: 2pm-5pm
☎ (0531) 32645

Dunluce & Rudd House
Lodge and Loch Roads
☎ (0531) 32645

De Beers Bulfontein Diamond Mine
Tours Monday-Friday:
9am and 11am
☎ (0531) 29651

Mafikeng
Lotlamoreng Tribal Village
Vryburg Road
Open daily
☎ (0140) 822095

Paarl
KWV Cellars
Kohler Street
☎ (02211) 73007

Oude Pastorie Museum
303 Main Road
Open Monday-Friday: 8am-5pm
Saturday: 10am-12noon
Sunday: 3pm - 5pm
☎ (02211) 22651

African Reptile Park
Babylon Storen Road
☎ (02211) 631142

Potchefstroom

Potchefstroom Museum
Corner of Wolmarans and Gouws Streets
☎ (0148) 2931611

Saldanha

Harbour Tours
☎ (02281) 31571

Stellenbosch

Village Museum
18 Ryneveld Street
Open Monday-Saturday: 9.30am-5pm
Sunday: 2pm-5pm
Closed: Christmas Day & Good Friday
☎ (021) 72902

Stellenryck Wine Museum
Corner Old Strand & Dorp Streets
Open Monday-Friday: 9am-5pm
Saturday: 10am-5pm
Sunday: 2pm-5pm
Closed for lunch: 12.45pm-2pm

Oude Meester Brandy Museum
Old Strand Road
Open Monday-Friday: 9am-5pm
Saturday: 10am-5pm
Sunday: 2pm-5pm
Closed for lunch: 12.45pm-2pm

The Bergkelder
Next to Railway Station
Open: daily except Sunday
☎ (021) 887 2440

The Van Ryn Brandy Cellar
Van Ryn Road
Vlottenberg
Open: weekdays only
☎ (021) 881 3875

Oude Libertas Amphitheatre
Stellenbosch Farmers Winery Centre
off R210 towards Cape Town
☎ (021) 808 7911 ext. 2473

Sun City

Valley of the Waves
Open daily: 10am-6pm September to April
Closes 5pm: May to August
☎ (011) 780 7800

Kwena Gardens Crocodile Farm
Rustenberg
Open daily: 10am-6pm

Tulbagh

Oude Drotsdy
Van der Stel Street
Tours daily: 10am & 3pm except Sunday

NATIONAL AND PROVINCIAL PARKS

Cape Town

Kirstenbosch Botanical Gardens
Rhodes Drive, Newlands
Open daily: 8am-6pm, (7pm in summer)
☎ (021) 762 1166

Cape of Good Hope Nature Reserve
Cape Point
Open daily: 7am-5pm

Cedarberg

Cedarberg State Forest
PO Box X1, Citrusdal 7340
☎ (022) 9212289

Kalahari Gemsbok National Park

Private Bag X5890
Gemsbok Park over Upington 8800
Open daily: 7am-6pm (longer in summer)
☎ (0020) ask for Gemsbok 901

Langebaan

West Coast National Park
PO Box 25, Langebaan 7357
Open: 9am-5pm August and September
☎ (02287) 22144

Pilanesberg

Pilansberg Nature Reserve
☎ (01465) 55356

Rustenberg

Rustenburg Nature Reserve
☎ (01421) 31050

Springbok

Goegab Nature Reserve
Open daily: 8am-4pm
☎ (0251) 21880

TRANSPORT

Cape Town

Cape Town International Airport
☎ (021) 936223

Blue Train Reservations
☎ (021) 405 2672

Trains
(021) 405 3871

Tuk-tuk
☎ (021) 245325

Greyhound
☎ (021) 418 4312

Kimberley

Trains
☎ (0531) 882060

Greyhound
☎ (0531) 811062

LOCAL TOURIST AUTHORITIES

Cape Town

Tourist Rendezvous Travel Centre
Adderley Street
Open Monday-Friday: 8am-5pm
Saturday & Sunday: 8.30-5pm
☎ (021) 418 5214

Flower Hotline
☎ (021) 216274

Franschoek

Information Office
Main Road
☎ (02212) 3603

Kimberley

Tourist Information Office
Corner Old Main Street & Transvaal Road
Open Monday-Friday: 7.45am-4.30pm
Saturday: 9am-11.30am
☎ (0531) 806264/5

Kuruman

☎ (01471) 21095

Mafikeng

Information Office
Martin Street
☎ (0140) 843040

Mmabatho

North West Tourism
Suite 10, Borekelong House
Lucas Mangope Highway
☎ (0140) 843040

Nieutwoutdville

Information Office
☎ (02726) 81052/81041

Paarl

Information Office
216 Main Road
☎ (02211) 24842

Saldanha

West Coast Publicity Association
Van Riebeeck Street
☎ (02281) 42088

Springbok

Tourist Information
Old Anglican Church
Namaqua Street
☎ (0251) 22071

Stellenbosch

Information Centre
30 Plein Street
Open: Monday-Saturday
☎ 02231 833584

Facts for Visitors

FACTS FOR VISITORS

ACCOMMODATION

South Africa offers a wide variety of accommodation ranging from low budget campsites through to luxury game lodges and five-star hotels. Homes and farms in most towns offer reasonably-price bed and breakfast accommodation. The Publicity Associations in each area can provide details. The South African Tourism Board (SATOUR) publishes a country-wide accommodation guide with star ratings. There are also agencies which specialise in specific areas. A number of official and unofficial youth hostels are located throughout the country and can be found in most resorts. They are very cheap, well located and can provide a useful information for budget travellers.

As camping is a popular form of holidaying for South Africans, most towns, however small, have a campsite or caravan park. Tent and rucksack hire is reasonably priced and major camping shops can provide details. Most resorts also have self-contained chalets and rondavels (traditional circular thatched houses) which sleep up to four people and are usually inexpensive. However as the demand for 'ethnicity' increases, the prices are rising.

Timeshare complexes offer fully-equipped standard and luxury properties. These make excellent alternatives for out-of-season visitors staying longer than two nights. Letting or estate agencies usually handle timeshare rental in their area. A popular, but sometimes expensive form of accommodation are the private game lodges which are very beautiful and offer a nature-based holiday in luxury, style and comfort.

Housesitters run a franchise operation which finds people to stay in South African's homes whilst the owners are away. Depending on the time of year, stays range from a week to a month or more, and this can make for a cheap and different form of lodging during peak periods when accommodation is in short supply.

When arranging a trip it is important to take into account that South Africa is a year-round holiday destination with complex seasonal tariffs. In the high season accommodation is expensive and difficult to find, and this is the worst time to visit without advance bookings.

The high season runs from 1 December to mid-January and the Easter holiday period, otherwise the seasons fluctuate in each province depending on school holidays.

There are a variety of hotels aimed at the budget traveller including the Formule One chain which offers cheap facilities without any frills.

Sun International is one of the largest and most prestigious hotel and casino groups on the African continent offering luxurious accommodation in superb settings.

Central Reservations
3 Sandown Valley
Crescent Sandown
PO Box 784487, Sandton 2146
Telephone: (011) 780 7800
Fax: (011) 780 7726
They also have reservations offices in the United Kingdom, USA, Germany, France and Japan for advance reservations or further information.

United Kingdom
Badgemore House
Gravel Hill, Henley on Thames
Oxfordshire RG9 4NR
Tel: (01491) 411222
Fax: (01491) 576194

United States of America
915 NE. 125 Street North, Miami
Florida 33161
Tel: (305) 891 2500
Fax: (305) 891 2682

The **Southern Sun Group** owns and manages a chain of sixty hotels in prime sites throughout Southern Africa. These include Southern Sun Inter-Continental hotels, Holiday Inn Crowne Plaza, Holiday Inn, Holiday Inn Garden Court, Sun Game Lodges and Formule One.

The Inter-Continental hotels are five-star properties conveniently located in major cities offering luxury accommodation and fine cuisine.

Southern Sun Resorts provide the perfect holiday experience for all the family with an excellent range of facilities including sports, watersports and entertainment.

Holiday Inn Crowne Plaza hotels are four-star deluxe hotels offering a superior standard of hotel designed to satisfy the demands of the discerning business and leisure traveller.

Holiday Inn Garden Court hotels provide quality facilities and essential services at unbeatable value. The properties are located in all major cities and prime beachfront locations.

Sun Game Lodges have three exceptional lodges in South Africa, all of which demonstrate a commitment to conservation, ecotourism and the local community. Their recently constructed Tau Game Lodge utilized traditional skills from local tribes to create a unique holiday environment.

The lodge is situated in the Madikwe Game Reserve which is home to the largest-ever game relocation programme in Africa where large numbers of endangered species have been translocated during the past five years.

Southern Sun Head Office:
7th Floor, Twin Towers, Sandton City
PO Box 782553
Sandton 2146
Tel: (011) 780 0155
Fax: (011) 780 0259
Central Reservations (011) 780 0101

United Kingdom and Europe
Southern Sun Group
Bray Business Centre
Weir Bank, Bray-on-Thames
Berkshire, SL6 2ED
Tel: (01628) 77 8722
Fax: (01628) 23908
United States and Canada
P.R.I.
1100 East Broadway
Glendale, California 91205
Tel: (818) 507 1151

The Conservation Corporation operates eco-tourism initiatives which help to ensure the development of Africa's wilderness areas. Their luxury lodges include the Londolozi Game Reserve in Mpumalanga, Singita Game Reserve which borders the magnificent Kruger National Park, Phinda Nyala Lodge and Forest Lodge and the Ngala Game Reserve which is the only private lodge within the Kruger National Park.
PO Box 1211
Sunninghill Park 2157
Central Reservations (011) 803 8421
Fax: (011) 803 1810

All star-rated hotels, game reserves and self-catering accommodation is graded according to the South African Tourism Board (Satour) national grading and classification scheme. The star programme allows members to have their facilities graded by stars according to the range of services they provide. All members of the scheme are required to indicate their membership by grading plaques which enable visitors to easily identify the status.

The National Parks Board Reservation Offices are under National Parks.

**Bed 'n' Breakfast
and Stay on a Farm Association**
Tel: (012) 482 2206

Holiday Inn Garden Court
Tel: (011) 780 0200

Protea Hotels
Tel: (011) 484 1717
Toll free 0800 11 9000

Stocks Hotels and Resorts
Tel: (011) 806 4192/3
Fax: (011) 806 4105

Aventura Resorts
Tel: (012) 346 2277

Leading Hotels of Southern Africa
Tel: (011) 884 3585
Fax: (011) 884 0676

Portfolio of Places
Tel: (011) 880 3414

Hostels Association of South Africa
Tel: (021) 419 1853

Housesitters Johannesburg
Tel: (011) 789 1250

Housesitters Durban
Tel: (031) 86 5010

HOTELS IN SOUTH AFRICA

The list of hotels is broken down into the following provinces:-
Eastern Cape, Mpumalanga, Free State, Gauteng, KwaZulu-Natal, Northern Cape, Northern Transvaal, North-West, Western Cape.

Eastern Cape

ADDO
Zuurberg Inn *
PO Box 12, Addo 6105
Mountain hideaway with sweeping views over the Addo Elephant Park.
Tel: (0426) 40 0583
Fax: As above (ask for fax)

ALIWAL NORTH
Thatcher's Spa Hotel **
PO Box 297, Aliwal North 5530
Ideal for both the commercial traveller and tourist with an excellent restaurant.
Tel: (0551) 2772
Fax: (0551) 42008

Umtali Motel **
PO Box 102, Aliwal North 5530
Comfortable accommodation in a friendly environment.
Tel: (0551) 2400
Fax: As above (ask for fax)

CRADOCK
New Masonic Hotel **
PO Box 44, Cradock 5880
Tel: (0481) 3115/3159
Fax: (0481) 4402

EAST LONDON
Dolphin Hotel **
PO Box 8010, Nahoon 5210
Old-world charm with easy access to the Nahoon River and Beach.
Tel: (0431) 351435
Fax: (0431) 354649

Esplanade Hotel **
Beachfront
PO Box 18041, Quigney
Comfortable accommodation on the main beachfront. Ideal for both the business and holiday traveller.
Tel: (0431) 22518
Fax: (0431) 23679

Holiday Inn Garden Court ***
PO Box 1255, East London 5200
Prime position on East London's Eastern beach promenade.
Tel: (0431) 27260
Fax: (0431) 4`37360

Hotel Majestic **
21 Orient Road
PO Box 18027, Quigney 5211
Friendly hotel near to the beach and city.
Tel: (0431) 437377
Fax: As above (ask for fax)

Hotel Osner ***
Esplanade
PO Box 334, East London 5200
Tel: (0431) 433 433
Fax: As above (ask for fax)

Kennaway Protea Hotel ***
Esplanade
PO Box 583, East London 5200
Good quality accommodation at reasonable prices.
Tel: (0431) 25531
Fax: (0431) 21326

King David Hotel ***
25 Interleith Terrace
Quigney, PO Box 1582
East London 5200
Fine accommodation minutes away from the seafront and city.
Tel: (0431) 23174
Fax: (0431) 436939

Fort Beaufort
Savoy Hotel **
53 Durban Street
PO Box 46, Fort Beaufort 5720
Charming accommodation in a warm friendly environment.
Tel: (04634) 31146
Fax: (04634) 32082

Graaff-Reinet
Drostdy Hotel ***
30 Church Street
PO Box 400, Graaff-Reinet 6280
Enjoy all the elegance, warmth, hospitality and charm of a bygone era with modern and efficient service.
Tel: (0491) 22161
Fax: (0491) 24582

Grahamstown
Cathcart Arms Hotel **
PO Box 6043, Grahamstown 6140
Charming country-style hotel with fourteen individually-furnished bedrooms.
Tel: (0461) 27111
Fax: As above (ask for fax)

Grahamstown Protea Hotel ****
PO Box 316, Grahamstown 6140
This elegant hotel is located near to Rhodes University. Excellent cuisine specialising in game dishes.
Tel: (0461) 22324
Fax: (0461) 22424

Settlers Inn ***
N2 Highway
PO Box 219, Grahamstown 6140
A warm, friendly hotel in the heart of Settler country.
Tel: (0461) 27313
Fax: (0461) 24951

Hogsback
Hogsback Inn **
PO Box 63, Hogsback 5721
Tel: (045) 962 1006
Fax: (045) 962 1015

Jeffrey's Bay
Savoy Protea Hotel ***
16 Da Gama Road
PO Box 36, Jeffrey's Bay 6330
A quiet country resort hotel ideally situated for the beach. Quality service and an excellent restaurant.
Tel: (0423) 931 106/7
Fax: (0423) 932 445

King William's Town
Grosvenor Lodge ***
PO Box 61, King William's Town
A friendly hotel with a homely atmosphere.
Tel: (0433) 21440
Fax: (0433) 24772

Lady Grey
Mountain View Country Inn **
PO Box 14, Lady Grey 5540
A delightful, owner-managed inn. Elegantly decorated, serving excellent cuisine in a spectacular mountain setting.
Tel: (05552) 112
Fax: (05552) 114

PORT ALFRED
Fish River Sun
PO Box 232, Port Alfred 6170
Situated on a remote and beautiful beach, this Polynesian-style casino resort offers excellent facilities.
Tel: (0405) 661101
Fax: (0405) 661115

The Halyards
PO Box 7814
Newton Park, Port Elizabeth 6055
Perfectly appointed between Port Elizabeth and East London in the prestigious Royal Alfred Marina. Luxurious bedrooms are stylishly-decorated. The Upper Deck restaurant offers fine international cuisine using a variety of fresh, local produce.
Tel: (0464) 42410
Fax: (0464) 42466

**Kowie Grand Hotel **
PO Box 1, Kowie West
Beautifully situated, country-style hotel with character and charm, offering personal attention and excellent cuisine.
Tel: (0464) 41150
Fax: (0464) 43769

**Victoria Protea Hotel **
PO Box 2, Port Alfred 6170
Well equipped hotel with cosy rooms and excellent facilities.
Tel: (0464) 41133
Fax: (0464) 41134

PORT EDWARD
Wild Coast Sun
PO Box 23, Port Edward 4295
Set on a dramatic stretch of rugged coastline this resort offers luxurious rooms, dazzling entertainment and an incredible selection of dining to suit all tastes.
Tel: (0471) 59111
Fax: (0471) 52778

PORT ELIZABETH
City Lodge Port Elizabeth *
Corner Beach & Lodge Roads
Summerstrand, PO Box 13352
A friendly value-for-money lodge offering comfortable accommodation overlooking Humewood Beach.
Tel: (041) 56 3322
Fax: (041) 56 3374

Holiday Inn Garden Court Port Elizabeth
(Kings Beach) ***
La Roche Drive
PO Box 13100, Humewood 6013
Clean and comfortable accommodation overlooking Kings Beach.
Tel: (041) 52 3720
Fax: (041) 55 5754

Holiday Inn Garden Court Port Elizabeth
(Summerstrand) ***
Marine Drive
Summerstrand, PO Box 204
Comfortable hotel with good facilities.
Tel: (041) 53 3131
Fax: (041) 53 2505

Marine Protea Hotel *
Summerstrand, PO Box 501
Fabulous ocean views only minutes from safe bathing, surfing and diving.
Tel: (041) 53 2101
Fax: (041) 53 2076

The Beach Hotel*
Summerstrand
PO Box 319, Port Elizabeth 6000
Close to Hobie Beach with excellent sports facilities.
Tel: (041) 53 2161
Fax: As above (ask for fax)

SHAMWARI GAME RESERVE
PO Box 7814,
Newton Park, Port Elizabeth 6055
This fabulous game reserve has been extensively restocked with lion, elephant, leopart, rhino, buffalo and antelope. Long Lee Manor is a gracious Edwardian mansion with twelve stylish bedrooms and Shamwari Lodge has five double en-suite bedrooms and two self-contained restored historic settler homes. Dinner is served under the stars or in the traditional dining rooms of the lodges.
Tel: (042) 851 1196
Fax: (042) 851 1224

STORMS RIVER
**Tsitsikamma Lodge **
PO Box 10, Storms River 6308
Luxurious en-suite log cabins set amidst a forest setting.
Tel: (042) 750 3802
Fax: (042) 750 3702

Tsitsikamma Forest Inn **
Darnell Street, Storms River 6308
Enchanting hideaway in the heart of the forest.
Tel: (042) 541 1711
Fax: (042) 541 1669

UMTATA
Holiday Inn Garden Court Umtata ***
East London Road
PO Box 334, Umtata 5100
Excellent value for money for both the business and leisure traveller.
Tel: (0471) 37 0181
Fax: (0471 37 0191

Mpumalanga

DULLSTROOM
Critchley Hackle Lodge
Teding van Berkhout Street
PO Box 141, Dullstroom 1110
Charming stone-built lodge with warm hospitality and personal service.
Tel: (01 325) 40415
Fax: (01 325 40246

Walkersons Country Manor
Off Dullstroom/Lydenburg Road
PO Box 185, Dullstroom 1110
An exclusive and peaceful country retreat offering an experience in pleasurable living.
Tel: (01 325) 40246
Fax: (01 325) 40260

HAZYVIEW
Bohm's Zeederberg ***
District Hazyview
PO Box 94,
Sabie 1260
Situated in the beautiful Sabie Valley near to the Kruger National Park, this charming property provides the ideal setting for complete relaxation in the country. Guests are accommodated in delightful chalets set in lush gardens and rolling lawns.
Tel: (01 317) 68101
Fax: (01 317 68193

Casa Do Sol ****
Farm Abele
PO 57, Hazyview 1242
A unique owner-managed establishment offering fine service, excellence and charm.
Tel: (01 317) 68111
Fax: (01 317 68166

Hazyview Protea Hotel ***
Burgers Hall
PO Box 105, Hazyview 1242
Luxury hotel and self-catering apartments just ten minutes from Kruger National Park.
Tel: (01 317) 67332
Fax: (01 317 67335

Karos Lodge ****
Sabie River/Kruger Gate
PO Box 54, Skukuza 1350
A warm and charming hotel on the Sabie River at the main entrance to the Kruger National Park.
Tel: (01 311) 65671
Fax: (01 311) 65676

Sabi River Sun ****
PO Box 13, Hazyview 1242
Luxurious accommodation just moments away from the Kruger National Park.
Tel: (01 311) 67311
Fax: (01 311) 67314

KOMATIPOORT
Border Country Inn ***
PO Box 197, Komatipoort 1340
Tel: (01 313) 50328
Fax: (01 313) 50100

LONDOLOZI GAME RESERVE
PO Box 1211
Sunninghill Park 2157
Three exclusive camps are operated in this private game reserve on the banks of the Sand River. The Main Camp caters for just twenty-four guests who are taken on private game drives for close encounters with leopard and other big game.
Tel: (011) 803 8421
Fax: (011) 803) 1810

MALELANE
Malelane Lodge ****
PO Box 392, Malelane 1320
Located on the Crocodile River close to the Kruger National Park's Malelane Gate. Each luxurious chalet is beautifully designed to complement the sub-tropical environment. The Kingfisher restaurant serves delicious gourmet meals or alternatively guests may dine around an open fire.
Tel: (01 313) 30331
Fax: (01313) 30145

Nelspruit

Crocodile Country Inn *
Schagen (next to N4)
PO Box 496, Nelspruit 1200
A charming country inn set in sub-tropical gardens in the glorious Lowveld.
Tel: (01 311) 63040
Fax: (01 311) 64171

Paragon Hotel *
19 Anderson Street
PO Box 81, Nelspruit 1200
Tel: (01 311) 53205
Fax: As above (ask for fax)

Ngala Game Lodge
PO Box 1211
Sunninghil Park 2157
Situated within the boundaries of the Kruger National Park, Ngala offers luxury facilities in an exquisite setting. All air-conditioned chalets have been constructed to recreate the elegance of a bygone era with antique bedsteads and ensuite bathrooms. The exclusive Safari Suite has a living room and sundeck overlooking a waterhole. The magnificent surroundings of indigenous gardens have a unique swimming pool cascading into a natural waterhole.
Tel: (011) 803 8421
Fax: (011) 803 1810

Pilgrim's Rest

Mount Sheba Hotel **
PO Box 100, Pilgrim's Rest 1290
This charming hotel is situated within hills and rainforest in a private nature reserve close to Pilgrim's Rest.
Tel: (01315) 81 241
Fax: (01315) 81 248

Singita Game Lodge
PO Box 1211
Sunninghill Park 2157
This intimate lodge nestles amidst giant ebony trees above the banks of the Sand River. Accommodating just sixteen people, Singita offers the ultimate in intimacy and exclusivity. The main lodge offers sweeping views over the river and plains beyond. Each luxurious room is equipped with air-conditioning, ensuite bathroom, plus a private outside shower.
Tel: (011) 803 8421
Fax: (011) 803 1810

White River

Cybele Forest Lodge **
PO Box 346, White River 1240
A charming exclusive retreat from which to explore the nearby Kruger National Park. Thirty guests are accommodated in beautiful rooms, some with private sitting rooms or walled private patios. The four spacious Paddock Suites have two bathrooms, a private living room, swimming pool and sun terrace. Dinner is served in a beautiful, candlelit dining room.
Tel: (01 311) 50511
Fax: (01 311) 32839

Glory Hill Guest Lodge *
PO Box 24, White River 1240
A delightful experience in a beautiful countryside location.
Tel: (01 311) 33217
Fax: (01 311) 33218

The Winkler Hotel **
PO Box 12, White River 1240
A comfortable country hotel set in the tranquil surroundings of Mpumalanga's Lowveld. All spacious bedrooms overlook the verdant lawns.
Tel: (01 311) 32317
Fax: (01 311) 31393

Pine Lake Sun **
PO Box 94, White River 1240
This resort offers extensive facilities and first-class service.
Tel: (01 311) 31186
Fax: (01 311) 33874

Free State

Bloemfontein

City Lodge Bloemfontein *
Corner Voortrekker Street & Parfitt Avenue
PO Box 3552, Bloemfontein 9300
A warm and friendly, value-for-money lodge with comfortable accommodation.
Tel: (051) 47 9888
Fax: (051) 47 5669

Holiday Inn Garden Court *
Corner Zastron Street & Melville Drive
PO Box 12015, Brandhof 9324
Comfortable hotel a few kilometres from the city centre.
Tel: (051) 47 0310
Fax: (051) 30 5678

Holiday Inn Garden Court
Bloemfontein/Naval Hill ***
1 Union Avenue
PO Box 1851, Bloemfontein 9300
Good facilities close to the city centre
Tel: (051) 30 1111
Fax: (051) 30 4141

Hotel Bloemfontein **
East Burger Street, Sanlam Plaza
PO Box 2212, Bloemfontein 9300
Luxurious accommodation in the heart of
the business centre.
Tel: (051) 30 1911
Fax: (051) 47 7102

BOSHOF
Boshof Hotel **
Jacob Street
PO Box 13, Boshof 8340
Comfortable and clean accommodation.
Tel: (0541) 0091
Fax: As above (ask for fax)

FICKSBURG
Franshoek Mountain Lodge **
PO Box 603, Ficksburg 9730
A country hideaway in a secluded mountain
valley. Ideal for horse-riding enthusiasts,
rock climbers and anglers.
Tel: (05 192) 3938/2828
Fax: As above (as for fax)

Nebo Holiday Farm **
PO Box 178, Ficksburg 9730
A beautiful guest farm set amidst a rose-
scented English mountain garden.
Tel: (05192) 3947/3286
Fax: As above (ask for fax)

LADYBRAND
Travellers Inn **
PO Box 458, Ladybrand 9745
Delightful stopover in the Eastern Free
State highlands
Tel: (05 191) 40191/3
Fax: As above (ask for fax)

VREDE
Langberg Hotel **
Marina Dam
PO Box 166 , Vreede 2455
Luxury thatched hotel with fine restaurant.
Tel: (01334) 32080
Fax: (01334) 31414

WELKOM
Welkom Hotel **
283 Koppie Alleen Road
PO Box 973, Welkom 9460
Charming service in a comfortable hotel.
Tel: (057) 51411
Fax: As above (ask for fax)

Welkom Inn**
PO Box 887, Welkom 9460
Private hotel close to the business and
commercial centres.
Tel: (057) 357 3361
Fax: (057) 352 1458

ZASTRON
Maluti Hotel **
PO Box 2, Zastron 9950
Comfortable hotel and good restaurant.
Tel: (05 542) 107
Fax: (05 542) 379

Gauteng

EDENVALE
City Lodge Jan Smuts Airport **
PO Box 448, Isando 1600
A friendly value-for-money lodge offering
comfortable accommodation close to
Johannesburg's International Airport
Tel: (011) 392 1750
Fax: (011 392 2644

Hotel Duneden **
46 Van Riebeeck Avenue
Edenvale
Comfortable rooms just minutes from
Johannesburg's International Airport.
Tel: (011) 453 2002
Fax: (011 453 7677

FERNDALE
Hotel Chambery **
PO Box 871, Ferndale 2160
Old-world style in quality surroundings.
Tel: (011) 886 7387
Fax: As above (ask for fax)

JOHANNESBURG
Holiday Inn Garden Court / Milpark **
Corner Empire & Owl Streets
Auckland Park
Quality accommodation with an extensive
range of facilities.
Tel: (011) 726 5100
Fax: (011 726 8615

Devonshire Hotel *
Corner Melle & Jorissen Streets
PO Box 31197, Braamfontein 2017
Luxurious accommodation with modern, full-service amenities.
Tel: (011) 339 5611
Fax: (011) 403 2495

Parktonian All Suite Hotel **
112 De Korte Street
PO Box 32278 , Braamfontein 2017
Excellent and luxurious accommodation is provided in this convenient hotel.
Tel: (011) 403 5740
Fax: (011) 339 7440

Carlton Hotel ***
Main Street, PO Box 7709
The hotels are connected by escalator and skybridge. The Carlton has 460 rooms and magnificent suites, while the Carlton Court has 63 bedrooms and suites each with its own jacuzzi, private bar and private fax. For the best in haute cuisine and fine wines, the Three Ships restaurant is a worthy choice. The lively El Gaucho serves South American specialities.
Tel: (011) 331 8911
Fax: (011) 331 3555

Karos Johannesburger Hotel *
Corner Twist and Wolmarans Streets
PO Box 23566, Joubert Park 2044
Situated in the heart of Johannesburg with facilities for the tourist and business traveller.
Tel: (011) 725 3753
Fax: (011) 725 6309

Linden Hotel *
Corner 7th Street & 4th Avenue
Linden 2195
Traditional style hotel with hospitable service. Situated near to the Rosebank business centre.
Tel: (011) 782 4905
Fax: As above (ask for fax)

Rosebank Hotel **
Corner Tyrwhitt & Sturdee Avenue
PO Box 52025, Saxonwold 2132
A comfortable surburban hotel offering three restaurants and conference facilities.
Tel: (011) 447-2700
Fax: (011) 447 3276

Sunnyside Park Hotel **
PO Box 31256, Braamfontein 2017
This hotel offers the peace and tranquillity of the countryside with the convenience of being only minutes from the city.
Tel: (011) 643-7226
Fax: (011) 642-0019

**Holiday Inn Garden Court
Johannesburg International Airport ***
Kempton Park 1627
The ideal stopover, just one kilometre from the airport.
Tel: (011) 392 1062
Fax: (011) 974 8097

**Holiday Inn
Johannesburg International Airport ****
Jan Smuts Airport
PO Box 388, Kempton Park 1620
Comfortable accommodation situated at Johannesburg International Airport.
Tel: (011) 975 1121
Fax: (011) 975 5846

Sandton Sun and Towers ***
PO Box 784902, Sandton 2146
A luxurious five-star hotel in the heart of Sandton offering first-class facilities, restaurants and elegant rooms.
Tel: (011) 780-5000
Fax: (011) 780-5002

Balalaika Protea **
20 Maud Street
PO Box 783372, Sandton
Comfortable hotel in the centre of Sandton.
Tel: (011) 322 5000
Fax: (011) 322 5021

Karos Indaba Hotel **
Hartebeespoort Dam Road
PO Box 67129, Bryanston 2021
Excellent hotel in the northern suburb of Sandton. All 210 air-conditioned rooms are comfortably furnished.
Tel: (011) 465 1400
Fax: (011) 705 1709

Holiday Inn Crowne Plaza Sandton **
Corner Grayston and Rivonia Roads
PO Box 781743, Sandton
A fine hotel in a beautiful garden setting.
Tel: (011) 783-5262
Fax: (011) 783-5289

KRUGERSDORP
Auberge Aurora *
PO Box 145, Krugersdorp 1740
Tranquil country house with seven luxury rooms thirty minutes from Johannesburg.
Tel: (011) 956 6307
Fax: (011) 956 6089

MAGALIESBURG
Magaliesburg Country Hotel *
PO Box 4, Magaliesburg 2805
A perfect country getaway only forty minutes from Johannesburg.
Tel: (0142) 771109
Fax: As above (ask for fax)

Mount Grace Country House Hotel **
PO Box 251, Magaliesburg 2805
A delightful country lodge with first-class facilities only one hour from Johannesburg. Three clusters of thatch and stone cottages provide luxurious accommodation which overlook charming gardens.
Tel: (0142) 77 1350
Fax: (0142) 77 1202

Valley Lodge **
PO Box 13, Magaliesburg 2805
A charming resort in a tranquil setting on the banks of the Magalies River. Charming bedrooms have been decorated to create a warm and cosy ambience. There are thirty-five standard rooms and twenty luxury river-front rooms. The nature reserve and bird sanctuary are excellent additions to the many facilities.
Tel: (0142) 771391
Fax: (0142) 771306

MULDERSDRIFT
Heia Safari Range *
Swartkop
PO Box 1387, Honeydew 2040
A luxurious escape to a nature reserve where animals roam freely.
Tel: (011) 659 0605
Fax: (011) 659 0709

PRETORIA
Arcadia Hotel ***
PO Box 26104, Arcadia
A charming hotel with a good reputation for friendly service.
Tel: (012) 326 9311
Fax: (012) 326 1067

Bentley's Country Lodge *
PO Box 16665, Pretoria North 0116
A tropical retreat in the foothills of the Magaliesberg.
Tel: (012) 542 1751
Fax: (012) 542-3487

Best Western Cresta Pretoria Hotel *
PO Box 40663, Arcadia 0007
Excellent value for money combined with warm hospitality and good service.
Tel: (012) 341 3473
Fax: (012) 341 2258

Holiday Inn Crowne Plaza **
PO Box 40694, Arcadia 0007
An ideal base for both the tourist and business traveller.
Tel: (012) 341-1571
Fax: (012) 341-4641

Holiday Inn Garden Court *
Cnr Van der Walt & Minnaar Streets
PO Box 2301,
Pretoria 0001
An ideally-located hotel for the business and holiday traveller.
Tel: (012) 322 7500
Fax: (012) 322 9429

The Farm Inn Hotel *
Lynwood Road at Silverlakes Golf Course
PO Box 71702, Die Wilgers 0041
A tranquil retreat amidst a private game sanctuary.
Tel: (012) 809 0266
Fax: (012) 809 0146

Karos Manhatten Hotel *
247 Schelding Street
PO Box 26212, Arcadia 0007
Close proximity to main routes, shopping centres and sports venues.
Tel: (012) 322 7635
Fax: (012) 322 1252

KwaZulu-Natal

BERGVILLE
Cavern Berg Resort **
Private Bag X 1626, Bergville 3350
An owner-run resort set in a tranquil mountain wilderness offering guided hikes and horse riding.
Tel: (036) 438 6270
Fax: (036 438 6334

Little Switzerland *
Private Bag X1661, Bergville 3350
Fine hospitality and excellent cuisine in a wonderful setting overlooking the Amphitheatre in the Drakensberg.
Tel: (036) 438 6220
Fax: As above (ask for fax)

The Drifters Inn
Oliviershoek Pass
PO Box 1417, Harrismith 9880
A delightful stone and organ pipe building. The inn offers breathtaking views and is situated on the crest of Oliviershoek Pass.
Tel: (0364) 386 130

BOTHA'S HILL
Rob Roy Hotel *
PO Box 10, Botha's Hill 3660
Superb cuisine and spacious rooms in a fairytale location.
Tel: (031) 777 1305
Fax: (031) 777 13564

DURBAN
Beach Hotel *
107 Marine Parade, PO Box 10305
Situated directly on the beachfront at the centre of Durban's Golden Mile.
Tel: (031) 37 5511
Fax: (031) 37 5409

City Lodge Durban *
PO Box 10842
A good value, friendly lodge offering comfortable accommodation in landscaped surroundings. Close to the beachfront.
Tel: (031) 32 1447
Fax: (031) 32 1483

Elangeni Sun **
63 Snell Parade, PO Box 4094
This fine quality hotel is situated opposite North Beach and offers excellent restaurants and facilities.
Tel: (031) 37 1321
Fax: (031) 37 5527

Holiday Inn Garden Court Durban/North Beach *
83/91 Snell Parade, PO Box 10592
Comfortable hotel overlooking the Indian Ocean and North Beach.
Tel: (031) 37 7361
Fax: (031) 37 4058

Holiday Inn Garden Court Durban/Marine Parade *
167 Marine Parade, PO Box 10809
Situated just 400 metres from the beach with excellent sea-facing rooms.
Tel: (031) 37 3341
Fax: (031) 37 9885

Royal Hotel ***
267 Smith Street
PO Box 1041
Voted the best city hotel in South Africa for five consecutive years. This luxurious property offers four cocktail bars, six excellent restaurants, 272 luxuriously appointed rooms and suites many of which overlook Durban's yacht basin. The Royal Grill is acknowledged as one of the best restaurants in the country.
Tel: (031) 304 0331
Fax: (031) 307 6884

The Palace Protea Hotel *
211 Marine Parade, PO Box 10539
This hotel offers fine accommodation in a stylish and comfortable setting.
Tel: (031) 32 8351
Fax: (031) 32 8307

HLUHLUWE
Zululand Tree Lodge
PO Box 3960, Hluhluwe
An oasis of luxury close to the Ubizane Game Reserve. Guests stay in twin-bedded luxury tree houses with ensuite bathrooms and private view decks. Each tree house is thatched in local patterns while interior walls are clad with locally woven mats. Enjoy sundowner cocktails on the view deck before enjoying a traditional meal and local Zulu dancing.
Tel: (035) 562 1020
Fax: (035) 562 1032

HIMEVILLE
Sani Pass Hotel and Leisure Resort *
Sani Pass Road
PO Box 44, Himmeville 4585
Charming resort situated in the heart of the breathtaking Drakensberg mountain range on the banks of the Mkhomozana River. Excellent sporting facilities including trout fishing, hiking, golf and swimming.
Tel: (033) 702 1320
Fax: (033) 702 0220

HOWICK
Old Halliwell Country Inn ***
Currys Post Road
PO Box 201, Howick 3290
Constructed in the 1800s, this elegant inn offers old-fashioned luxury in the heart of the Midlands. Each of the fifteen suites has its own fireplace and private patio overlooking the picturesque Karkloof valley. Cocktails are served in the historical Steven's Bar in front of a roaring log fire and the menus are superb.
Tel: (0332) 30 2602/30
Fax: (0332) 30 3430

ILLOVO BEACH
Karridene Protea Hotel *
Old Main South Coast Road
PO Box 20, Illovo Beach 4155
Tel: (031) 96 3321
Fax: (031) 96 4093

LADYSMITH
Royal Hotel *
PO Box 12, Ladysmith 3370
Well-appointed rooms in a comfortable environment.
Tel: (0361) 22176
Fax: As above (ask for fax)

MKUZE
Ghost Mountain Inn *
Old Main Road
PO Box 18, Mkuze 3965
This charming country hotel offers excellent cuisine and fine accommodation in the heart of the bush.
Tel: (035) 573 1025
Fax: As above (ask for fax)

MONT-AUX-SOURCES
Karos Mont-aux-Sources Hotel *
Private Bag X1670, Bergville 3350
A warm and welcoming hotel in a tranquil environment.
Tel: (036) 438 6230
Fax: As above (ask for fax)

NEWCASTLE
Holiday Inn Garden Court Newcastle *
PO Box 778, Newcastle 2940
Comfortable rooms and an attractive restaurant.
Tel: (03 431) 28151
Fax: (03 431) 24142

PIETERMARITZBURG
Imperial Hotel *
224 Loop Street, Pietermaritzburg 3200
Highly recommended hotel in the city centre with seventy-two ensuite rooms.
Tel: (0331) 42 6651
Fax: (0331) 42 9796

RICHARD'S BAY
Karos Bayshore Inn *
The Gulley
PO Box 51, Richard's Bay 3900
A comfortable hotel close to the sea.
Tel: (0351) 31246
Fax: (0351) 32335

Karos Richards Hotel *
Hibberd Drive
PO Box 242, Richard's Bay 3900
A warm and friendly hotel suited to both the tourist and business traveller.
Tel: (0351) 31301
Fax: (0351) 32334

SOUTHBROOM
San Lameer Estate Hotel **
Main Road
PO Box 88, Southbroom 4277
The ultimate tropical paradise with accommodation in either a deluxe hotel or fully-equipped luxury villas.
Tel: (03 931) 30011
Fax: (03 931) 30157

ULUNDI
Holiday Inn Garden Court Ulundi *
Princess Magogo Street
PO Box 91, Ulundi 3838
Central located close to shops, museums and historic buildings. Quality rooms and good restaurant and bar.
Tel: (0358) 21 121
Fax: (0358) 21 721

UMHLALI
Shortens Country House **
Compensation Road
PO Box 499, Umhlali 4390
This old colonial homestead built in 1903 has been restored to its former glory and accommodation in the form of individually appointed chalets have been built in the award-winning gardens.
Tel: (0322) 71140/1/2/3
Fax: (0322) 71144

UMHLANGA ROCKS
Beverly Hills Sun *****
PO Box 71, Umhlanga Rocks 4320
This luxurious hotel is situated at the finest location on the North Coast. Excellent cuisine is served in both the two elegant restaurants within the hotel and specialise in serving freshly-caught seafood for which the Natal coast is famous.
Tel: (031) 561 2211
Fax: (031) 561 3711

Oyster Box Hotel ***
PO Box 22, Umhlanga Rocks 4320
Gracious hospitality in colonial comfort. This charming hotel has a perfect beach-front location amidst charming gardens.
Tel: (031) 561 2233
Fax: (031) 561 4072

UNDERBERG
Drakensberg Gardens Golf & Leisure Resort ***
Drakensberg Gardens, Underberg 4590
This premier resort is situated in the spectacular Drakensberg mountains. The property offers an eighteen-hole golf course and extensive sports and leisure facilities.
Tel: (033) 701 1355
Fax: As above (ask for fax).

UVONGO
Brackenmoor Hotel ***
Lot 2013, PO Box 518
St. Michael's on Sea, Uvongo 4265
A gracious and charming country hotel with an elegant and hospitable restaurant.
Tel: (03 931) 75165
Fax: (03 931) 75109

VRYHEID
Stilwater Protea Hotel ***
Private Bag X9332, Vryheid 3100
The ideal base from which to tour the northern historical battlefields.
Tel: (0381) 6181
Fax: As above (ask for fax)

WINTERTON
Cathedral Peak Hotel ***
PO Winterton, Winterton 3340
Escape to the peace and tranquillity of this fine resort in the Drakensberg mountains.
Tel: (036) 488 1888
Fax: As above (ask for fax)

Cayley Lodge ***
PO Box 241, Winterton 3340
A fine lodge located close to the magnificent Drakensberg mountains. All bedrooms are equipped with a dressing room, private bathroom and boast unrivalled views of the mountains. Guests can relax on a sunset cruise on the dam below the hotel and enjoy the unsurpassed essence of nature.
Tel: (036) 468 1222
Fax: As above (ask for fax)

Drakensberg Sun ***
Cathkin Peak
PO Box 335, Winterton 3340
A superb mountain resort situated in the Cathkin Peak area of the Drakensberg mountain range.
Tel: (036) 468 1000
Fax: (036) 468 1224

Northern Cape

Hanover
Hanover Lodge Hotel **
PO Box 88, Hanover 5960
Owner-managed hotel halfway between Cape Town and Johannesburg on the N1.
Tel: (053 642) 19
Fax: (053 642) 53

KAKAMAS
Waterwiel Protea Hotel ***
PO Box 250, Kakamas 8870
A warm friendly welcome in a well-equipped hotel.
Tel: (054) 431 0838
Fax: (054) 431 0836

KAMIESKROON
Kamieskroon Hotel **
Old National Road
PO Box 19, Kamieskroon 8241
A family-owned country hotel in the heart of Namaqualand specialising in eco-tourism and photographic workshops.
Tel: (0257) 614
Fax: (0257) 675

KIMBERLEY
Diamond Protea Lodge **
124 Du Toitspan Road
PO Box 2068, Kimberley 8300
Comfortable hotel at reasonable prices.
Tel: (0531) 81 1281
Fax: (0531) 81 1284

Holiday Inn Garden Court Kimberley ***
PO Box 635, Kimberley 8300
Impressive hotel situated in the heart of Kimberley.
Tel: (0531) 31751
Fax: (0531) 21814

Hotel Kimberlite ***
162 George Street, Kimberley 8301
This modern hotel offers excellent rooms in a peaceful setting.
Tel: (0531) 81 1967/8
Fax: (0531) 81 1967

KURUMAN
Eldorado Motel ***
PO Box 313, Kuruman 8460
An oasis in the Kalahari offering home-from-home facilities.
Tel: (05 373) 22191
Fax: As above (ask for fax)

KORANNABERG PRIVATE NATURE RESERVE
The Lodge *****
16km off Hotazel/Van Zyls Road
Kuruman 8460
An oasis of opulence which offers an unparalleled wilderness experience.
Tel: (05 375) 215/521
Fax: (05 375) 234

SPRINGBOK
Kokerboom Motel **
PO Box 340, Springbok 8240
Enjoy Namaqualand hospitality at its best. This cool, spacious hotel and friendly staff ensure a pleasant stay.
Tel: (0251) 22685
Fax: (0251) 22257

Springbok Hotel **
PO Box 46, Springbok 8240
A charming base in the very heart of Namaqualand.
Tel: (0251) 21161
Fax: (0251) 22257

UPINGTON
Oasis Protea Lodge **
26 Schroder Street
PO Box 1981, Upington 8800
A comfortable stay is guaranteed at this well-equipped hotel.
Tel: (054) 31 1125
Fax: (054) 2 2232

Northern Transvaal

LOUIS TRICHARDT
Bergwater Hotel ***
5 Rissik Street
PO Box 503
Louis Trichardt 0920
Top-quality service in a charming hotel.
Tel: (015) 516 0262/3
Fax: As above (ask for fax)

Clouds End Hotel ***
Private Bag X2409, Louis Trichardt 0920
Good value-for-money in a delightful atmosphere. The hotel has been Swiss-owned and run since 1968.
Tel: (015) 517 7021
Fax: (015) 517 7187

Ingwe Ranch Motel ***
PO Box 433, Louis Trichardt 0920
Charming country-style hotel with friendly staff.
Tel: (015) 517 7087
Fax: (015) 517 7122

MAGOEBASKLOOF
Glenshiel Country Lodge ****
Magoebaskloof
PO Box 1
Haenertsburg 0730
Peaceful hotel where the owner-managers will ensure a relaxed and stress-free stay.
Tel: (015 276) 4335
Fax: As above (ask for fax)

Magoebaskloof Hotel ***
Road R71, Magoebaskloof 0730
A friendly base for those looking to explore the area.
Tel: (015 276) 4276
Fax: (015 276) 4280

Troutwaters Inn **
Road R71, Magoebaskloof 0730
A delightful inn with large family rooms.
Tel: (015 276) 4245/6
Fax: As above (ask for fax)

MESSINA
Kate's Hope River Lodge
PO Box 2720, Cresta 2118
Luxury lodge where game drives, river cruises and gracious hospitality are the order of the day.
Tel: (011) 476 6217

NYLSTROOM
Shangri-La Country Lodge ***
PO Box 262, Nylstroom 0510
An idyllic retreat offering the comfort and
style of a bygone era. Guests stay in either
luxury, thatched rondavels or executive
suites.
Tel: (01470) 2381/2071
Fax: As above (ask for fax)

PIETERSBRUG
Holiday Inn Garden Court Pietersburg ***
PO Box 784, Pietersburg 0700
Conveniently situated close to all amenities
and city centre.
Tel: (0152) 291 2030
Fax: (0152) 291 3150

The Ranch ***
PO Box 77, Pietersburg 0700
A family-owned hotel with a long tradition of
warm hospitality. Set in fifteen hectares of
lush gardens.
Tel: (0152) 293 7180
Fax: (0152) 293 7188

TZANEEN
Coach House Hotel *****
Old Coach Road
PO Box 544, Tzaneen 0850
Country hospitality at the highest level is
provided in this 45-bedroom property with
panoramic views across the valley towards
distant mountain peaks. The historic bar is
charming and the menu makes use of the
wonderful fresh local produce from the
surrounding farms.
Tel: (0152) 307 3641
Fax: (0152) 307 1466

Karos Tzaneen Hotel ***
PO Box 1, Tzaneen 0850
A peaceful haven surrounded by the
splendid scenery of the Drakensberg
foothills.
Tel: (0152) 307 3140
Fax: As above (ask for fax)

WARMBATHS
Mabula Game Lodge ***
Private Bag X1665, Warmbaths 0480
8,000 hectares of private game reserve
only two hours north of Johannesburg.
Tel: (011) 463 4217
Fax: (011) 463 4299

North-West Province

BAKUBUNG GAME LODGE
PO Box 294, Sun City
Top class accommodation is provided
within the splendour of the Pilanesberg
National Park. Guests can stay in either
luxurious appointed hotel rooms or private
self-catering accommodation.
Tel: (01465) 21861
Fax: (01465) 25 5711

KWA MARITANE GAME LODGE
PO Box 39, Sun City 0316
This ninety-room complex is set within the
fabulous Pilanesberg National Park and
offers comfortable accommodation in either
duplex cabanas or five/eight sleeper
chalets. Each have their own private patio
facing the rolling hills.
Tel: (01465) 21820
Fax: (01465 21147

MAFIKENG
Molopo Sun
PO Box 3355, Mmabatho 8681
Set in the heart of Mmabatho, the hotel
offers comfortable accommodation with a
fabulous array of entertainment including
casino, live entertainment and sports.
Tel: (0140) 24184
Fax: (0140) 23472

Morula Sun
PO Box 59401 , Karenpark 0118
A sparkling casino resort with seventy
comfortable rooms and two suites. The
resort is famous for its casino and slot
machines which is reputed to be the largest
in Africa.
Tel: (01461) 23320/9
Fax: (01461) 24662

SUN CITY
The Cascades
PO Box 7, Sun City 0316
This beautiful hotel offers a fantasy world of
cascading water and tropical lagoons which
are home to flamingos and swans. The
Grotto bar has an exotic swim-up bar and
the bedrooms range from luxurious double
rooms to magnificent suites with private
balconies and jacuzzis.
Tel: (01465) 21000
Fax: (01465) 73442

Mmabatho Sun
PO Box 600, Mafikeng 8670
This elegant hotel offers guests luxurious accommodation and sparkling entertainment. Facilities include a casino, two pool decks and various sports.
Tel: (0140) 89 1111
Fax: (0140) 86 1661

The Palace of the Lost City
PO Box 308, Sun City 0316
Throughout the 338-room Palace, the architecture and decor recall an era of opulence and splendour. Delightful food is served in the Villa del Palazzo Restaurant with its magnificent ceiling frescoes of jungle scenes.
Tel: (01465) 73000
Fax: (01465) 73111

Sun City Hotel
PO Box 2, Sun City 0316
A jet-set playground set amidst sub-tropical gardens and a man-made lake. The elegant bedrooms have views across the pool towards the Pilanesberg mountains. The Harlequin Restaurant and Supper Club serves delightful meals and fine cocktails. The huge casino features a disco.
Tel: (01465) 21000
Fax: (01465) 74210

Tshukudu Game Lodge
PO Box 294, Sun City 0319
Nine select chalets are situated in the heart of the Pilanesberg National Park each with luxuriously-appointed facilities including a sunken bath with its own private view of the waterhole, fireplace and private bar.
Tel: (01465) 21861
Fax: (01465) 21621

Potchefstroom
Elgro Hotel *
PO Box 1111, Potchefstroom 2520
Tel: (0148) 297 5411
Fax: (0148) 297 5411

Rustenburg
Karos Safari Hotel *
PO Box 687, Rustenburg 0300
A sub-tropical resort for both the business and leisure traveller.
Tel: (0142) 97 1361
Fax: (0142) 97 1220

Olifantsnek Country Hotel **
Olifantsnek, PO Box 545
Family-run atmosphere and a natural environment give this hotel a unique appeal.
Tel: (0142) 92208
Fax: (0142) 92100

Sparkling Waters Holiday Hotel **
Rietfontein Farm
PO Box 208, Rustenburg 0300
Gourmet food, a friendly atmosphere and fine surroundings ensure a special stay.

Westwinds Country House **
Westwinds Farm, Rustenburg District
PO Box 56, Kroondal 0350
Tel: (0142) 750560
Fax: (0142) 75 0032

Tau Game Lodge
Sun Game Lodges
PO Box 782553, Sandton 2146
Located in the southern sector of Madikwe Game Reserve, this unique private lodge offers twenty-six luxury thatched chalets spread out around a vast waterhole. Each chalet has an individual sundeck allowing guests to experience the bush in privacy.
Tel: (011) 780 0100
Fax: (011) 780 0106

Vryburg
International Hotel **
PO Box 38, Vryburg 8600
Homely accommodation with good food and friendly service.
Tel: (05 391) 2235
Fax: As above (ask for fax)

Western Cape

Albertinia
Albertinia Hotel **
PO Box 85, Albertinia 6795
A lovely country hotel with old-fashioned hospitality.
Tel: (02 934) 51030
Fax: (02 934) 51495

Beaufort West
Oasis Hotel **
66 Donkin Street
PO Box 115, Beaufort West 6970
Comfortable hotel in the heart of the Karoo.
Tel: (0201) 3221
Fax: As above (ask for fax)

Wagon Wheel Motel **
North End on N1, Beaufort West 6970
Friendly and affordable accommodation.
Tel: (0201) 2145
Fax: As above (ask for fax)

BELVILLE
Belville Inn ***
PO Box 233, Belville 7535
Good rooms and meals at reasonable rates.
Tel: (021) 948 8111
Fax: (021) 946 4425

BREDASDORP/ARNISTON
Arniston Hotel ***
PO Box 126, Bredasdorp 7280
A charming hotel in a quaint 200-year-old
fishing village. Each of the rooms and suites
are beautifully furnished, and nine rooms
have private balconies overlooking the
Indian Ocean. The dining room offers a fine
blend of French and Cape cuisine.
Tel: (02 847) 5 9000
Fax: (02 847) 5 9633

Hotel Victoria **
PO Box 11, Bredasdorp 7280
Spotless full-equipped rooms in a friendly
hotel offering excellent country cuisine.
Tel: (02 841) 41159
Fax: (02 841) 41140

BRENTON-ON-SEA
Brenton-on-Sea Hotel **
Agapanthus Avenue, Brenton-on-Sea
Hotel and self-catering accommodation
situated on the beach.
Tel: (0445) 81 0081
Fax: As above (ask for fax)

CALEDON
Alexandra Hotel **
PO Box 3, Caledon 7230
Intimate atmosphere in a centrally-located
position.
Tel: (0281) 23052
Fax: (0281 41102

The Overberger Country Hotel & Spa ***
PO Box 480, Caledon 7230
Situated in the lush tranquillity of the rolling
wheatlands, this charming hotel makes a
perfect getaway.
Tel: (0281) 41271
Fax: (0281) 41270

CAPE TOWN
The Ambassador Hotel &
Executive Suites ****
34 Victoria Road, Bantry Bay
Luxurious twenty-four hour personal care in
this fabulous property surrounded by
breathtaking views.
Tel: (021) 439 6170
Fax: (021) 439 6336

The Bay Hotel *****
Victoria Road, Camps Bay 8040
A beach hotel of matchless elegance, run
with dignity and charm.
Tel: (021) 438 4444
Fax: (021) 438 4455

Cape Sun Hotel *****
Strand Street
PO Box 4532, Cape Town 8000
A luxury five-star hotel situated in the centre
of Cape Town.
Tel: (021) 23 8844
Fax: (021) 23 8875

Capetonian Protea Hotel ****
Pier Place, Heerengracht
Comfortable rooms with charming Cape
hospitality.
Tel: (021) 21 1150
Fax: (021) 25 2215

Carlton Heights Hotel **
88 Queen Victoria Street, 8001
A city-centre hotel with self-catering
facilities overlooking Table Mountain.
Tel: (021) 23 1260
Fax: (021) 23 2088

Holiday Inn Garden Court
Greenmarket Square ***
PO Box 3775
Situated on cobbled Greenmarket Square,
the hotel reflects a strong European
influence.
Tel: (021) 23 2040
Fax: (021) 23 3664

Holiday Inn Garden Court
St. George's Mall ***
Trustbank Building, PO Box 5616
Elegant hotel close to the business and
entertainment centre of Cape Town.
Tel: (021) 419 0808
Fax: (021) 419 7010

Town House Hotel ****
60 Corporation Street, PO Box 5053
A hotel with the peace of a private house
offering fine accommodation and service.
The restaurant is known for its exquisite
meals and memorable wines.
Tel: (021) 45 7050
Fax: (021) 45 3891

Tulbach Protea Hotel ***
PO Box 2891, Cape Town 8000
A country-style hotel in the city centre.
Tel: (021) 21 5140
Fax: (021) 21 4648

**The Cellars — Hohenort Country
House Hotel** *****
PO Box 270, Constantia 7848
An elegant property situated in charming
landscaped gardens in the Constantia
Valley. Fifteen spacious suites and 38
lovely bedrooms have spectacular views
from the slopes of Table Mountain. The
Cellars restaurant is renowned for its fine
English and French cuisine with emphasis
on locally-caught fish and the superb local
produce of the Cape.
Tel: (021) 794 2137
Fax: (021) 794 2149

Cape Swiss Hotel ***
PO Box 21516, Cape Town 8000
An elegant hotel situated at the foot of
Table Mountain commanding magnificent
mountain and city views.
Tel: (021) 23 8190
Fax: (021) 26 1795

Mount Nelson Hotel *****
PO Box 2608, Cape Town 8000
Traditional luxury nestling in the shadow of
Table Mountain.
Tel: (021) 23 1000
Fax: (021) 24 7472

The Vineyard Hotel ****
PO Box 151, Newlands 7725
Set in six acres of parkland with sweeping
views of Table Mountain, this hotel offers
old-world charm and tranquillity. Each
bedroom is stylishly-appointed in period
decor and the dinner is served in the
romantic candlelit dining room.
Tel: (021) 683 3044
Fax: (021) 683 3365

Villa Belmonte ***
Oranjezicht, Cape Town 8001
Relax in a stylish atmosphere close to Table
Mountain, Lion's Head and Devil's Peak.
Tel: (021) 462 1576
Fax: (021) 462 1579

Karos Arthur's Seat Hotel ****
Arthur's Road, Sea Point 8001
This Mediterranean-style hotel is regarded
as one of the finest properties in Cape Town
with scenic views of Table Bay and Table
Mountain. The hotel boasts 123 luxuriously
furnished rooms with ensuite facilities.
Tel: (021) 434 1187
Fax: (021) 434 9767

The Peninsula All-Suite Hotel ****
PO Box 17188, Sea Point 8060
Superbly located just five minutes from the
Waterfront, this all-suite hotel offers luxury
accommodation overlooking Table Bay.
Jackson's Restaurant and Bar is one of the
finest restaurants in the Cape with cuisine
derived from Provence, Italy, Morocco and
New Orleans.
Tel: (021) 439 8888
Fax: (021) 439 8886

The Portswood ****
Victoria & Alfred Waterfront, PO Box 6221
Comfortable friendly service and excellent
accommodation are offered within this
luxurious hotel. The 102 rooms offer views
of the harbour and Table Mountain.
Tel: (021) 418 3281
Fax: (021) 419 7570

Victoria and Alfred Hotel ****
Waterfront, PO Box 50050
Victorian elegance combined with modern
top quality rooms — this hotel offers
superior accommodation in the traditional
style of colonial Cape Town.
Tel: (021) 419 6677
Fax: (021) 419 8955

CITRUSDAL
Cedarberg Hotel **
PO Box 37, Citrusdal 7340
Situated in the Olifants River valley, this
hotel offers comfortable accommodation
and good home cooking.
Tel: (021) 921 2221
Fax: (021) 921 2704

CLANWILLIAM
Strassberger's Hotel Clanwilliam ✱✱
PO Box 4, Clanwilliam 8135
A cosy getaway with reasonably-priced accommodation.
Tel: (027) 482 1101
Fax: (027) 482 2678

FRANSCHOEK
Franschoek Mountain Manor ✱✱✱
PO Box 54, Franschoek 7690
A charming country hotel with excellent facilities situated in a far corner of the Franschoek Valley.
Tel: (02 212) 2071
Fax: (02 212) 2177

Huguenot Hotel ✱✱
PO Box 27, Franschoek 7690
Pleasant accommodation, centrally-located in the Franschoek Valley.
Tel: (02 212) 2092

GEORGE
Far Hills Protea Hotel ✱✱✱
PO Box 10, George 6530
Country hospitality in a unique and beautiful setting.
Tel: (0441) 71 1925
Fax: (0441) 71 1951

Hawthorndene Hotel ✱✱
PO Box 1, George 6530
A peaceful and tranquil hotel with friendly service and excellent cuisine.
Tel: (0441) 74 4160
Fax: As above (ask for fax)

GORDON'S BAY
Van Riebeeck Hotel ✱✱✱
PO Box 10, Gordon's Bay 7150
This charming hotel offers a memorable stay beside the sandy beaches of the Indian Ocean.
Tel: (024) 56 144
Fax: (024) 56 1572

GRABOUW/HOUHOEK
Houwhoek Inn ✱✱
PO Box 95, Grabouw 7160
Established in 1834, this historical inn offers Cape charm, country cooking, log fires and a memorable experience.
Tel: (02 824) 49646
Fax: (02 824) 49112

HERMANUS
The Marine Hotel ✱✱✱
PO Box 9, Hermanus 7200
Relax in old-English style overlooking the spectacular Walker Bay.
Tel: (0283) 70 0150
Fax: (0283) 70 0160

The Windsor of Hermanus ✱✱
PO Box 3, Hermanus 7200
Traditional hospitality in comfortable surroundings.
Tel: (0283) 23727
Fax: (0283) 22181

HOUT BAY
Hout Bay Manor ✱✱
PO 27035, Hout Bay 7872
A small intimate hotel situated under old oak trees within a short walk to unspoilt beaches.
Tel: (021) 790 5960
Fax: (021) 790 4952

KNYSNA
Knysna Protea Hotel ✱✱✱
PO Box 33, Knysna 6570
Conveniently situated on the Garden Route with excellent accommodation.
Tel: (0445) 22127
Fax: (0445) 23568

KOMMETIJIE
The Kommetijie Inn ✱✱✱
PO Box 48156, Kommetjie 7975
Excellent accommodation and a seafood speciality restaurant make this charming hotel a comfortable break.

LAMBERT'S BAY
Marine Protea Hotel ✱✱✱
Voortrekker Street
PO Box 249, Lambert's Bay 8130
The Marine boasts a fine reputation for seafood and comfortable accommodation.
Tel: (027) 432 1126/7
Fax: (027) 432 1036

Raston Gashaus ✱✱✱
24 Riedeman Street
PO Box 20, Lambert's Bay 8130
Pleasant individually decorated rooms in a charming older-style hotel.
Tel: (027) 432 2431
Fax: (027) 432 2422

MATIJIESFONTEIN
Lord Milner Hotel **
Logan Road, Matijiesfontein 6901
Elegant hotel with charming ambience in
the wilds of the Karoo.
Tel: (02 372) ask for 5203
Fax: (02 372) ask for 5802

MONTAGU
Avalon Springs Hotel ***
PO Box 110, Montagu 6720
Great holiday resort and health spa in a
magnificent mountain setting
Tel: (0234) 41150
Fax: (0234) 41906

MOSSEL BAY
Eight Bells Mountain Inn ***
PO Box 436, Mossel Bay 6500
Charming family-run inn on the Garden
Route amidst magnificent scenery. All
rooms, rondavels and alpine chalets are
delightfully furnished.
Tel: (0444) 95 1544/5
Fax: (0444) 95 1548

Rose and Crown Hotel ***
PO Box 302, Mossel Bay 6500
A family-run hotel with a charming and
welcoming atmosphere.
Tel: (0444) 91 1069
Fax: (0444) 91 1426

MUIZENBERG
Shrimpton's Manor
19 Alexander Road, Muizenberg 7945
Serving excellent cuisine, this intimate
manor house offers ageless charm.
Tel: (021) 788 1128
Fax: (021) 788 5225

OUDTSHOORN
Caves Motel **
PO Box 125, Oudtshoorn 6620
A friendly farm atmosphere with modern
facilities.
Tel: (0443) 22 2511
Fax: As above (ask for fax)

Holiday Inn Garden Court ***
PO Box 52, Oudtshoorn 6620
Centrally located comfortable hotel set in
charming landscaped gardens.
Tel: (0443) 22 2201
Fax: (0443) 22 3003

PAARL
Grande Roche Hotel *****
PO Box 6038, Paarl 7620
Situated in the heart of the winelands
amidst fertile vineyards, this fabulous
property at the foot of the gleaming Paarl
Rock offers a luxurious and unforgettable
stay. A member of the Relais et Chateaux,
the accommodation has been carefully
restored and converted into seventeen
sumptuous suites. Twelve new vine-clad
terrace suites are scattered amongst the
vineyards. Bosman's Restaurant is located
in the beautiful, restored manor house and
serves fine gourmet cuisine. The award-
winning wine list features 300 wines.
Tel: (02211) 63 2727
Fax: (02211) 63 2220

Zomerlust ****
PO Box 92, Paarl 7620
A stylish and elegant hotel steeped in the
history and romance of a bygone era.
Tel: (02 211) 22 117
Fax: (02 211) 28312

PLETTENBERG BAY
Hunter's Country House ****
Pear Tree Farm
PO Box 454, Plettenberg Bay 6600
Gracious living in individual thatched suites
amidst beautiful gardens and orchards,
overlooking magnificent forests. The hotel
caters for thirty guests in elegant antique-
furnished suites each with fireplace and
private patio. Dinners are served in the
baronial dining rooms of the main house.
Tel: (04 457) 7818
Fax: (04 457) 7878

Stromboli's Inn **
PO Box 116
Plettenberg Bay 6600
A country getaway in the heart of the
Garden Route.
Tel: (04 457) 7710
Fax: (04 457) 7823

The Crescent Hotel
PO Box 191, Plettenberg Bay 6600
Close to the beaches of Plettenberg Bay,
this charming hotel offers personal
attention and service.
Tel: (04 457) 34490
Fax: (04 457) 34491

The Plettenberg ****
PO Box 719, Plettenberg Bay 6600
A country hotel of unsurpassed elegance and excellence on this idyllic stretch of coast. Twenty-six exquisitely furnished rooms provide delightful accommodation, and the restaurant offers superb cuisine specialising in seafood and lamb.
Tel: (04 457) 32030
Fax: (04 457) 32074

PRINCE ALBERT
Swartberg Hotel and Lodge **
PO Box 6, Prince Albert 6930
Comfortable accommodation and country cooking at the foot of the famous Swartberg Pass.
Tel: (04 436) 332
Fax: (04 436) 383

ROBERTSON
Avalon Grand Hotel **
PO Box 171, Robertson 6705
A charming Victorian hotel which combines fine meals with cosy, country hospitality.
Tel: (02 351) 3272
Fax: (02 351) 61158

SALDANHA BAY
Saldanha Bay Protea Hotel ***
PO Box 70, Saldanha Bay 7395
A tranquil watersport resort, sixty minutes from Cape Town.
Tel: (02 281) 41264
Fax: (02 281) 44093

SIMON'S TOWN
The Lord Nelson Inn ***
58 St. George's Street, Simon's Town 7995
Beautiful ensuite rooms and a memorable restaurant ensure an unforgettable visit.
Tel: (021) 786 1386
Fax: (021) 786 1009

SOMERSET WEST
Lord Charles Hotel *****
PO Box 5151, Heiderberg 7135
Casual elegance combined with gracious hospitality. Charming accommodation with the emphasis on privacy and tranquillity is provided in elegant rooms. The Garden Terrace Restaurant serves an imaginative menu of fresh Cape produce.
Tel: (024) 44 1040
Fax: (024) 55 1107

STELLENBOSCH
Devon Valley Protea Hotel ***
PO Box 68, Stellenbosch 7600
A delightful hotel situated in the heart of the winelands.
Tel: (021) 882 2012
Fax: (021) 882 2610

D'Ouwe Werf Herberg ***
30 Church Street, Stellenbosch
PO Box 3200, Coetzenburg 7602
Gracious luxury living in a tranquil environment close to the heart of the town.
Tel: (021) 887 4608
Fax: (021) 887 4626

Guest House 110 Dorp Street ***
110 Dorp Street, Stellenbosch 7600
A gracious national monument which combines Cape history with twentieth-century luxury.
Tel: (021) 883 3555
Fax: As above (ask for fax)

Lanzerac Hotel ****
PO Box 4, Stellenbosch 7599
A country hotel of ageless charm in the heart of the winelands near Stellenbosch. Thirty beautifully-appointed suites each have direct access to the gardens.
Tel: (021) 887 1132
Fax: (021) 887 2310

Stellenbosch Hotel ***
PO Box 500, Stellenbosch 7600
A wonderful find in the heart of historic Stellenbosch.
Tel: (02 131) 887 3644
Fax: (02 131) 887 3673

SWELLENDAM
Swellengrebel Hotel ***
PO Box 9, Swellendam 6740
A popular hotel in the heart of the historic town of Swellendam.
Tel: (0291) 41144
Fax: (0291) 42453

WILDERNESS
Fairy Knowe Hotel **
PO Box 28, Wilderness 6560
An ideal family resort situated on the banks of the Touw River.
Tel: (0441) 877 1100
Fax: (0441) 877 0364

Holiday Inn Garden Court Wilderness *
N2 National Garden Route Highway
PO Box 26, Wilderness 6560
Comfortable hotel overlooking miles of unspoilt beaches and the Indian Ocean.
Tel: (0441) 877 1104
Tel: (0441) 877 1134

Karos Wilderness Hotel **
N2 National Road
PO Box 6, Wilderness 6560
A beautiful winter and summer holiday resort set amidst secluded lagoons, waterfalls and lush forest overlooking the beautiful Wilderness coast. The 160 deluxe bedrooms offer privacy and tranquillity, and guests may dine in the excellent restaurant on fresh seafood.
Tel: (0441) 877 1110
Fax: (0441) 877 0600

WITSAND/PORT BEAUFORT
Breede River Lodge **
Port Beaufort
PO Witsand
6761
A charming fishing lodge at the mouth of the Breede River. The restaurant specialises in fresh seafood and oysters.
Tel: (02 935) 631
Fax: (02 935) 650

WORCESTER
Cumberland Hotel *
2 Stockenstroom Street
PO Box 8, Worcester 6850
Friendly hospitality and comfortable rooms in this well-equipped conference hotel.
Tel: (0231) 72461
Fax: (0231) 73613

SELF-CATERING FACILITIES

Eastern Cape

KENTON ON SEA
Kariega Park **
PO Box 35, Kenton on Sea 6191
Luxurious lodges in a private game park. Swimming, hiking and abundant wildlife.
13 three-bedroom units, 6 four-bedroom units.
Tel: (0461) 31 1049
Fax: (0461) 2 3040

ST. FRANCIS BAY
Cape St. Francis Resort **
PO Box 139, St. Francis Bay 6312
The resort fronts onto three kilometres of pristine beach and offers access to surfing, hiking and fishing.
4 two-bedroom units, 8 three-bedroom units.
Tel: (0423) 94 0420
Fax: (0423 94 0409

Mpumalanga

BADPLAAS
Aventura Badplaas *
PO Box 15, Badplaas 1190
A popular and picturesque resort with healing springs.
69 one-bedroom units, 80 two-bedroom units.
Tel: (01 344) 4 1020
Fax: (01 344) 4 1391

GRASKOP
Log Cabin Village *
PO Box 77, Graskop 1270
A relaxing environment in the heart of scenic Mpumalanga.
3 one-bedroom units, 5 two-bedroom units.
Tel: (01 315) 7 1974
Fax: (01 315) 7 1975

HAZYVIEW
Eagle's Nest Chalets *
PO Box 719, Hazyview 1242
Just minutes from the Kruger National Park close to scenic places of interest.
10 one-bedroom units, 2 two-bedroom units.
Tel: (01 317) 68434.
Fax: As above (ask for fax)

Kruger Park Lodge ****
PO Box 989, Hazyview 1242
Spacious self-catering chalets with full resort facilities and a golf course on the Sabie River close to Kruger National Park.
2 one-bedroom units, 24 two-bedroom units and 31 three-bedroom units
Tel: (01 317) 67 021
Fax: (01 317) 67 386

PILGRIM'S REST
Crystal Springs Mountain Lodge ***
PO Box 10, Pilgrim's Rest 1290
An elevated and beautiful haven above the restored town of Pilgrim's Rest with luxury lodges situated within a game reserve.
53 one-bedroom units, 99 two-bedroom units, 12 three-bedroom units
Tel: (01 315) 8 1153
Fax: As above (ask for fax)

Trout Hideaway ***
PO Box 880, Lydenburg 1120
Self-catering units close to Pilgrim's Rest.
1 one-bedroom unit, 2 two-bedroom units, 1 three-bedroom unit, 1 four-bedroom unit
Tel: (01 314) 8 1347
Fax: As above (ask for fax)

Free State

Aventura Maselspoort ***
Private Bag X20519, Bloemfontein 9300
A charming resort for holiday-makers of all ages on the banks of the Madder River.
22 two-bedroom units
Tel: (051) 41 7848
Fax: (051) 41 7865

BLOEMFONTEIN
Reyneke Park **
PO Box 2245, Bloemfontein 9300
Modern, luxurious self-catering chalets close to the centre of town.
6 one-bedroom units
Tel: (051) 2 3888
Fax: (051) 2 3887

GARIEP DAM
Aventura Midwaters ***
Private Bag X10, Gariep Dam 9922
Comfortable self-catering resort.
6 one-bedroom units, 39 two-bedroom units and 15 three-bedroom units
Tel: (052 172) 45
Fax: (052 172) 135

Gauteng

VEREENIGING
Club Koppisol Holiday Resort **
PO Box 93, De Deur 1884
Self-catering resort only forty minutes from Johannesburg International Airport
6 two-bedroom units
Tel: (016) 56 1112
Fax: (016) 56 1155

KwaZulu-Natal

ILLOVO BEACH
Karridene Timeshare ***
PO Box 20, Illovo Beach 4155
Modern self-catering flats close to the beachfront, twenty minutes from Durban.
18 two-bedroom units, 6 three-bedroom units
Tel: (031) 96 3331
Fax: (031) 96 4033

MARGATE
Margate Sands ****
PO Box 653, Margate 4275
Luxury air-conditioned three-bedroomed flats overlooking Margate beachfront.
63 three-bedroom units
Tel: (03931) 21541
Fax: As above (ask for fax)

Marine Terrace ***
PO Box 653, Margate 4275
Nice apartments close to the beach.
9 two-bedroom units
Tel: (03931) 4075
Fax: (03931) 3753

Palm Park ***
PO Box 653, Margate 4275
Spacious apartments a short stroll from Margate's Golden Beach.
10 two-bedroom units, 3 three-bedroom units
Tel: (03931) 22542
Fax: (03931) 73753

MTUNZINI
Umlalazi Nature Reserve **
PO Box 234, Mtunzini 3867
An ideal family resort with twenty kilometres of unspoilt beaches, a beautiful lagoon and a variety of activities.
13 two-bedroom units.
Tel: (0353) 40 1836
Fax: (0353) 40 1607

Northern Transvaal

WARMBATHS
Aventura Warmbaths *
PO Box 75, Warmbaths 0480
An internationally-renowned spa with modern facilities and accommodation.
17 one-bedroom units, 87 two-bedroom units
Tel: (01473) 62200
Fax: (01473) 4712

Sondela Nature Reserve **
PO Box 22, Warmbaths 0480
Tranquil bushveld hospitality amidst unspoilt nature and farm culture.
27 two-bedroom units
Tel: (014) 736 4304
Fax: (014) 736 4310

North-West Province

BRITS
Magalies Park Country Club*
PO Box 3138, Brits 0250
On the banks of the Magalies River, luxury self-catering facilities for all the family.
40 one-bedroom units, 17 two-bedroom units, 66 three-bedroom units.
Tel: (01 207) 7 1315
Fax: (01 207) 7 1373

CHRISTIANA
Aventura Vaal Spa *
PO Box 19, Christiana 2680
Modern chalets with facilities for the family.
10 one-bedroom units, 72 two-bedroom units
Tel: (0534) 2244
Fax: (0534) 2354

Western Cape

Cape Town
The Place on the Bay **
Camps Bay, Cape Town 8001
Luxury and personal service overlooking Camps Bay Beach.
11 one-bedroom units, 10 two-bedroom units
Tel: (021) 438 7060
Fax: (021) 438 2692

DURBANVILLE
Brass Bells Self-Catering Cottages *
7 Biccard Street, Durbanville 7550
Charming self-catering cottages.
4 one-bedroom units, 1 two-bedroom unit
Tel: (021) 96 8758
Fax: (021) 96 9838

CAPE TOWN — FISH HOEK
Tudor House by the Sea *
43 Simonstown Road, Fish Hoek 7975
Spectacular views from every apartment.
2 one-bedroom unit, 1 two-bedroom unit
Tel: (021) 782 6238
Fax: (021) 782 5027

CAPE TOWN — MOUILLE POINT
Amalfi Holiday Apartments *
PO Box 51025, Waterfront 8002
Just one hundred metres from the sea close to the Victoria and Alfred Waterfront. Modern, fully equipped services apartments.
38 one-bedroom units
Tel: (021) 439 4920
Fax: (021) 439 9346

Lions Head Lodge *
PO Box 41563, Sea Point 8060
Centrally situated for the beach, waterfront and restaurants.
17 one-bedroom units, 1 two-bedroom unit
Tel: (021) 434 4163
Fax: (021) 439 3813

Zeanor All-Suite Apartments *
PO Box 154, Sea Point 8060
5 one-bedroom units, 1 two-bedroom unit. Serviced and elegantly designed apartments with open-plan kitchens.
Tel: (021) 434 4970
Fax: (021) 439 0245

CERES
Kagga Kamma *
PO Box 7143, Northern Paarl 7623
A unique private nature reserve with breathtaking views and rock formations.
9 three-bedroom units
Tel: (02 211) 63 8334
Fax: (02 211) 63 8383

KNYSNA
Old Drift Forest Lodge *
PO Box 461, Knysna 6570
Charming self-catering accommodation offering luxury, tranquillity and privacy in a forest and river setting just six kilometres from Knysna.
1 one-bedroom unit, 3 two-bedroom units, 3 three-bedroom units
Tel: (0445) 21 994
Fax: As above (ask for fax)

NOORRDHOEK CAPE
Monkey Valley Beach Nature Resort **
PO Box 114, Noordhoek Cape 7985
Luxury thatched cottages located in a milkwood forest overlooking the beach.
3 two-bedroom units, 13 three-bedroom units, 1 four-bedroom unit
Tel: (021) 789 1391
Fax: (021) 789 1143

PLETTENBERG BAY
Aventura Keurbooms **
Private Bag X1000, Plettenberg Bay 6600
A magnificent nature resort situated near the mouth of the Keurbooms River.
6 one-bedroom units, 8 two-bedroom units, 16 three-bedroom units.
Tel: (04 457) 9309
Fax: (04 457) 9912

Keurbooms Hotel and Chalets *
PO Box 889
Plettenberg Bay 6600
Ideally situated coastal resort just seven kilometres from Plettenberg Bay.
3 one-bedroom units, 5 two-bedroom units, 2 three-bedroom units.
Tel: (04 457) 9311
Fax: (04 457 9362

SOMERSET WEST
Zandberg Farm *
PO Box 5337, Heiderberg 7135
Comfortable cottages in the lush gardens of a wine farm.
4 one-bedroom units
Tel: (024) 842 2945
Fax: As above (ask for fax)

SWELLENDAM
Milestone Cottages *
PO Box 265, Swellendam 6740
Fully equipped cottages in the historic town of Swellendam.
5 one-bedroom units
Tel: (0291) 4 2137
Fax: As above (ask for fax)

AIRPORT TAX

There is an arrivals tax of R20 included in the price of an international airline ticket, R5 in the price of a domestic ticket. A tax of R40 is collected on arrival at Skukuza airport, if visiting a private game reserve, less if staying in the Kruger National Park.

BANKING

Banks are open from 9am to 3.30pm from Monday to Friday and from 8.30am to 11am on Saturdays. (See Currency, Banking and Credit Cards).

CAR HIRE

Car hire is probably the best way to experience most of the country and most international car hire companies are well represented in South Africa. Dolphin Europcar offices are country-wide and for a slightly higher excess, they will reduce the minimum age requirement to 21 years, instead of 25 years. Their toll free number is 08000 11344. Avis offices are represented at 94 locations throughout the country including all national and secondary airports. They offer a special unlimited mileage rate for overseas visitors on car hire of three or more days. Contact either their International sales consultants on (011) 974 2571 or fax: (011) 974 2683 or call their toll free number at 08000 21111.

Imperial Care Hire is one of the larger car hire organisations, as are Budget, Interrent and Sun Cars.

The minimum age requirement for driving is eighteen regardless of the type of driving licence held. Anybody wishing to hire a vehicle must have an international driving licence, but a licence in English (or with a certified English translation) is sufficient for visitors driving a vehicle on loan.

The wearing of motorbike helmets

and seat belts in both the front and back is compulsory.

There is no unleaded fuel and most vehicles take 93 premium in the northern areas and 97 when you are at the coast. Only cash or locally issued fuel credit cards may be used at service stations. It is not possible to use standard credit cards i.e. Visa, Mastercard, Diners, Amex so it is essential to carry enough cash.

Filling stations are in most locations and offer a fully service. It is customary to give a small tip to attendants who wash the windscreen and check the oil and water.

CLIMATE

The seasons in the southern hemisphere are the opposite to those in the northern hemisphere, meaning that December and January is the peak holiday season in South Africa. At this time, flights and accommodation are expensive, the resorts are crowded and the weather is extremely hot. October, November, February, March and April are better times to visit in terms of both weather and prices.

In the central and northern areas of the country, the winters are very cold at night with cool, sunny days. The weather in the Cape is typically Mediterranean with wet, cool winters and warm, sunny summers. Durban is hot and humid in the summer and warm in winter.

CURRENCY, BANKS AND CREDIT CARDS

The unit of currency is the rand and one rand is equal to 100 cents. Exchange rates and commissions vary between each bank so it is worth checking around.

Most banks have the facility to process cash advances from Visa and Mastercard, and First National Bank and Standard Bank also handle American Express and Diners. Bank hours vary slightly but standard hours are from 9am-3.30pm during the week and 8am-11am on Saturday.

There is a 24-hour automatic currency exchange machine at Johannesburg International Airport

Average maximum temperatures in degrees Celcius

	Jan	Feb	Mar	Apr	May	June	July	Aug	Sep	Oct	Nov	Dec
Cape Town	26.5	27.1	25.8	23.0	19.9	18.5	17.2	18.1	19.1	21.5	24.0	25.5
Pretoria	28.8	28.1	26.8	25.1	22.5	20.2	19.1	22.7	25.7	28.3	28.1	28.7
Johannesburg	26.3	25.6	24.3	22.1	19.1	16.5	16.4	19.8	22.8	25.0	25.3	26.1
Port Elizabeth	25.4	25.5	24.6	22.8	21.9	20.1	19.5	19.9	20.1	20.9	22.4	24.0
East London	25.2	25.6	24.7	23.5	22.6	20.9	21.0	21.3	21.4	21.6	22.8	24.0
Durban	27.2	27.5	26.9	25.6	24.1	22.5	22.0	22.4	22.9	23.6	24.9	26.2
Bloemfontein	29.8	28.3	26.3	22.8	19.0	16.6	16.4	19.6	22.8	25.8	27.5	29.2
Kimberley	32.5	31.0	28.4	25.3	21.2	18.6	18.5	21.8	24.6	28.3	29.9	31.7
Kruger	31.4	30.6	30.1	28.6	27.0	25.0	25.0	26.0	28.5	29.0	30.0	30.0

and the airport banking services are open 24-hours a day. Automatic Teller Machines (ATM) are situated outside most banks and most accept Visa and Mastercard withdrawals with a PIN number.

Foreign currency may be exchanged at commercial banks and American Express, Rennies Foreign Exchange offices, and all of the large hotels have their own foreign exchange facilities. The rand is accepted at hotels, shops and restaurants, as are major credit cards and travellers cheques.

Whilst there is no black market, many South Africans are keen to exchange rands for dollars and sterling for a slightly better rate than the bank.

Lesotho

In Lesotho the unit of currency is the Loti (plural Maloti) and one Maloti is equal to 100 lisente. It is equivalent in value to the South African rand which is accepted widely.

Swaziland

In Swaziland the unit of currency is the Lilangeni (plural Emalangeni), and is also equivalent in value to the rand.

CUSTOMS, IMMIGRATION AND HEALTH REGULATIONS

Visitors arriving within six days of leaving a risk area will require a yellow fever vaccination certificate. Malaria tablets are available on arrival and should be taken by visitors travelling to the Northern Transvaal, Mpumalanga, northern KwaZulu-Natal and the Kalahari Gemsbok National Park.

Gifts with a maximum value of R500 may be imported duty free and an additional R10,000 worth of goods are charged at a rate of twenty per cent duty. The duty free allowance is one litre of spirits (including liqueurs), two litres of wine, 50ml of perfume or toilette water, 400 cigarettes or 50 cigars or 250g of tobacco.

All plant and animal products are prohibited, as is pornography and illegal narcotics. Visitors should carry a doctor's prescription for any medication they may be carrying and if in any doubt, should check with their local embassy before travel.

There is no limit on the import of foreign currency, but a maximum of R500 may be brought into South Africa.

It is prohibited to take alcohol from South Africa to Lesotho, but each visitor may bring a maximum of one litre of wine, one litre of spirit or any other alcoholic beverage, 400 cigarettes or 50 cigars and 300ml perfume. No dangerous weapons, pornographic material or illegal narcotics may be taken into Lesotho.

Swaziland allows duty-free import of up to 400 cigarettes, 250g tobacco, two litres of wine, 500ml perfume, 250ml toilet water and one litre of spirit.

DISABLED VISITORS

With tourism still in its relative infancy, facilities for the disabled compared with international standards are somewhat limited.

Satour produces an accommodation guide to the Free State for the disabled, and Captour prints symbols in its guide to the Cape to attractions where disabled facilities are available.

Most new shopping centres have toilets for the disabled as well as lifts and specially assigned parking bays.

DOCUMENTS/VISAS

A temporary residence permit for a period not exceeding ninety days is issued on arrival to tourists and business visitors from the United Kingdom, Australia, New Zealand,

Canada, United States of America and Israel. All other passport holders should check visa requirements with their local South African embassy or consulate before travel. For visitors planning to travel to Lesotho or Swaziland, it is advisable to have a multiple entry visa, otherwise it will be necessary to have a re-entry visa issued at the Department of Home Affairs in South Africa, which can sometimes take up to seven days.

Lesotho

There is some confusion surrounding visa requirements for Lesotho. Some officials maintain that United States of America, Australian and Canadian passport holders do not require visas are required and others deem it necessary. It is advisable to check with a local Lesotho representative before travel (see Travel Information).

Citizens of the United Kingdom, New Zealand and Israel do not need a visa.

Swaziland

It is advisable to check before travel but basically United States of America, Canadian and Australian passport holders do not need a visa and entry permits for United Kingdom and New Zealand citizens can be obtained at the border.

DRIVING

The roads in South Africa range from a spaghetti of highways and flyovers to gravel roads and dirt tracks. The network of roads is excellent and driving is on the left.

An international driving licence is generally required, although some care hire companies will accept a British licence.

The speed limit in urban areas is 60kph (37mph) and on the highways is a maximum of 120kph (75mph). Traffic police are everywhere and there are numerous speed traps — so beware as fines are issued on the spot for offenders. The traffic police are also vigilant on illegally-parked vehicles, so it is always worth having plenty of loose change available for parking meters.

Cash only can be used to pay for fuel. In major centres many filling stations are open twenty four hours a day, although most are generally open from 7am to 7pm. In rural areas filling stations may operate on a more limited service and there may be lengthy distances to cover between towns. It is advisable to fill up at every opportunity.

There are road tolls on some roads in South Africa, usually on main highways. Visitors travelling around by car should keep coins or small denomination notes with them.

AA members are entitled to use the AA Travel Services in South Africa. They can also make reservations for accommodation throughout the country and provide route planning maps free of charge for all areas.

Telephone: toll free 0800 111 999 or visit one of their travel centres.

ELECTRICITY

Mains electricity is supplied at between 220 to 230 volts AC and sockets with three-pronged plugs are used.

However in Pretoria the supply is 250 volts AC. Visitors with European or American appliances will need an adaptor which can be obtained from electrical supply shops.

EMERGENCIES

Dial: 10111 for the police or flying squad
Dial: 998/999 for the fire brigade
AA 24-hour breakdown service is toll free 0800 010101

INTERNATIONAL ARRIVALS

Johannesburg International Airport is fourteen miles from the city centre. Cape Town is twelve miles and Durban is ten miles. Many hotels provide courtesy buses and there are buses in to the city centres. Taxis are easily available and fairly inexpensive.

MEDICAL

It is essential to take out a medical insurance policy prior to travel. While treatment in clinics and hospitals is of a high standard, it is also extremely expensive and there is no cheap medical cover available to non-residents.

Pharmacists are extremely helpful and knowledgeable and can provide medication for most general ailments without a prescription.

Doctors are listed under *medical* in the telephone directory.

LANGUAGE

There are eleven official languages in South Africa all of which are used to a different degree in broadcasting and the media. Many signs in Afrikaans can still be found, but this will gradually change in the future. To bridge the gap many people are using English but this has brought strong opposition from the staunch Afrikaners.

Afrikaans is a dialect of Dutch and the only Indo-European language to have originated in Africa and is only spoken in South Africa. The African languages include the Nguni language group which consists of Swati, Zulu, and Xhosa and the Sotho group which incorporates Sesotho saLebowa, southern Sotho and Setswana. To bridge the gap, particularly in the mines, the basic language of Funagalô has evolved which uses different phrases from of these languages.

Useful Afrikaans phrases

Afrikaans, along with English, is still the most widely-used official language. It is worth knowing a few basic Afrikaans words and phrases, particularly for visitors who will be travelling through the more rural parts of the country. It is the first language to many coloureds and is the only language spoken by some people away from the main towns. It is basically a simplified version of Dutch, which leaves out the complicated grammar and uses words from other languages, including English, French, as well as African and Asian languages. It sounds quite guttural and remember that 'v' is pronounced like 'f 'and 'w' like 'v'. So the popular surname Van der Merwe is pronounced *fan der merver*.

Numbers

1	*een*
2	*twee*
3	*drie*
4	*vier*
5	*vyf*
6	*ses*
7	*sewe*
8	*agt*
9	*nege*
10	*tien*
11	*elf*
12	*twaalf*
13	*dertien*
14	*veertien*
15	*vyftien*
16	*sestien*
17	*sewentien*
18	*agtien*
19	*negentien*
20	*twintig*
30	*dertig*
40	*veertig*
50	*vyftig*
60	*sestig*
70	*sewentig*
80	*tagtig*

90	negentig
100	honderd
200	twee honderd
300	drie honderd
1000	duisend

Days of the Week

Sunday	Sonda or So
Monday	Maandag or Ma
Tuesday	Dinsdag or Di
Wednesday	Woensday or Wo
Thursday	Donderdag or Do
Friday	Vrydag or Vr
Saturday	Saturdag or Sa

Months

January	Januarie
February	Februarie
March	Maart
April	April
May	Mei
June	Junie
July	Julie
August	Augustus
September	September
October	Oktober
November	November
December	Desember

Useful phrases

Yes	ja
No	nee
Please	asseblief
Thank you	dankie
Hello	hallo
Goodbye	totsiens
Good morning	Goeie-môre
Good evening	Goeie-naand
Good night	Goeie-nag
How are you?	Hoe gaan dit?
Do you speak English?	Praat u/jy Engels?
What is your name?	Wat is jou naam?
Sorry	Jammer/Ekskuus
I want....	Ek wil...hê
Where is...?	waar is...?
Waiter	kelner
Post office	die postkantoor
Tourist office	toeristeburo

museum	museum
Bus station	busstasie
Toilet	Toilet
Ladies/Gents	Dames/Mans/Here
Do you have...?	Het u/het jy?
A single room	'n singel kamer
A double room	'n dubbel kamer
With bath	met 'n bad
With shower	met stortbad
Hotel	hotel
Shop	Winkel
Market	mark
bank	bank
How many	hoeveel
How much does it cost	wat kos dit?
Open/closed	oop/toe or gesluit
Stamps	seëls
Envelope	koevert
One kilo	een kilo
apples	appels
oranges	lemoene
tomatoes	tamaties
cucumber	komkommer
lettuce	blaarslaai
potatoes	aartappels
Doctor	Doktor
Hospital	Hospitaal
Police	Polisie
Enquiries	Navrae
Information	Inligting
Office	Kantoor
Pharmacy	Apteek
ticket	kaartjie
am	vm
pm	nm
left	links
right	regs
exit	uitgang
city	stad
city centre	middestad
avenue	laan
street	straat
road	weg
traffic light	verkeerslig/robot
beach	strand
arrival	aankoms
departure	vertrek
viewpoint	uitsigpunt
hot	warm

cold	koud
water	water
tea	tee
coffee	koffie
beer	bier
wine	wyn
menu	spyskaart
steak	biefstuk
fish	vis

Zulu

Zulu is a sub-group of the Nguni shared language group which means that a Xhosa speaker will understand the basic phrases given below. The main difference between the two languages lies in the strength of the 'click'. Basically the Zulus click on the letter c, q, x and it is achieved by clicking the tongue on the roof of your mouth. The Xhosa 'click' is more pronounced and comes from the back of the throat and is most pronounced on the letters q and x.

Numbers

1	-nye
2	-bili
3	-thathu
4	-ne
5	-hlanu
6	isithupha
7	isikhombisa
8	isishiyagalombili
9	ishishiyagalolungye
10	ishumi
11	ishumi nanye
12	ishumi nambili
13	ishumi nantathu
14	ishumi nane
15	ishumi nanhlanu
16	ishumi nesithupha
17	ishumi nesikhombisa
18	ishumi nesishiyalombili
19	ishumi neshishiyagalolunye
20	amashumi amabili
21	amashumi ambabili nanye
30	amashumi amathathu
50	amashumi amalanu
100	ikhulu

Days of the Week

Sunday	Sonto
Monday	uMsombuluko
Tuesday	oLwesibili
Wednesday	oLwesithathu
Thursday	oLwesine
Friday	oLwesihlanu
Saturday	Mbgibelo

Months

January	uJanuwari
February	uFebruwari
March	uMashi
April	uApreli
May	uMeyi
June	uJuni
July	uJulayi
August	uAgasti
September	uSeptemba
October	uOkthoba
November	uNovemba
December	uDisemba

Useful phrases

Yes	Yebo
No	Cha
Please	Jabulisa
Thank you	Ngiyabonga
Hello (to one person)	Sawubona
Hello (to a group)	Sanibona
Goodbye (as you leave)	Sala kahle
Goodbye (as they leave)	Hamba kahle
What is it?	Yani?
How are you?	Unjani?
How are you all?	Ninjani?
How much is it?	Malini?
Water	Amanzi
I don't know	Angazi
Excuse me	Uxolo
I am sorry	Ngiyadabuka
My friend	Mngane wami!
Help!	Siza!
What (is it)?	Yini?
Where	Kuphi?
Toilet	indlu encane

Everyday South African English

boerwors	a popular spicy sausage
howzit	hello, how are you doing?
izit?	is that so?
just now	something that will happen imminently
soon soon	very soon
jol	to party or a party
bakkie	a pick-up truck
location	a township
lekker	very good
takkie	sports shoe
shame	response to good or bad news
robot	traffic lights
traffic circle	roundabout
haw haws	creepy crawlies
larney	expensive, up-market
sis	horrible! unpleasant!
full full	very full

LEGAL ADVICE

There are Citizen's Advice Bureaux in most major cities who can give legal advice concerning South African legislation, or alternatively contact either your embassy or representative in Pretoria and they will be able to assist.

NATIONAL HOLIDAYS

Christmas Day	25 December
Day of Goodwill	26 December
New Years Day	1 January
Human Rights	21 March
Good Friday	
Family Day	17 April
Constitution Day	27 April
Workers Day	1 May
Youth Day	16 June
National Women's Day	9 August
Heritage Day	24 September
Day of Reconciliation	16 December

Lesotho Public Holidays

New Year's Day	1 January
Moshoeshoe's Day	12 March
National Tree Planting	21 March
Good Friday	
Easter Monday	
King's Birthday	17 July
Ascension Day	
Family Day	First Mon in July
Sports Day	First Mon in Oct
Independence Day	4 October
Christmas Day	25 December
Boxing Day	26 December

Swaziland

New Years Day	1 January
Good Friday	
Easter Monday	
King's Birthday	19 April
National Flag Day	25 April
Public Holiday	22 July
Independence Day	6 September
Christmas Day	25 December
Boxing Day	26 December
Incwala Day	December/January

NATIONAL PARKS

The National Parks Board maintains seventeen parks which offer accommodation ranging from camping, through to rustic huts, and fully-equipped chalets. Except in the high season, it is not necessary to make advance reservations for camping, but other accommodation should be booked prior to travel. The National Parks Board handles all reservations except for those in the KwaZulu-Natal area which are under the authority of the Natal Parks Board.

PO Box 787
Pretoria 0001
Tel: (012) 343 1991

PO Box 7400
Rogge Bay 8012
Tel: (021) 22 2810

The Natal Parks Board administers over sixty nature reserve and parks in the province KwaZulu-Natal has a separate board to deal with its many game parks and nature reserves.

Natal Parks Board
PO Box 1750
Pietermaritzburg 3200
Tel: (0331) 471981

MEDIA

The Weekly Mail, the Sunday Times and the Sunday Independent are the national newspapers, and there are a variety of regional daily newspapers; mainly in English and Afrikaans. Editions of major international newspapers and magazines are available in newsagents in the major cities. A good alternative are the weekly International Telegraph or International Express which are widely available.

South African Broadcasting Corporation (SABC) offers four channels with news and entertainment programming. There is also a private channel (M-Net) which has been in operation since 1986 and is broadcast in a many hotels throughout the country.

CNN and Sky TV are both shown daily for international news.

PHOTOGRAPHIC TIPS

Standard 100 ASA film is widely available throughout the country, but it is generally more difficult to purchase anything out of the ordinary. Fuji are well-established here and Kodak have returned in the last couple of years since sanctions were lifted. There are plenty of one-hour photo processing labs but the developing costs can be expensive. It may be difficult to find a reliable laboratory to develop black-and-white film inexpensively.

The sunlight in South Africa can be extremely harsh and it worth using an ultraviolet or sunlight filter to cut down the glare, along with a faster exposure. A telephoto lens is strongly recommended for visitors planning to visit a game reserve and it is worth remembering that the harsh light between 11am and 3pm will give very poor photographic results.

It is prohibited to photograph any military installations and visitors should respect the local people's religions and customs by asking their permission first to take their photograph. The Swazi's are extremely sensitive over the photographing of their ceremonies and it is not permitted to photograph the King's palace.

Nowadays, many shopping centres and buildings pass hand luggage through x-ray machines as a security precaution. It is therefore advisable to remove any photographic equipment and spare film as not all the machines are 'film safe'.

RELIGION

South Africa is a primarily a Christian nation with a wide range of denominations including the Afrikaner NG Kerk, Catholic, Methodist, Baptist and a range of Afro-Christian churches like the Zionists who combine Christianity with their ethnic beliefs

Pentecostal and Evangelical Christianity is becoming increasingly popular and hyper churches are emerging to cope with congregations of 5,000 or more worshippers at one time. These churches have played an important role in the creation of the new South Africa as they tend to be the most mixed congregations.

Less than five per cent of the population make up the Hindu, Muslim and Jewish faiths. There are a number of mosque around Cape Town which can be visited although it is advisable to dress modestly. There are also Buddhist retreats in some parts of the country.

SHOPPING

Shopping has altered significantly during the last decade as large modern shopping complexes have been constructed in many suburbs throughout South Africa. There has also been a huge increase in the number of flea markets where it is possible to buy unusual gifts and African specialities. Woolworth is a large chain store which sells good quality clothing, footwear, luggage and a fine selection of food.

Store hours are generally 8.30am to 5pm Monday to Friday, 9am to 1pm on Saturday and Sunday. However, shopping hours have recently become more flexible and most large city stores now open all day Saturday. There are numerous late night cafes and supermarkets in most towns. Bottle shops (off licences) are open from Monday to Friday until 6.30pm and until about 1pm on Saturday.

VAT is charged at fourteen per cent on most purchases, meals and accommodation. A VAT refund is available to non-residents on items costing over R250 which will be exported at the end of a trip. It is necessary to provide proof of purchase when claiming and VAT desks are at most points of exit from South Africa.

TIPPING

A service charge is rarely added to restaurant bills and it is customary to leave between a ten and fifteen per cent gratuity. Tips should be given to porters (R1-1.50 per item), hairdressers (R5) and shampooists (R2).

TELEPHONES AND POSTAGE

There are plenty of telephone booths in all major centres including shopping complexes, restaurants and airports. There are also a number of telephone/fax agencies which provide a service for dialling both local and international calls from a private booth in their bureau, which is billed after the call. Whilst this is more convenient, they charge a higher rate than standard telephone boxes. The main post offices in all large cities are open 24-hours a day for both local and international calls.

Telephones are fully automated with direct dialling to most places in the world. A table of rates and international codes is given at the front of the telephone directory.

1023 for local enquiries
1025 for national numbers.
10118 for the Electronic Yellow Pages
0900 and 0903 for the operator to call collect (reverse charge call).

It is also possible to hire cellular telephones from major airports.

Phone cards are a convenient way of making calls and an increasing amount of telephones in the cities offer this facility. The cards can be purchased from any shops displaying a 'phonecard' sign and this is a convenient and cheap way of making calls. Photocopies can be made at many businesses and pharmacies for a small charge.

Mail can be sent to all major post offices throughout the country addressed as follows:-
Poste Restante
GPO
City Name
American Express offices will also hold mail and the service is free to cardholders.

There are specially-priced stamps for postcards and aerogrammes can be sent to anywhere in the world for a flat rate.

Post offices are open from 8am-4.30pm Monday to Friday and until 1pm on Saturday. Some smaller branches close for lunch between 1-2pm.

PUBLIC CONVENIENCES

Toilets are free and can be easily found at shopping centres, hotels, restaurants and service stations. Some of the newer ones have both facilities for the disabled and baby-changing areas. However, this is only in the major cities and is a relatively new concept.

UNSAFE AREAS

A visit to a township is often a high priority for overseas visitors and is an fascinating and educational experience. It is inadvisable to visit a township alone, as it is possible to encounter dangerous situations unless accompanied by a resident of the area. There are regular tour bus trips or education tours which are detailed in each chapter.

TRAVEL INFORMATION

Since the lifting of sanctions, many airlines have established a regular service into South Africa from destinations throughout the world. British Airways and South African Airways (SAA) operate daily flights from the UK and Alitalia, KLM, Sabena, Lufthansa and Egyptair are competitively priced, but usually require a plane change en route. Air Namibia, Air Zimbabwe, Zambia Airways and Ethiopian Airlines also have connecting flights from Europe via their hubs in Africa. Quantas operates from Australia and New Zealand, and Singapore Airlines, Cathay Pacific and China Airlines connect Johannesburg with points across Asia. Alitalia and KLM tend to offer the best service and fares from Canada and the United States.

The South African Tourism Board (SATOUR) is the official tourism body for South Africa and produces excellent printed material and maps on the entire country. Whilst most brochures are provided free-of-charge, there is a nominal fee required for others. Their Travel Guide to South Africa is a comprehensive guide with maps of cities and provinces countrywide and where to find the attractions.

There are tourist information bureaux or publicity associations in every town across the Republic and the major ones are listed at the end of each chapter. They provide local maps and information on points of interest, accommodation and restaurants.

There are already three Tourist Rendezvous Travel Centres established in Pretoria, Johannesburg and Cape Town where the Satour office, the local publicity office, a travel agent and National Parks Board reservations are all located under one roof.

WHAT TO WEAR

In the summer in South Africa lightweight informal clothing is generally worn. In the winter a sweater or coat will be needed, particularly in the cool evening air.

Some establishments require a jacket and tie for the evening, but most restaurants are informal and relaxed, although smart casual is generally preferable.

At game reserves it is advisable to wear neutral colours i.e. khaki or beige as bright colours can disturb the game. It can be cold in the early morning or after dusk, so it is worth taking a sweater or jacket.

Always wear a hat to avoid sunstroke and take a swimsuit for the afternoons to relax around the pool.

There are opportunities to go on walking safaris, so take sensible shoes and socks.

Always pack plenty of insect repellent to ward off mosquitos. It is worth packing a pair of binoculars and a torch.

Satour Offices Worldwide

Australia and New Zealand
Level 6, 285 Clarence Street
Sydney
N.S.W. 2000
Tel: (2) 261 3424
Fax: (2) 261 3414

Austria
Stefan Zweig Platz 11
A-1170, Vienna
Tel: (1) 4704 5110
Fax: (1) 4704 5114

Benelux Countries
Parnassustoren
Locatellikade 1, 7E Etage
1076 AZ Amsterdam
Tel: (20) 664 6201
Fax: (20) 662 9761

Canada
4117 Lawrence Avenue East
Suite 2
Scarborough, Ontario MIE 2S2
Tel: (416) 283 0563

France
61 rue La Boetie
75008 Paris
France
Tel: (1) 4561 0197
Fax: (1) 4561 0196

Germany
Alemannia Haus
An der Hauptwache 11
D-60313 Franfurt/Main 1
60019 Frankfurt
Tel: (69) 2 0658
Fax: (69) 28 0950

Israel
14th Floor
Century Towers
124 lbn Gvirol Street
Tel Aviv 61033
Tel: (3) 527 2950/2351
Fax: (3) 527 1958

Italy
Via Durini 24, 20122 Milan
Italy
Tel: (2) 79 4100
Fax: (2) 79 4601

Japan
Akasaka Lions Bulding 2nd Floor
1-1-2 Moto Akasaka
Minato-ku
Tokyo 107
Tel: (3) 3 478 7601
Fax: (3) 478 7605

Switzerland
Seestrasse 42
CH 8802 Kilchberg/Zurich
Switzerland
Tel: (1) 715 1815/6/7
Fax: (1) 715 1889

Taiwan/Hong Kong
Room 1204
12th Floor, Bank Tower Building
205 Tun Hua North Road
Taipei 10592
Tel: (2) 717 4238
Fax: (2) 717 1146

United Kingdom
Republic of Ireland/Scandinavia
No 5-6 Alt Grove
Wimbledon, London SW19 4DZ
Tel: (0181) 944 8080
Fax: (0181) 944 6705

USA (Eastern)
500 Fifth Avenue, 20th Floor
New York N.Y. 10110
Tel: (212) 730 2929
(1-800) 822 5368
Fax: (212) 764 1980

USA (Western)
Suite 1524
9841 Airport Boulevard
Los Angeles, California 90045
Tel: (310) 641 8444
(1-800) 782 9772
Tel: (310) 641 5812

To check up-to-date visa requirements and specific information, contact either the South African embassy or Consulate-General in the country of origin.

South African Embassies Worldwide

Australia/New Zealand
Rhodes Place
State Circle
Yarralumla
Canberra
ACT 2600
Tel: (6) 2732424/5/6/7
Fax: (6) 2733543

UK (including Ireland)
SA House
Trafalgar Square
London
WC2N 5DP
Tel: (71) 9304488
Fax: (71) 3210834

USA
3051 Massachusetts Avenue NW
Washington DC 20008
Tel: (202) 2324400
Fax: (202) 2651607

Canada
15 Sussex Drive
Ontario
Ottawa KIM IM8
Tel: (613) 744 0330
Fax: (613) 7411639

Israel
16th floor
Top Tower
50 Dizengoff Street
Tel Aviv
Tel: (3) 5252566

Transport

There are a number of domestic airlines who offer flights to destinations throughout South Africa, Lesotho and Swaziland. Reservations made three months in advance will guarantee excellent discounts on fares. Alternatively, there are also good savings available on bookings made a minimum of fourteen days before departure. Tickets can be purchased at travel agents within South Africa or before arrival in the Republic.

Rail

Contact the local Transnet/Spoornet office for details of rail services and timetable information. Although more expensive than coaches, the train is an excellent way to see the country. There are three different price levels according to class, third class being most comparable to coach fares. Sleeper accommodation is available for overnight journeys and the price of the bert is included in the fare. An inter-city timetable can be picked up from any main line station and details of local services can be obtained from main stations within each area.

There are also a number of rail services which add a special magic to a journey.

The Blue Train is a luxury express which travels between Pretoria, via Johannesburg to Cape Town and return. A route to the Lowveld, Pretoria to Nelspruit and return is also available. There is also a service which runs from Cape Town, via Johannesburg to Victoria Falls. Passengers travel in air-conditioned comfort and the train travels through some of the most beautiful parts of the country.

Rovos Rail has revived the golden age of steam travel with their 'Pride of Africa' service. The 1920s restored coaches travel on various routes including an overnight journey between Pretoria and a three-night Mpumalanga Tour which includes 24-hours at a private game reserve; a 24-hour journey from Pretoria to Cape Town (or vice-versa) which includes stops at Kimberley and Matjiesfontein. They also run an annual twelve-day journey between Cape Town and Dar es Salaam in Tanzania.

The Shamwari Rail Safari runs a luxury service from Johannesburg to Boesmanspoort to transport visitors to their Shamwari Game Reserve.

The Banana Express steam train operates two-and-a-half hour round trips between Port Shepstone and Izotsha, in KwaZulu-Natal, travelling through the banana and sugar cane plantations.

The Outeniqua Choo-Tjoe is an old steam train which travels through the most scenic areas of the Garden Route.

Union Limited offers fourteen-day steam safaris along various fascinating routes including one from Johannesburg via Mpumalanga to Zimbabwe and the Victoria falls and returning via the Northern Transvaal.

Other special trains include the Umgeni Steam Train, the Magaliesberg Express, the Neerail North West Cape Railway, the Ostrich Express and the Midmar Steam Railway.

Bus/Coach

Within South Africa coaches are generally cheaper than trains.

Springbok Atlas operates scheduled coach tours with guaranteed departure day tours and long distance tours from Cape Town, Durban, Johannesburg, Port Elizabeth and George.

Translux has recently launched a range of coach travel passes and holidays which include:

The Lux Pass which offers unlimited travel on the entire network of Translux for either seven, ten, fifteen, twenty-one or thirty days. The passholder may disembark and board at as many of the designated stopover points and backtrack as required.

The Tourlink Pass offers a variety of routes which allow up to six months travel along specified routes stopping at specified destinations for as long as the passenger requires.

The Hotel Pass offers passengers the opportunity to pre-purchase accommodation at guaranteed rates along a series of six unescorted coach holidays.

TIME

Lesotho, Swaziland and South Africa are on the same time which is two hours ahead of Greenwich Mean Time; seven hours ahead of Eastern USA Standard Time and eight hours behind Australian Standard Time. There is no Daylight Saving.

VAT

VAT is charged at the rate of fourteen per cent on most items and services including hotel accommodation, goods and transport and tours. VAT can be claimed back on goods exceeding R250 at the international departure point.

WATER

Tap water is safe to drink in all areas, but *bilharzia* exists in certain rivers and streams and caution should be taken in some areas. Local and imported mineral water is widely available. Water purifying tablets are widely available if in doubt.

Index